THE POLITICS OF NATURE

Does green political theory provide plausible answers to the central problems of political theory – problems of justice and democracy, of individual rights and freedom, and of human nature and gender?

The contributors to this book, who come from a range of disciplines – philosophy, political science, sociology and economics – and a range of political backgrounds, explore this question from a variety of perspectives. They look at the relationship between green political ideas and liberalism, anarchism, feminism, social democracy, individualism, critical theory and christianity.

Green political theory shares some basic ideas with anarchism, feminism and German critical theory. Yet it can and should be reconciled, according to some authors, with liberalism or social democracy. Christianity, which is often perceived by greens as part of the problem rather than part of the solution, is also shown to have some affinity with green thought.

Additionally, some chapters focus on issues which seem peculiar to green thought: the critique of industrialization and economic growth; holism and ecocentrism. Not all chapters are purely theoretical; one chapter deals with social policies, another with forms of direct democracy.

The Politics of Nature presents a uniquely comprehensive and balanced survey of current green political ideas. It is directed to those with academic interests in the environment, but the chapters that deal with practical issues will be of equal relevance to those with professional interests in the area.

THE POLITICS OF NATURE

Explorations in green political theory

Edited by
Andrew Dobson and
Paul Lucardie

London and New York

First published 1993
by Routledge
11 New Fetter Lane, London EC4P 4EE

New in paperback 1995

Simultaneously published in the USA and Canada
by Routledge
29 West 35th Street, New York, NY 10001

Typeset in Baskerville
by Pat and Anne Murphy, Highcliffe-on-Sea, Dorset
Printed and bound in Great Britain by
Mackays of Chatham PLC, Chatham, Kent

British Library Cataloguing in Publication Data
A catalogue record for this book is available from
the British Library
ISBN 0–415–08593–4 (hbk)
ISBN 0–415–12471–9 (pbk)

Library of Congress Cataloguing-in-Publication Data
The Politics of nature: explorations in green political theory /
edited by Andrew Dobson and Paul Lucardie.
p.   cm.
Simultaneously published in the USA and Canada.
Includes bibliographical references and index.
ISBN 0–415–08593–4 (hbk)
ISBN 0–415–12471–9 (pbk)
1. Green movement.   I. Dobson, Andrew.
II. Lucardie, Paul, 1946–
JA75.8.P65   1993   322.4′4–dc20
92-46098 CIP

CONTENTS

FIGURES

CONTRIBUTORS

Wouter Achterberg holds the chair of Humanist Philosophy at the University of Wageningen and teaches philosophy at the University of Amsterdam.

Ted Benton is Reader in the Department of Sociology at the University of Essex.

Alan Carter is Lecturer in Philosophy at Heythrop College, University of London.

Andrew Dobson is Senior Lecturer in Politics at the University of Keele.

Frank Dietz teaches Economics at the Department of Public Administration of the Erasmus University at Rotterdam.

Judy Evans is Lecturer in Politics at the University of York.

John Ferris is Lecturer in Social Policy in the Department of Social Policy and Administration at the University of Nottingham.

Keekok Lee is Lecturer in the Department of Philosophy at the University of Manchester.

Paul Lucardie is Research Associate at the Documentation Centre of Dutch Political Parties at the University of Groningen.

Michael Saward is Lecturer in the Department of Social Policy at the Royal Holloway and Bedford New College of the University of London.

Jan van der Straaten lectures in the Department of Social Economics at Tilburg University.

Michael Watson is Senior Lecturer in the Department of International Politics at the University College of Wales at Aberystwyth and **David Sharpe** is preparing a doctoral dissertation at the same department.

Marcel Wissenburg is preparing a doctoral dissertation at the Department of Politics of the University of Nijmegen.

INTRODUCTION

The authors of this book met in a workshop on green political theory at the European Consortium for Political Research sessions at the University of Essex in 1991. They shared a keen interest in green ideas but came from different disciplines and diverse political families – some considered themselves 'green', others did not. While disagreements were rife, the consensus was that green political theory is undertheorized and demands further investigation.

Most authors discuss only fragments of such a theory, but to some degree or other the fragments fit together. We have arranged them in four sections: ethical foundations; green politics: the state and democracy; green society: economics and welfare; green political theory: the boundaries.

Environmental ethics constitutes the core or the foundation of green political theory, as we understand it. Traditional political theory assumes a moral community consisting of all (rational) 'men', whilst green theory expands this community to include animals, plants, and possibly even the Earth itself. All green theorists seem to agree on this, even if they disagree about the implications. The moderates – 'light greens' or 'shallow ecologists' – remain anthropocentric: human rights may be extended to 'higher' animals, but human values and interests retain hegemony in any moral discourse. (Moreover, the 'higher animals' are held to be higher precisely because they approximate in some sense or other to human beings.) The structure of their discourse may still be traditional – inspired by Bentham, Kant or Aristotle. Radicals, 'dark greens' or 'deep ecologists' perceive man as a rather young and arrogant member of the Community of Life whose claim to a leading part in the play should be rejected.

This radical notion of Nature as a moral community cannot be reconciled easily with traditional ethical theories. As Marcel Wissenburg argues in his contribution to this volume, it may be impossible to found a theory of justice on this idea. Justice can only be applied by moral subjects to other moral subjects. A moral subject has to be a sentient being which can suffer harm; hence Wissenburg includes animals but excludes plants and minerals. Even so, he argues that human beings are 'more equal' than animals. In the end, his position remains anthropocentric and individualistic. Nature can be an object but not a subject of moral discourse; or in his words: Nature can be seen as a resource or a recipient, but not a distributor of justice. Holistic conceptions of Nature as a god-like subject (Gaia) are incompatible with the idea of distributive justice and lead to quietism or totalitarianism.

Whereas Wissenburg looks from a traditional individualist perspective at the problem of environmental ethics, Paul Lucardie starts from the other side: how do ecocentric or biocentric ethical theorists deal with individualism? They do not all reject it in favour of a 'Gaian' holism, as one might have expected. In fact, many of them have come to realize that 'strong' forms of holism or organicism lead – as Wissenburg argued – to morally or logically untenable conclusions. However, 'strong' individualism seems equally unacceptable to Lucardie. A perfect way out would be a mystical union between the individual and the Community of Life, as deep ecologists claim to experience. However, if one fails to realize this experience, one should strike a compromise between 'weak' holism and 'weak' individualism. We can communicate with other human beings and also with mammals; some of us even with plants. So we may widen our moral community step by step, without giving up individual autonomy altogether.

The expansion of our moral community has political implications, of course. 'Politics' itself becomes a broader notion. Some of the implications are discussed in the second part of this volume. A daring attempt to construct a full-fledged green political theory is made by Alan Carter. Though he admits to being inspired by anarchism, socialism and feminism, he claims to present a green theory of politics. In his model, the political has primacy: the state and its dominant actors control the economy by selecting and stabilizing the relations of economic control that correspond with their rational self-interest. The relations of economic control determine the development of the forces of production. Yet the forces of production support the forces of defence needed by the state and its dominant actors. Thus the circle is closed: while the political sphere determines the economic sphere, the latter 'empowers' the former. A centralized and authoritarian state tends to stabilize competitive and inegalitarian economic relations that support nationalistic and militaristic coercive forces (nuclear arms, for example), and those that damage the environment. In Carter's opinion, most existing states fit this model. Hence he calls for a decentralized, participatory democracy that would select egalitarian, co-operative economic relations that would support non-violent defence and benign relations with the environment.

This association of environmental protection – the green imperative – with participatory or direct democracy is questioned by Michael Saward. According to him, the two are not logically related and may even be incompatible. An authoritarian state would be more in line with the green imperative. If this seems undesirable, greens should strive for a semi-direct democracy based on interactive communication technology rather than on face-to-face communication. Direct democracy is in his eyes not a desirable option, as it would invite manipulation and demagogy.

Like Michael Saward, Wouter Achterberg perceives a tension between the environmental crisis and democracy. A structural solution of the crisis would require sustainable development – that is, development that does not compromise the ability of future generations of human beings, and possibly of other creatures, to meet their needs. This would imply considerable sacrifices by the present generation; for instance, a reduction of (auto-) mobility, limited economic growth and interference with the market economy. One may well wonder if people will agree to these sacrifices – not only in a direct democracy, as discussed by Saward, but even in a liberal democracy. Does not liberalism require a neutral state that does not interfere with private decisions concerning the use of a private car? A liberal state cannot prescribe a 'good' (green) way of life to its citizens, but has to accept a pluralism of values. However, Achterberg suggests that Rawls's idea of an overlapping consensus might offer a solution here. People with different conceptions of the good life could agree on certain procedures and principles that are not incompatible with their conceptions. Rawls suggested two principles (equal rights and the greatest-benefit-of-the-least-advantaged), Achterberg adds a third one: 'we should not hand the world on to our successors in a worse shape than we received it'. The principle seems quite compatible with liberalism. Therefore, sustainable development can be justified even in a liberal democracy. A concrete example can be found in The Netherlands, where parliament has approved a fairly radical National Environmental Policy Plan. Hence one could speak of hypothetical general consent in this case; which should satisfy liberal democrats. Green democrats might strive for direct, explicit consent, of course. Even they would be hard put, however, to obtain such a consent from all members of our moral community, human as well as non-human.

Hence the green theory of democracy seems incomplete, if not non-existent. It borrows ideas either from anarchists (direct democracy) or from liberals (indirect democracy/tacit consent) without adding much of its own. But if, as on this reading, there are no specific green ideas about the political framework there might still be green ideas about political contents: the kind of society Greens should strive for. If not, then Greens should drop any pretension to be different from environmentally conscious liberals, socialists or whatever.

A coherent green model of society is defended by Keekok Lee. She presents a radical critique of industrial society based on ecological as well as social arguments. Her list of arguments looks impressive: industrialization degrades nature and especially animals, exhausts non-renewable resources and produces too much waste; it results in mass unemployment and concentration of power and wealth in the hands of a few, while a large part of the world can never reach an advanced level of industrialization – because of environmental limits – and has to remain poor; supply-led production ignores non-profitable wants and stimulates profitable wants; paid work, but also household work and daily life in general, becomes less skilled and more mechanical – for example, pre-packaged food and entertainment do not require active skills but only the manipulation of a microwave oven or a video display. Therefore, it would be better for human as well as non-human nature if we de-industrialized and revived artisanal skills as well as traditional, labour-intensive agriculture. Inspired by Ruskin and Gandhi, Lee sketches the outlines of a green society that might look romantic and unrealistic in the eyes of sceptical liberals; but it has the merit of coherence.

The economists Frank Dietz and Jan van der Straaten do not provide us with a model of a green economy, but show the need for it in a critical survey of dominant economic theories from a green point of view. Before 1850, classical economists like Ricardo and Malthus gave natural resources a central place in their theories and saw nature and economy as integrated in a closed system. Their neo-classical and Marxist successors, however, perceived the economy as an open system and reduced nature to externalities. Recently, neo-classical economists have recommended internalizing externalities, but Dietz and Van der Straaten consider this practically impossible: we lack sufficient knowledge concerning individual preferences and the ecological consequences of aggregated preferences. Therefore, economists are urged to return to the classical notion of a closed system – or in more contemporary terms: sustainable development. Whether this can be reconciled with a market economy remains to be seen; at least considerable government intervention will be required to overcome opposition from vested interests, labour as well as capital. Thus Dietz and Van der Straaten seem to open up a 'third way' in economic thinking, neither socialist nor liberal – even if they do not go as far as Lee or Carter.

None of them advocates a *rapprochement* between socialism and ecologism, as John Ferris does. He rejects all green claims to a coherent political vision of an alternative society as unrealistic. At best, Greens can claim an ecological rationality which they apply to all sorts of political and social problems. Though they have developed ideas about specific problems such as housing, poverty and health, these do not add up to a unified vision or model of welfare. Perhaps the construction of a new political theory is even impossible in our time of transition. Hence Ferris advises the Greens to adopt the socialist or social democratic welfare model, stripped of its *étatist* excesses, rather than to seek refuge in 'fundamentalism' of anarchist or conservative inspiration – traditions which both lack 'social rationality' in his eyes. In other words, ecological rationality should be complemented by social rationality.

While John Ferris sees complementary relations between socialism and ecologism, Ted Benton observes a structural congruence between the two. In his very original contribution he focuses on animal rights. Animal rights theories tend to start from liberal-individualist assumptions, which may weaken the impact of these theories. Even if formal rights were claimed for animals, their enforcement would be obstructed by the social context – as in the case of women workers, only more so. Benton develops this argument in a penetrating analysis of the social relations between animals and human beings, at home (pets), in a laboratory (animal experiments) and in a 'factory farm'. Especially in 'factory farms', relations between farm workers and animals have to be instrumental and amoral. But even if the relations were to be moral and communicative, the epistemic limits to communication might cause 'benevolent harm' to powerless animals. To prevent this, the autonomy of the animals ought to be maximized – the opposite of what intensive stock-rearing implies! In this respect, animals should not be compared to infants or mentally disabled human beings who would not benefit much from maximized autonomy. In another sense, however, animals are social beings like people. If they have rights, they should enjoy them in a proper social and species-specific context. Perhaps enforcement of animal rights as well as human rights ought to be supplemented by a socialist transformation of the social relations between human beings and (other) animals – and vice versa: socialism should not neglect individual rights either.

More sympathy for liberal ideas can be detected in the contribution of Judy Evans. Writing as a feminist, she wants to call liberalism's bluff, rather than follow the ecofeminists in their essentialist and potentially conservative ventures. Evans takes issue with theorists like Mary Daly, Andrée Collard and Ynestra King, and also with Carol Gilligan. Women are not more 'natural' than men; nor do they practise a different, more ecological ethic. However, they still receive different treatment because of different socialization patterns – and that ought to stop.

To call liberalism's bluff has also been the purpose of Critical Theory, as developed by Horkheimer, Adorno and Marcuse. Like green theorists, the Critical Theorists reject the domination of nature taken for granted by liberals as well as other inheritors of the Enlightenment. Andrew Dobson points out other similarities as well as differences between the two schools of thought. Green theorists should resist the temptation to renounce modernity and Enlightenment altogether, he concludes, but concentrate on two challenges to (post-)modern capitalism: post-materialism and the intrinsic value of the environment.

Both challenges are taken up not only by the Greens but also by Christians, as Michael Watson and David Sharpe show. The World Council of Churches developed a programme on 'Justice, Peace and the Integrity of Creation' in the 1980s which comes close to ecologism. Its theocentrism might not appeal to biocentric deep ecologists, but definitely goes beyond the anthropocentrism that prevailed in western Christianity until recently. Whereas eastern (orthodox) churches retained a theocentric view of nature – as a permanent, ongoing creation of God through the Holy Spirit – western Christianity emphasized human, individual salvation and considered creation to be a completed process. So Lynn White and other critics were partly right: in western Europe, Christianity contributed to our present ecological crisis, even if only indirectly, by desanctifying nature. Nevertheless, it might also contribute to a solution of the crisis.

But so might socialism, if we believe Ferris and Benton; and liberalism, if we agree with Achterberg; and anarchism, Carter might add. Is there still need – and room – for a green theory, different from other traditions?

Though all our authors show at least some sympathy for green values – who does not, these days? – many of them tend to give a negative answer to this question. They deny the existence as well as the feasibility of a green theory of democracy (Saward), justice (Wissenburg), feminism (Evans) or welfare (Ferris). One could regard them as 'light green' at best.[1] The somewhat 'darker green' authors would concede that green theory is far from complete, but emphasize its originality – in its critique of industrial society (Lee) and of modern economic theories (Dietz and Van der Straaten), its conception of the 'relations of political control' (Carter), its ecological holism (Lucardie) and its critical reception of modernity (Dobson). Thus, I would conclude, if green political theory does not yet exist, it is *in statu nascendi*. It may turn out to be a miscarriage. Nevertheless, the editors of this volume would like to think of themselves here as midwives rather than abortionists – but we should let the reader judge, of course.

Paul Lucardie
University of Groningen, 1993

NOTE

1 Wissenburg prefers to call himself 'grue', green + blue; 'blue' stands for (conservative) liberal, at least in The Netherlands!

Part I

ETHICAL FOUNDATIONS

1

THE IDEA OF NATURE AND THE NATURE OF DISTRIBUTIVE JUSTICE[1]

Marcel Wissenburg

INTRODUCTION

When I wrote the first draft of this text, Iraq was threatening to set fire to Kuwait's oil wells. And so they did. There are at least two philosophical points of interest in this disaster, both relating to the possibility of a green political theory. In the first place, it reminds us of the fact that environmental catastrophes, though they have happened all through the geological history of the earth, seem to happen more often since man took over the world – and more of them seem to be caused by man. Whether causal responsibility for the mutilation of nature implies that we can speak of harming or benefiting nature, of treating nature justly and unjustly, is one of the themes I shall discuss in this chapter.

Secondly, the reactions to the Kuwait fires illustrate the fact that different people interpret the world differently. Those who stressed the ecological repercussions of the battle, rather than the political, social, or economic consequences, were a minority. On the view that language games are sets of rules for selecting and mixing facts and values concerning the way the world fares and ought to fare, the Greens seem to be playing a different game. (I will use the word 'Green' to denote all variants of the environmentalist and ecologist persuasions.)

This last observation will serve as my point of departure. I am not interested – at least not here – in the question: 'What is to be done, given the ecological crisis?' For the sake of argument I shall suppose that this is a legitimate question with a definite answer. I thus assume that there is an ecological crisis in a malleable world, that this crisis can perhaps be controlled in some way or other, and that we should control it if we can. My question is rather: 'Given a necessary course of action directed towards the environmental crisis, can we defend it in terms of distributive justice?'

Hence I am engaged in the distributive justice language game rather than in the green language game. I am, in particular, interested in the basic questions concerning the theoretical side-constraints of green theories of distributive justice. Unlike most writers on green distributive justice (for example, Wenz

3

1988, Singer 1988, Taliaferro 1988), I will ask whether, and not how, the concept of justice can be applied in green political theory. I shall make no proposals for new principles or theories of distributive justice, and there will be little discussion of the proposals made by green thinkers in this field. I do however intend to follow them in presupposing that we want a green theory of justice to be defensible in the terms of the debate on distributive justice as it has been going on for the last twenty-odd years. The phrase 'in terms of' will be taken in a literal sense to catch hold of some categories essential to the debate: those of distributor, distributed benefits and burdens, and recipient of the distributed resources[2] or goods and what Orwell would call ungoods. I plan to go some way towards discovering which ethical and ontological assumptions about nature are compatible with the categories of distributive justice. In short, my subject is the idea of nature and the nature of distributive justice.

Now why would this be a problem worth discussing? Consider my heuristic device (see Figure 1.1). Ecologism or environmentalism, far from being a unified movement, is a collection of controversies between more and less radical positions at various levels of abstraction. A radical position at one level does not necessarily exclude a more moderate position at another.

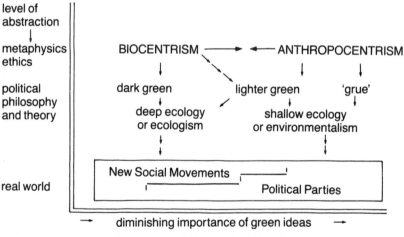

Figure 1.1 Varieties of green thought

Strongly oversimplified, the questions we are dealing with here are those of tensions between new social movements and political parties, tensions between darker and lighter shades of environmental concern, tensions between ecologism in a broad sense and 'grue' political theories, and finally a fundamental conflict between anthropocentrism and biocentrism. Grue, a combination of the words green and blue, stands for theories that used to be thought of as non-green in the days when concern about the environment was not 'in', but which turned green when the tide changed: socialism, conservatism, leftish liberalism, and some variants of Marxism.

What interests us is whether a green language game can generate a political theory. But what is political theory? The simplest definition of politics talks about who gets what, when, and how. Political theory is that and a little more. It is the 'Why?' question about who gets what, when, and how:

Y (who-what-when-how)?

My approach, one of the possible Ys, starts out from within the theory of distributive justice and is directed towards the essentially new part of green movements, that is, not their concern with pacifism, feminism, socialism, anarchism, or sometimes even Luddism – let us call that old news – but with the element of nature and the intrinsic value of nature. I suppose a green political theory would be incomplete and therefore not totally convincing without a satisfactory answer to this Y-question.

In contrast to my talk of justice, the ecologists play a totally different language game. To make the difference clear, let me focus on an ideal type of what, following Arne Naess's terminology, has been called deep ecology. The points deep ecologists stress are also the main issues of the whole green debate. Whether a so-called shallow ecology (aka environmentalism) exists as a school, or whether it is defined only by criticism of deep ecological theories – as in the bad old days, when Marxist critics of True Marxism were by definition bourgeois traitors – is another question.

Deep ecology is not concerned with justice but with nature in relation to man. Man is considered to be a danger to the whole of nature, and ultimately, as part of nature that totally depends on it, also as a danger to mankind – though the deepest ecologists seem to be a trifle less worried about the last aspect. Some, like Rudolf Bahro (Bahro 1980: 87–115, 179–81), blame capitalism, industrialism, consumerism or humanism; others blame egoism or individualism, regardless of the structure of society. Garrett Hardin's 'Tragedy of the Commons' (Baden and Hardin 1977) is of course the best-known and most often quoted source for this approach. All end up with the same conclusion: we are heading for an ecological disaster that can only be prevented if we develop a new way of life, an alternative society and social consciousness, in which individual responsibility and a harmonious relation with the totality of nature are the most important values.

The essential difference between deep and shallow ecology is philosophical. Unlike shallow ecologists, deep ecologists propose a fundamental change of mentality – often described as biocentrism or ecocentrism – away from traditional anthropocentrism. We ought to judge our actions from the point of view of nature as a whole, rather than from the partial position of man, because 'mother Nature knows best', because nature is the first and most important condition of human existence, or – the mainstream position – because nature has intrinsic value. Consequently, deep Greens do, and shallow Greens do not necessarily, defend a radically new society, a kind of Ecotopia.[3]

Greens of all kinds are aware of the need to convince others of the rationality of their proposals, and one of the ways in which they try to do so is by appealing to the idea of distributive justice. But can they? Can green policies be defended as just policies? My answer will amount to a qualified 'yes'.

Seen from the perspective of a scholar of distributive justice, there is no such thing as *the* environmental problem. There are environmental problem*s*, problems of different types, in which the idea of nature has different meanings, and which require that different environmental policies be justified in different ways. It all depends on whether we are dealing with rational, with sentient, or with living and inorganic nature, and on the different roles nature can play in the distributive justice language game: those of distributor, distributed good, and recipient of whatever is distributed. The differentiation I propose does not violate the rule of objectivity in distributive justice that equals be treated equally. I shall argue that there are sound reasons for treating different types of nature differently.

The next section is devoted to the translation of the idea of nature, as it is understood in environmental ethics into terms suitable for discussion within the framework of distributive justice. I will distinguish three types of nature: rational, sentient, and living or inorganic nature. Subsequently I will ask if and how these three types can function as legitimate variables in a metric of distributive justice – that is, if they are compatible with the categories of distributor, distributed resource, and recipient. Finally, in the last section, I shall discuss whether an alternative biocentric approach to distributive justice is possible, and what it takes to justify a green theory of distributive justice.

CONCEPTIONS OF NATURE

'Nature' is a vague and promiscuous term. It fits all sorts of things: those green things outside, or everything that is not man-made, either including or excluding humanity itself, or the essence of things, or even, as in Spinoza's *Ethics*, everything that exists (*Deus sive Natura*). Consequently, 'nature' is also a term with a certain rhetorical value. Politicians can and do often use it to build up credit: being known as a friend of the earth is politically wise, nowadays.

The meaning in which I will use the term 'nature' in this essay is closely related to both Spinoza and deep ecology. Roughly speaking, nature is the interconnected system of all that exists and for its existence depends on everything else – in the vicinity of this planet. The difference from Spinoza is the restriction to earth, which is simply meant to focus attention on ecology rather than on metaphysics. The difference from deep ecology is more important: my nature explicitly includes artefacts like factories, poems, WordPerfect macros, and artificial diamonds, which are only implicitly included in the deep green image of nature. Whether it is, all in all, a more adequate conception than that of the (deep) ecologists is a question I cannot answer here – though I think it makes little sense to talk about the interconnectedness of everything, and everything's dependence on everything else, while at the same time disconnecting artefacts.

In terms of the variables used in theories of distributive justice, nature is conceived of as having three roles. Politicians and ecologists often talk about it as a resource of mankind – that is, as a source of rest and healing, or as a source for economic use, or even, according to Ernest Partridge, as a moral resource: respecting nature for the sake of nature would be a moral act (Partridge 1984: 101). Others think of nature or parts of it as a recipient of distributive justice. Animals, for instance, are supposed to have the need or right not to be hunted and tortured, not to be robbed of their means of existence, or not to be eaten (by humans); ecosystems should not be destroyed or harmed for human- as well as nature-centred reasons; species must be protected against extinction. A third party, the Diggers among the deep ecologists, stress the role of nature as the ultimate distributor, giving and taking life and whatever comes with it: Gaia, the goddess of earth, an idea borrowed from James Lovelock (Lovelock 1979).

It is a broadly if not unanimously accepted axiom in the theory of distributive justice, ever since Aristotle introduced the idea in his *Ethica Nicomachea* (1959: $1134^{b}9$, $1138^{a}11$), that it makes no sense to talk about distributive justice when there is only one party involved: a person cannot be unjust to herself or her possessions, nor can she distribute things 'over' herself – except metaphorically. The same goes for nature. If nature is the distributor, then it cannot distribute itself justly or unjustly to itself. If nature is a recipient, it cannot be distributed. Finally, if nature is a resource, there is no one to distribute it to. So if we want to think about distributive justice with regard to nature, nature must be cut into parts. It does make sense to say that some part of nature distributes another part, justly or unjustly, to a third part.

There is no answer in the structure of theories of distributive justice to the question of how to cut up nature. An answer could come from environmental ethics, where several models are offered.

First, there are theories which deny the possibility of valuing different parts of nature differently. Let us call these theories varieties of the Gaia hypothesis. As they deny Aristotle's axiom, they cannot answer our question and thus, by implication, cannot be defended in terms of distributive justice. Even if we disregard this fact they must be hard to defend at all. They do not have a basis in the considered judgements or practices of most cultures, and therefore lack an intuitive moral justification. It is doubtful whether a contractarian theory in which all of nature decides can defend any other principle than that the lion must lie peacefully next to the lamb; and like problems confront an ideal observer. The remaining possibilities are absolutist: that is, referring to a true view independent of human consent – but to be practical and convince non-believers they still need that consent.

Second, there are theories which differentiate between degrees of nature; theories that, I think, all have their roots in the Greek model of stages of existence with decreasing moral importance: God, demons, mankind,

7

animals, plants and inorganic nature. Differences between these modern theories derive from disagreement about the reasons for the distinctions rather than about the distinctions themselves. In our modern picture of the world the model has been simplified by leaving out all beings higher than man, whereas at the lower levels more precise distinctions (borrowed from biology) are made – for example, between mammals and other higher and lower animals, plants, bacteria, microbes, viruses, water, clay, and so forth (cf. Singer 1988: 224, Wenz 1988). For my argument, three categories will suffice, broadly made up of mankind, animals, and a residual category which I will call living and inorganic nature.

Finally, theories of what is called biodiversity, which are borrowed from ecology, offer alternatives to the Greek model by distinguishing different subsystems of nature: individual (living) beings, biospheres, and ecosystems (cf. Devall and Sessions 1984: 312). Such theories may or may not offer a viable alternative, depending on whether these subsystems can be analysed as, and reduced to, aggregates of the various degrees of existence distinguished by the classic model – as multi-species, multi-degree societies for instance. Though I feel that this is possible, I shall have to leave biodiverse theories aside because I think they are irrelevant to our subject. The arguments I am about to present can, *mutatis mutandis*, be just as easily applied to the categories biodiversity might distinguish.

Instead, I shall hold to my version of the classical view, and defend the view that a green political theory, in order to justify itself in terms of distributive justice, must divide nature into three parts: mankind, or at least rational nature; animals, or non-rational but sentient nature; and non-rational, non-sentient, living and inorganic nature. Because we only discuss nature as Greens generally define it, the category of artefacts will not be explicitly discussed though it is part of inorganic nature.

VARIABLES IN METRICS OF DISTRIBUTIVE JUSTICE

So far we have established that the idea of nature can be translated into terms compatible with the structure of theories of distributive justice. Our next problem is to find out if the debate on distributive justice offers reasons for talking about nature in moral terms, and especially in terms of justice. I will first discuss (more) reasons why nature cannot be understood as a distributor, and why we have to restrict ourselves to conceptions of nature as a resource and nature as a (collection of) recipient(s). Subsequently, the moral importance of the three parts of nature distinguished earlier, and some reasons for holding on to exactly these distinctions, will be considered.

The distributor

Nature as a distributor – Gaia in particular – is not only incompatible with the structure of theories of distributive justice, it is also incompatible with the whole idea of distributive justice in itself. 'Gaianism' is a modern variant of philosophical determinism. It supposes that everything depends in varying degrees on everything else, that all of nature is one whole (hence its (w)holism), that the whole rules itself, and that no part of it is autonomous. Gaianism necessarily leads to one of three courses of action: quietism, totalitarianism, or 'anything goes'.

If Gaia can take care of herself and does not need man's help or co-operation, no action whatsoever is prescribed: anything goes. Gaianism then has little to say about distributive justice, and theorists of distributive justice have little to say about Gaia. The debate on distributive justice asks us what humans should do to justly distribute whatever can and may be distributed – a question irrelevant to Gaia – but has no opinion about the behaviour of gods and goddesses.

If, on the other hand, Gaia depends on the passive support of the human species, and prescribes a life and distribution in accordance with nature – as the stoics called it – then, by implication, it prescribes quietism. If we follow Gaia's rules, all is well; if we do not, Gaia will ultimately know how to heal herself. In this version of Gaianism we cannot authoritatively or autono-mously influence our environment. At best we have a say in what constitutes our private nature – that is, our character, inclinations, preferences, etc.

Finally, if Gaia really depends on the active support of mankind for its maintenance (thus making man partly a distributor), then Gaianism leads to totalitarianism, to the subjection of all human interests to one non-human, external goal: the preservation of nature. We could call this one step beyond the *raison d'état* a *raison de nature*.

There is only one possibility for Gaianism to escape this last charge, and for that reason I introduced Spinoza earlier: it must at the same time distinguish between human (short-term, life-plan) interests and the aspect of eternity, thus allowing human autonomy, and harmonize the eternal and the tem-porary. One way to do so would be to let the *raison de nature* work for the benefit of the members of nature, just as the *raison d'état* of Spinoza and like-minded humanist philosophers was conceived of as working in the interest of the citizens by guaranteeing their peace and security. But that is, I think, a problem lying beyond the scope of this essay. The point to be noted is that whatever solution we may find, it cannot be 'blind' Gaia, it must be 'smart' mankind, which distributes – given the rules of the distributive justice game.

Recipients

This brings us to the problem of the relative moral importance of man, animals, and plants and inorganic nature. Let me start with what looks like an easy question: What makes man a recipient, why are man's interests morally relevant? This question of course presupposes that there is such a thing as moral relevance, and a definite and positive answer to the eternal 'why should I be moral?'[4] Theories of distributive justice generally give two reasons for qualifying man as exclusively or especially worthy of moral treatment. In the first place we can identify ourselves (as subject) with others (as object), and second, we do so because we recognize in them a shared capacity to be moral and have a rational plan of life. Being moral means, among other things, being able to make promises and keep them, and being free to act consciously; having a plan of life means that one can be concerned about what happens to one's resources and to one's life in general.

The implications of this theory for our relation with nature are striking: neither animals, nor plants, let alone inorganic parts of nature, have a plan of life or care for their lives – as far as we know, of course. Consequently, we do not have reasons to assign them rights, nor to believe that their needs, if they have any, matter. Causing an ecological disaster would not be unjust to animals or 'lesser' parts of nature, as no promises are broken and no plans of life disrupted. There would be no injustice except for the harm done to human interests. Causing the death of an individual animal – killing it – would not be any more unjust than its natural death would be. Whether an animal dies from one cause or another, at one time or another, in greater or lesser pain, is of no relevance to it or to us.

The idea of distributive (in)justice towards the rest of nature – which we, in so far as we are Greens, intuitively feel to exist – apparently cannot be built into a green political theory unless we find further sources of identification: that is, other characteristics of man which make humans morally relevant, which they share with other beings, and which can thus make these other beings morally relevant as well.

In environmental ethics, two concepts are proposed as deeper sources of identification: sentience and interaction. Let me start with the last option. Peter Wenz, following others, has argued that the more we interact with parts of nature, the more we make them depend on us and the more we are responsible for them – actually as well as ethically (Wenz 1988: 142). Consequently we would have a duty to treat animals justly.

Although I do feel that the idea of interaction must be part of every serious environmental ethics, it is not directly relevant to our subject, to that part of ethics called distributive justice. Responsibility resulting from interaction does not explain why we feel responsible for an animal as a recipient, a subject, rather than as an object, a means. It tells us more about the quantity of a relationship than about the quality. It we do not take the word interaction to mean what it means in social science – a combination of meaningful actions and meaningful reactions – but understand it only as a one-sided action, then any relationship between a human being and something outside of it (animals as well as paintings or a system of values) creates responsibility, and the more interaction there is, the more responsibility. This will get us nowhere: how much more unjust is it to kill a fox than to destroy the killer's gun? If, on the other hand, we take the word in the traditional sense, then responsibility depends on the meaningfulness of interactions, in which case we have to explain which quality of the other party makes the interaction meaningful – in other words, why interest goes with identification, with recognition of the object as a moral subject.

The concept of sentience as defended by Peter Singer (1976) comes closer to an answer. Singer is convinced that animals, as conscious beings able to experience pleasure and pain, are as relevant as man is to the calculation of happiness, or whatever it is utilitarians calculate. He has a point there: it can hardly be declined that sentience, and especially the cry of pain, the language of immediate needs, is the emotional basis of morality and justice. Yet Singer's theory cannot be accepted as it stands. For one thing, there may be more to life that makes it valuable, even for animals, than pleasure and pain. A more serious objection is that utilitarianism is always a safe bet for philosophically absurd but socially unacceptable dilemmas. Multi-species utilitarianism could well be even more cruel (to individual humans) than classical utilitarianism. It may, for instance, allow the sacrifice of some humans for the temporary (and soon forgotten) happiness of some animals, or the extinction of humanity for the future happiness of all other animals. Intuitively, few people can accept such conclusions, and no ethical theory however sceptical can do without the basic element of intuition in one form or another.

If we reject utilitarianism, perhaps prematurely, for not taking seriously the differences between individuals and between humans and other beings, we will however have to find other reasons for accepting sentience as a source of identification with animals. The easiest way out is probably a compromise with utilitarianism. The conscious experience of pleasure and pain could then be seen as a (one) necessary element in every rational plan of life, an element that is not the whole story of man's moral importance. The rest of the story – morality, rationality, the content of plans of life – still makes humans, to an as yet undefined degree, more important than animals. Nevertheless, according to this compromise, animals can legitimately be called recipients of distributive justice.

In his *Social Justice and the Liberal State*, Bruce Ackerman argues however that a creature can only take part in a society's debate on justice if it can, in principle, speak for itself and give sound and impartial reasons for its claim to a part of the resources (Ackerman 1980: 70–5). Whereas it is true that animals cannot satisfy this condition, humans can speak on their behalf – in any fictional contract situation or in the real world. Any serious theory of social justice allows paternalism on behalf of children and mentally disturbed people. In as far as we can identify ourselves with their interests, we can impartially represent them. So why would it be impossible to do the same for animals – in so far as we understand them?

At this point I should remark that we do not know to what degree we understand animals, and should not be too hasty in declaring that we can represent their points of view. Thomas Nagel reached this same conclusion in his *The View from Nowhere*, based on his tasteless adventures in a university toilet, where he killed a spider while trying to imagine its point of view (Nagel 1986: 208).

11

The more we learn about animals, the more we will – or may – understand them, but for the moment we are working under extreme uncertainty. I am working on the hypothesis that we can understand the physical pain of animals, but even that may be too presumptuous.

Ackerman is certainly right about one thing: whatever we do for animals and non-citizens in general is a voluntary gift, rather than a duty resulting from a reciprocal prior agreement. Reasons to endow benefits and burdens on strangers may be derived from the basic moral notion that we should treat equals equally, but humans are more equal than animals. There are relevant differences that allow us to treat animals differently – in some respects.

What plants share with humans and animals is life – whatever that may be. If we feel that life in itself has any moral importance, then plants should be recipients, in as far as we can influence their life chances. But I do not think that we can, or should, value life in itself.[5] Life is a necessary but not a sufficient condition for being a moral subject or for deserving moral treatment as a subject. A living thing that, unlike a foetus or a patient in coma, has no perspective or chance whatsoever, either in principle or actually, of being anything but living matter differs too much from us to be morally equal in any sense.

Plants, and the same goes for inorganic nature (with which we share nothing but existence), lack the relevant property of subjective consciousness, of consciousness as such. Plants cannot be harmed by, nor benefit from, anything that happens to them – at least not in our ordinary language game. The sun may cause a dandelion to grow, but the dandelion only *metaphorically* benefits from the sunshine; it cannot be aware of sunlight, unlike animals and man, and it cannot freely use it as a resource. In short: neither plants nor inorganic nature can consciously, let alone willingly, receive, and therefore they cannot be recipients.

Resources

Apparently plants and inorganic nature cannot play any part in theories of distributive justice other than as resources. They cannot value or appreciate other resources nor use them for self-defined ends. This implies that we can only approach this part of nature from a teleological standpoint. Ernest Partridge has denied this; he claims that nature, although it can be understood teleologically as a technical, scientific, economical and psychological resource, can and should nevertheless also be seen as a moral resource, valued for its own sake.

That last phrase of course brings to mind Kant's third formulation of the categorical imperative, not to use man only as a means but always at the same time as an end in itself. Partridge argues that we should do the same with regard to nature, but I think his argument fails for two reasons.

In the first place, the reason why Partridge claims that we should love nature for its own sake is that it follows from a self-transcending need to care, which would be an innate part of human psychology. The aspect of self-transcendence has to do, among other things, with our natural tendency to identify the things we personally value with things that would or should be valuable to all, and with the recognition of (personal) survival as a result of co-operation – giving and taking – in society. Caring for nature, according to Partridge, expresses a non-egoistic, self-transcending, concern for others, and in that perspective nature is a moral resource, an opportunity to behave morally (Partridge 1984: 117–22).

Now at best Partridge's associative and obscure reasoning shows that a self-transcending concern for nature is *not* the same as loving nature for nature's sake. Rather, it is loving nature for the sake of fellow-beings, humanity, society, or community – not as an end in itself, but as a resource, a means of survival.

Second, if there is such a thing as loving nature for the sake of nature, it cannot be like loving others for their sake, but rather something like loving art for art's sake. The reason why we love others, according to Kant and the whole of western philosophy since the stoics and long before, is that we recognize ourselves in the other, or to be more specific, we recognize our essence as rational, morally free, and responsible beings with plans, aims, and ends. According to the intuitive ethical rule that like cases should be treated alike, we should love others as ourselves. We cannot do such a thing with works of nature or works of art, as we cannot identify with either one to the same, or even any, extent. Provided there is an essence of art, we can love a piece of art or the making of art because of what it means to us as art, and not as an investment or as a way of being different from others. Perhaps we can do the same with nature – that is, love it as a work of non-human art, if that is the essence of nature.[6] Yet we will always love it because of what it means to us as a resource, not because of what it means to itself. It will always take a human being to turn whatever potential value a piece of nature has into actual value – if I may use these Aristotelian terms.

The point of my story is that to the extent that we can identify with another part of nature, we tend to see it as an end in itself, as a recipient of justice. To the extent that we cannot identify with a thing, it is either a means, a resource, or an obstacle, an ungood. Until we learn otherwise we may suppose that plants and inorganic nature lack all, and animals most, capacities to qualify as recipients.

Grim as all this sounds, it does not imply that nature is something that can just be grabbed and distributed among recipients in proportion to their merit, contribution, needs or rights. From the fact that talents are undeserved it does not follow that society has a right to decide who is to use his or her talents in what way – as Sandel remarked about Rawls's theory of justice; from the fact that a person and his or her labour power are not identical it does not follow that one is free to sell one's labour power, or that the buyer is free to use it at will or to resell it – as G. A. Cohen and other critics of Nozick have observed. From the fact that nature can actually be possessed, it does not follow that we rightfully own it.

13

Of course we cannot avoid using resources or using recipients as means: we have to eat and kill for our food, we have to use the grocer or the butcher to kill for us, we probably cannot have dogs or parents without trying to obtain protection or warmth from them. There is little sense in questioning the justice of the unavoidable – but there is in questioning the contingent. We can legitimately ask if we distribute the benefits and burdens of nature justly among ourselves and other members of our society, other societies, other animals, and, if they matter, future persons or generations. We should also ask whether nature and particular parts of nature can be legitimately distributed *at all* – and why. How this question is to be answered is not important now; what matters is that the question can and must be raised.

CONCLUSIONS AND PERSPECTIVES

In the previous sections I have sketched one line of argument along which it is possible to defend a green political theory in terms of distributive justice. The concept of nature, which I suppose must be a central point of reference for any green political theory, cannot be translated into anything applicable in the theory of distributive justice, unless we divide it to fit the structure of the debate. Sentient animals and humans, we saw, can be recipients of distributive justice, and all of nature can be a resource. Had we not divided nature in Greek but in biodiverse parts – biospheres, ecosystems, etc. – we would have come to the same conclusion: whether and to what degree something is a recipient or not depends on the presence of certain properties only individual humans and some animals have. We have also seen that the partial status of man and animal, and the exclusive status of the rest of nature, as resources does not imply that their distribution is a matter of convenience – quite the contrary.

On the other hand we should also admit that there are conceptions of nature which cannot be used in theories of distributive justice, and consequently that green political theories are imaginable which cannot be defended in terms of distributive justice. This is true of holistic conceptions of nature such as Gaianism, and it is true of theories in which nature is ascribed an intrinsic value.

Holism is completely incompatible with distributive justice, both in theory (as we saw above) and in practice. Though the environmental crisis may demand holistic policies, such policies cannot be defended as one plan, one whole. A sound defence has to differentiate between at least five types of nature: man and animals as recipients, and man, animals and the rest of nature as resources. In terms of distributive justice the use or abuse of each resource and the allocation of goods and ungoods to each individual recipient have to be accounted for. Only then can we do justice to the complexity of justice.

Intrinsic value theories may or may not be compatible with theories of justice, but in either case the hypothesis of intrinsic value is irrelevant.

Distributive justice is based on the needs or rights of recipients – in other words, on what is valuable to humans and animals. I think even a prominent intrinsic value theorist like Wouter Achterberg agrees with me on that point. In his contribution to this book he treats nature technically as a resource by proposing a kind of Zero Principle in addition to Rawls's two principles, roughly prescribing us to leave nature behind in a state no worse than when we found it.

Apart from an argument in favour of green justice, I have brought up, but avoided, a list of philosophical problems, designating them as beyond the scope of this essay. If defending a deep holistic green political theory in terms of distributive justice is impossible, how should deep Greens revise their ethical premises? What have other approaches to distributive justice to say about environmental justice – for instance, which principles should we apply, which existing theories of justice can be applied to environmental problems? Can a green political theory be defended if it analyses nature as a system of subsystems? Is life in itself worth anything? And so on and so forth.

In this last section I shall discuss the implications of some questions beyond the scope of this essay – namely, a way out for biocentric deep ecology, and the justification of green conceptions of justice.

First, let me make it clear that the distributive justice language game is not a decisive test for the ethical standing of a green political theory. Justice is concerned with the problem of no one taking too much of the good things in life, or too little of the unwelcome things. Where there is no giving or taking by morally conscious beings, the concept cannot be applied. The goodness or badness of an earthquake and its effects cannot be assessed in terms of justice (except perhaps by the writers of theodicies) – whereas human policies can be called just or unjust. Furthermore, the Anglo-Saxon debate on social justice is not the only one; there are other language games of distributive justice which I have not discussed, and which may come to other conclusions with regard to green political theory. And finally, the Anglo-Saxon conception of distributive justice is not infallible. Few writers in that tradition would appreciate building cathedrals at the expense of the poor, or subsidizing Rembrandt or Mozart instead of the orphanage, or protecting a beautiful landscape against an expanding city. There is little room in theories of distributive justice for the aesthetic value of life, for the idea of an intrinsic value of nature, and for values and virtues other than justice, like democracy or benevolence – things a perfectionist might want to see included in a conception of justice.

Back to the real world and abstract theories. As I have left out of the discussion all principles of justice, except for the Aristotelian demand to treat like cases alike, I have offered little more than an abstract account of what a green political theory can and cannot assert about nature if it wants to take justice seriously. What exactly a just green policy for the real world would be like was left in the dark.

My conclusions may sound trivial to most green thinkers, green voters, and green activists – and perhaps false, heretical and revisionist to deep ecologists.

But as a theoretical point they are not trivial. They illustrate that it is not only possible to express green concerns, convictions, demands, and considered judgements in the language of distributive justice, but that it is also legitimate.

There are, as we saw, some obstacles to such a legitimate discussion of green distributive justice. The most important one concerns the differences between the types of nature (rational, sentient, living or inorganic) on the one hand, and the dogma of identification on the other.

This dogma has been attacked from two sides, for similar reasons. Common-sense thinkers have argued that identification in itself implies a fully self-centred ethic. The more one can identify with a person or thing, the more moral importance he, she, or it, would have: one's brother is more important than one's neighbour, the latter being more important than one's community, and so on. And of course I am more important than anything else in the universe.

The solution would be to demand that identification be based on impartial characteristics – as, in fact, theorists of distributive justice try to do. But the model then remains anthropocentric: we would agree to attach less importance to animals, because they are less like man, but we could not intuitively accept a restriction of our own rights to the benefit of extraterrestrials, who claim to be better moral persons because of some more-than-human characteristic – not even if we could assess the truth of their claim (cf. Nozick 1974: 45–7). So how impartial are our ethics?

The same point has been raised by the French and Jewish philosopher Emanuel Levinas, who accuses western philosophy of not taking seriously the basic moral intuition of respect for, and recognition of, the Other as other-than-we. Western philosophy has, in his view, always denied the existence of the Other by trying to comprehend (in fact: colonize) her as a copy of the ethical subject's self.

Those critiques are relevant both to the theory of distributive justice and to green political theory: it would open up a way out for deep ecology, which cannot be defended on the basis of regular theories of distributive justice. Deep ecologists are noted for their efforts to replace the anthropocentric view of nature by a biocentric view. Yet I doubt if that attempt can really be successful. A biocentric view will always remain a man-made interpretation or language game of nature. Man decides what nature is and according to which theory it works; man defines what an animal is and what a human (cf. Tester 1991: 194–5); man defines what is good and just, what a problem is, and what a disaster is; and these concepts can make sense to man only. Is it really possible to conceive of nature in terms or concepts which we, and only we, understand, without epistemologically and ethically colonizing it?

Related to the matter of identification, anthropocentrism and biocentrism, is the question of how to justify a green theory of distributive justice. Somewhere human intuitions about justice and ethics are bound to creep in. No one will accept the conclusions of, say, an ideal observer if they absolutely contradict what we sincerely believe and cannot help believing. Nor will they

16

be accepted if they are deduced from a first principle, however plausible or intuitively attractive. Instead we will revise if not reject the first principle.

The most influential method of justification for theories of distributive justice among both green and non-green thinkers is contractual. Various contract situations have been designed, often on the basis of John Rawls's original position, in which identification would guarantee consideration for nature, or at the least for animals. Unfortunately there is a limit to what contracts can justify.

Take, for instance, Brent Singer (1988), Donald VanDeVeer (1979), and Peter Wenz (1988: 247–50). VanDeVeer (defended by Singer) and Wenz have both produced the same revisions of Rawls's original position: they 'thicken the veil of ignorance' by enlarging the uncertainty in the original position.[7] The people in the original position should not only be ignorant about their position in real society, their capacities, power, and character – but they should also be uncertain about whether or not they will turn out to be humans. As they do not like to take chances, they would accept principles that protect animals.

What is wrong with this picture is not that a contract made under such conditions is not valid, because animals cannot keep their promises (let alone make them). Nor will thickening the veil make it too difficult to 'calculate' the interests of the individual participants in the contract. Those are points that can be dealt with. We could, for instance, say that distributive justice – as opposed to commutative justice – does not necessarily presuppose reciprocity. We do not expect anything back from generations in the far future, and the famous or notorious dead do not receive the honour or blame we bestow on them. The other charge can be answered by pointing out that, even if the chance of turning out to be an animal complicates things, the original position does not have to meet a deadline.[8]

What is wrong is that this thickened veil of ignorance stretches the imagination too far. Supposing we find ourselves in the original position, we can imagine ourselves in the position of any human being in the real world,[9] provided that human being is as rational as we are – because otherwise we cannot make plans of life in that human being's place. We cannot imagine what it is like to be irrational or immoral, or even psychotic;[10] we certainly cannot think ourselves into the position of an animal.

What we can do is represent the interests of animals, just as Rawls allows the representation of the interests of children and mentally disturbed adults. There is absolutely no reason why we would not be able to acknowledge that some beings (even some human beings) are less equal to us than others, but still equal enough not to be seen as benefits or burdens only. That perspective is far less fantastic than totally identifying ourselves with whatever beings have something in common with us. After all, justice may be eternal, but human imagination, human intellectual flexibility, is limited. Improbable ideas about what justice towards nature requires are risky, however just they may seem. A viable theory of justice needs a basis in what Rawls called considered

17

judgements as a government needs support – or else it cannot function. As Brian Barry recently said: 'The question is if we *want* to be just. If the price is too high, then probably we won't' (Barry 1991).

SUMMARY

This chapter investigates the concept of nature from the point of view of distributive justice: can it be applied within the context of that language game? Three possible roles are open for nature: that of distributor, distributed benefit or burden, and recipient of whatever is distributed. To assess which roles are relevant, a distinction must be made between qualitatively differing parts of nature – for example, between humans, higher animals, and the rest of nature.

I argue that Nature (as an undivided whole) cannot be a distributor, because – among other things – it is useless to talk about distributive justice when there is only one party involved. Distributive justice only makes sense if man, as a responsible and autonomous being, distributes. Parts of nature can, however, be recipients of justice: man, and to a lesser extent animals. Whereas animals lack most characteristics that qualify man as a morally relevant object in a subject–object relation (such as freedom, morality, or the capacity to have a rational plan of life), the capacity of animals for sentience makes them equal enough to us to be regarded as recipients of justice. Finally, all parts of nature are, to a varying degree, resources (means or obstacles), even if nature can be loved for its own sake (like we love art for art's sake). However, this does not mean that we are free to distribute nature at will: possession and ownership are not the same. My conclusion is that holist ('dark green') environmental policies are indefensible, at least in terms of the modern theory of distributive justice. From that perspective, a green political theory can only be just if it is sophisticated – that is, it differentiates between the parts of nature and their interests and needs, and indicates what legitimizes the prima facie unjustifiable distribution and use of nature.

In the last section I ask whether it is possible to go beyond anthropocentric ethics and still have a viable green theory of distributive justice; and if the most popular method of justification, the contract theory, can sustain green justice.

NOTES

1 Based on a paper given at the ECPR Joint Sessions of Workshops, Workshop on Green Political Theory, University of Essex, Colchester, 22–8 March 1991. I am deeply indebted to Grahame Lock, Masja Nas, and Ellen Hulsebosch, as well as to the participants in this workshop, for their critique of earlier versions of this text and for their willingness to discuss my, often wild, ideas.
2 Though I am unhappy with the concept of resources, especially as it can only be applied in a strict sense to human beings with aims, ends, and plans, I will nevertheless conform to the vast majority of green thinkers in the field of distributive justice and speak only of resources.

3 For more elaborate descriptions of both deep and shallow ecology (ecologism and environmentalism), biocentrism and anthropocentrism, see, for example Andrew Dobson (1990), Ernest Partridge (1984), Bill Devall and George Sessions (1984), and Peter Wenz (1988).

4 For an original but very incomplete defence of moral behaviour, see Peter Wenz (1988: 338). By translating 'why should I be moral?' into 'why should I do what I should do?' – a question quite similar to the child's everlasting 'why?' – Wenz thinks he can avoid dealing with the conflicting claims of rationality (best-for-me) and morality (all-in-all-best). Compare also Paul Lucardie's contribution to this book.

5 Ronald Dworkin (1991) has recently argued for the same point from the slightly different perspective of the autonomous possessor of a life.

6 If, on the other hand, we reject essentialism, loving nature and loving others will be like loving Bambi: what we love in them is what we project on them. But even then I think my argument remains valid, as it depends on the possibility of identification and not on essentialism.

7 In Rawls's theory (Rawls 1972), principles of justice are certified as just, in the first place, if they conform to our 'considered judgements in reflective equilibrium', and in the second place, if they are acceptable in a contract situation (the 'original position') where the people designing the contract should in some respects be omniscient and in others suffer from amnesia. They have complete knowledge of the laws and facts of economy, sociology, politics, etc.; they know there is moderate scarcity; they have or know that they will have a sense of justice; they have emotional ties with the nearest future generations; but they do not have any knowledge of their position in society, their power, capacities, or character. The part they do not know is said to be shrouded by the 'veil of ignorance'. The veil, together with partial omniscience, guarantees an impartial judgement on principles – according to Rawls.

8 Cf. also Singer's perhaps too simple answer to these charges (Singer 1988: 223–6).

9 Though we cannot be or become any of them, unlike some of Rawls's critics have supposed. The people in the original position are not disembodied rational entities, but normal human beings who imagine themselves to be in an abnormal situation.

10 Cf. Singer (1988: 222, n. 12), who remarks that Rawls would object to including the chance of being a psychotic – but he does not ask why.

BIBLIOGRAPHY

Ackerman, B. (1980) *Social Justice in the Liberal State*, New Haven: Yale University Press.

Aristotle (1959) *Ethica Nicomachea*, Oxford: Oxford University Press.

Baden, J. and Hardin, G. (eds) (1977) *Managing the Commons*, San Francisco: W. H. Freeman.

Bahro, R. (1980) *Elemente einer Neuen Politik*, Berlin: Olle & Wolter.

Barry, B. (1991) Untitled paper given at Conference on the Concept of the State in Policy Analysis, The Netherlands Institute for Advanced Study in the Humanities and Social Sciences (NIAS), Wassenaar, January.

Devall, B. and Sessions, G. (1984) 'The development of nature resources and the integrity of nature', *Environmental Ethics* 6(4): 293–322.

Dobson, A. (1990) *Green Political Thought*, London: Unwin Hyman.

Dworkin, R. 'Your right to die', *New York Review of Books* 28(3): 14–17.

Lovelock, J. (1979) *Gaia: A New Look at Life on Earth*, Oxford: Oxford University Press.

Nagel, T. (1986) *The View from Nowhere*, Oxford: Oxford University Press.

Nozick, R. (1974) *Anarchy, State, and Utopia*, New York: Basic Books.

Partridge, E. (1984) 'Nature as a moral resource', *Environmental Ethics* 6(2): 101–30.

Rawls, J. (1972) *A Theory of Justice*, Oxford: Oxford University Press.

Singer, B. (1988) 'An extension of Rawls' theory of justice to environmental ethics', *Environmental Ethics* 10(3): 217–31.

Singer, P. (1976) *Animal Liberation*, London: Jonathan Cape.

Taliaferro, C. (1988) 'The environmental ethics of an ideal observer', *Environmental Ethics* 10(3): 233–50.

Tester, K. (1991) *Animals and Society*, London: Routledge.

VanDeVeer, D. (1979) 'Of beasts, persons, and the original position', *The Monist* 64(3): 368–77.

Wenz, P. (1988) *Environmental Justice*, Albany, N.Y.: State University of New York Press.

2

WHY WOULD EGOCENTRISTS BECOME ECOCENTRISTS?

On individualism and holism in green political theory

Paul Lucardie

> Here is a difficult ridge to walk: to the left we have the ocean of organic and mystic views, to the right the abyss of atomic individualism.
>
> Arne Naess,
> *Ecology, Community and Lifestyle: Outline of an Ecosophy*

INTRODUCTION

Individualism has penetrated practically all sections of western society, institutions, ideologies and practices. Local communities, classes, churches, families and other collective bodies have lost much of their normative binding force and social significance; so have collectivist ideologies such as socialism (Marxist as well as non-Marxist) or Fascism. Not only in Western and Southern Europe but even in China, Albania and Russia the masses are dying (sometimes literally) to become individualistic consumers and competitive producers on a market rather than class-conscious members of workers' co-operatives or agents of a socialist state. In most western societies trade-unions, churches and political parties tend to lose members and to shift their activities from collective rituals and celebrations to representation of individual interests, counselling and promotion of individual careers. Social scientists tend to follow suit and explain social behaviour in terms of rational choice by individuals rather than social norms or class interest. In ethics, individualism can take different forms: Kantian deontology, rights theories or utilitarianism. Everywhere, however, the supreme value of the individual is recognized. Even if extreme individualism may be criticized at times and the importance of social bonds admitted, attempts to subordinate the individual to a collective entity are condemned almost universally (Dumont 1983, Ketcham 1987, Lemaire and Van de Meulebroeke 1986).

Almost: while the old enemies of individualism suffer defeat upon defeat, in the Arabian desert as well as on Red Square, a new enemy rises in shining green armour to challenge the victor. Ecologism, especially in its 'dark-green', biocentric or ecocentric variety, implies subordination of mankind as a whole to the Community of Life, Earth (Gaia) or the ecosystem: so *a fortiori* it implies subordination of the human individual, one might infer.

However, at a closer look many green thinkers turn out to be half-hearted and inconsistent in their defence of holism. In fact, individualism seems to have already penetrated the armour of its new challenger. Though there are whole-hearted holists, of course, such as Holmes Rolston and J. Baird Callicott, even the father of deep ecology, Arne Naess, tries to reconcile individualism and ecologism through the concept of the 'Ecological Self'. Val and Richard Routley claim to transcend individualism and holism. Paul Taylor advocates a biocentric outlook that does not entail holism but respect for each individual organism in the world.

This ambivalence can be observed within green parties as well. Manon Maren-Grisenbach, a former president and ideologist of the *Grünen*, admits this quite clearly: 'We, Greens, experience this dilemma among ourselves, almost at every meeting: either my Ego in self-realization or . . . the community, a unity without boundaries. Either or. Yet we want both'[1] (Maren-Grisenbach 1982: 74). Within the small Dutch Green party (not the Green Left, but the 'dark green' *Groenen*) individualism has been defended by Evert Voogd whereas party leader Roel van Duijn argues for holism (Voogd 1990, Van Duijn 1984: 101–10).

In this chapter I would like to discuss the individualist as well as the holist varieties of (dark) green political theory. In order to limit the size of the chapter, I will try to isolate the holist–individualist debate from other issues as much as possible, without neglecting the ecological context of the debate. First I will look at the 'pure' holist case, as presented by Rolston and Callicott. In the second part of the chapter the biocentric individualism of Taylor will be dealt with. In the third part, attempts to avoid the two extreme positions will be discussed.

ECOLOGICAL HOLISM

Arguments in favour of ecological holism can be divided into three categories: ontological, psychological and ecological in the strict sense.

Ontological arguments for holism tend to be variations on the classical theme 'the whole is more than the sum of its parts'. J. Baird Callicott sums it up simply: 'the nature of the part is determined by its relationship to the whole' (Callicott 1989: 111). Individual organisms are determined by their ecological relationships; if they do not adapt to the environment or ecosystem they will die. But all things depend in a more fundamental physical sense on the 'flow of energy' in the world. Thus he quotes Morowitz, a biophysicist: 'the reality of individuals is problematic, because they do not exist per se but only as local perturbations in this universal energy flow' (Callicott, 1989: 108). The individual mind, as well as the individual body, depends on energy.

There is no room for Cartesian dualism here: 'human consciousness, including abstract rational thought, is an extension of the environment, just as the environment becomes fully actual, in the mind–body unity of the New Physics, only as it interacts with consciousness' (Callicott 1989: 113).

This metaphysical interpretation of physics may sound mystical, but Callicott rejects the oriental mystical view that all things are illusory manifestations of one undifferentiated Spirit, God or Brahman. Even so, he concludes that 'the world is, indeed, one's extended body'; and at one occasion he felt 'in a flash of self-discovery, that the river [Mississippi] was a part of me' (Callicott 1989: 113–14).

Callicott is not the only ecological holist to make this kind of argument. Holmes Rolston III also refers to the New Physics to prop up his holistic ethics: 'the evolving mind is also controlled by the matter it seeks to investigate' (Rolston 1986: 98). As the self has a 'semipermeable membrane', it cannot exclude itself from the natural objects it tries to observe as well as evaluate: both subject and object are part of a 'natural field'. In more personal and poetic terms, Rolston felt 'I am the sentient offspring of this rock' (1986: 233) and 'The waters of North Inlet are part of my circulatory system' (1986: 224).

Arne Naess expresses similar ideas in his 'ecosophy': all properties of objects are interdependent and related to our conception of the world; hence also 'our egos are fragments – not isolatable parts' (Naess 1989: 173). John Seed, an Australian activist and supporter of deep ecology, used more concrete terms:

'I am protecting the rain forest' develops into 'I am part of the rain forest protecting myself'. I am that part of the rain forest recently emerged into thinking. The thousands of years of separation are over and we begin to recall our true nature.

(Seed 1985: 243)

The terms 'separation' and 'true nature' betray a mystical way of thinking, which may go back to the Perennial Philosophy of antiquity: at some point we were all One, undifferentiated and unconscious, then mankind broke away from the One and started thinking; now at last we are One again, but consciously (Happold 1964: 18–45). Actually, a nature-mystic like Richard Jefferies who wrote 'I spoke in my soul to the earth', did not even feel as close to nature as Seed, Rolston and Callicott seem to have done (Happold 1964: 355). The way the latter overcome 'thousands of years of separation' in a sudden flash of insight seems almost too easy to convince a sceptical reader. No wonder many philosophers reject this way of thinking right away as irrational nonsense. However, the off-hand rejection of mysticism seems itself a trifle irrational. In fact, as Frits Staal has shown, mystical doctrines resemble science in their structure and are quite compatible with rationality (Staal 1975: 60–3; see also Zimmerman 1988). The differences between mysticism and science concern their assumptions and methods.

The main weakness of the ontological argument for holism may lie neither in its mystical connotations nor in its – sometimes dubious – reference to modern science, but in mixing these elements with ethical statements. They belong to different perspectives that in my opinion are all legitimate but should not be confused:

1 The 'spectator' or objectivist view of the world as object of investigation, to be observed, analysed and explained from a distance – as also New Physicists and ecologists try to do; thus the scientists may investigate even their own atoms, bodies and minds as distant objects.
2 The 'participant' or intersubjective perspective – we belong to the world like other participants and we interact and communicate with them on (more or less) equal terms, according to ethical or social norms.
3 The 'expressive' or subjectivist perspective, when I experience the world as a reflection of my subjective feelings, of my fear, love, sorrow or aggression.
4 The 'mystical', 'transcendent' or 'transsubjective' view of the world as the creation, incarnation or illusory appearance of a transcendent subject (God or Being, Spirit, Buddha-nature, *Gottheit*, World-soul) of which we are but alienated parts.

With Habermas (1982: 299–331) I tend to associate moral or ethical discourse with the intersubjective (participant) perspective. Of course, what we see as 'objective' spectators may inform our ethical discourse as participants. Moreover, Habermas would emphasize the intersubjective aspects of the objective and subjective perspectives too: both require the use of language, for one thing. Social values cannot be separated completely from observed facts. Yet they should not become indistinguishable, as Rolston seems to suggest with his statement: 'Subjectivity has eaten up everything, even the fact/value distinction' (Rolston 1986: 94). Hume's admonition that one cannot derive an 'Ought' from an 'Is' has not lost all validity, it seems to me.

Callicott seems to agree; at least he tries to conform to Hume's teaching. To his empirical premise: 'the natural environment is a community or society to which we belong', he adds an ethical premise: 'we all generally have a positive attitude toward the community or society to which we belong'; then the conclusion follows: 'we ought to preserve the integrity, stability and beauty of the biotic community' (Callicott 1989: 127). Even so he does not avoid the Is/Ought fallacy altogether, as has been pointed out also by Edward Johnson (1984: 352–4). Callicott's presumed ethical premise sounds more like a descriptive statement. Even if I have a positive attitude towards my community, I may not be convinced that this should be the case. If my community happens to be a Mafia family or a neo-Nazi party, perhaps I ought to change my positive attitude.

However, for the sake of the argument, let us grant Callicott his two premises. Does the conclusion follow logically? Why would a positive attitude towards a community entail preservation of stability or beauty? A community may exist very well without stability, as Andrew Brennan (1988: 92–156) has argued. Beauty seems an equally problematic quality, especially when we speak about a community. It may be easy to sing about 'America the beautiful', but impossible to reach an intersubjective consensus about the exact criteria of a beautiful country. If we reduce Callicott's argument to its bare essentials, he says that if one has a positive attitude towards one's community, one ought to preserve its integrity. This seems a plausible, but almost tautological argument; without integrity, a community will (by definition) disintegrate.

If we regard our planet or biosphere as one (mega) community, it seems self-evident that we should try to preserve its integrity – unless we have been convinced that the world is sinful beyond redemption and should be destroyed, of course. We tend to leave this final judgement to a transcendent subject, however, as self-interest may prevent us from passing an impartial judgement here.

Ecological holists often refer to self-interest, but widen its meaning to include spiritual or aesthetic satisfaction, self-realization and quality of life. This kind of argument, psychological rather than ontological, runs as follows: 'atomistic' and anthropocentric individuals are alienated from nature (and from each other, in so far as human beings belong to nature, too); they would lead more satisfying lives if they would feel part of nature – the Community of Life, Gaia, or more modestly, their bioregion. The psychological argument is especially popular with deep ecologists (Naess 1989: 29, 90, 177–82; Devall and Sessions 1985: 7, 110), but crops up occasionally in the writings of Rolston (1986: 133, 226) and Callicott (1989: 113) as well.

The validity of these psychological and other prudential arguments depends on empirical evidence more than on logical reasoning. However, two comments can be made a priori. In the first place, psychological arguments appeal to individuals, by definition. They presuppose that the individual can freely choose between a (more satisfying) life in agreement with nature or a (less satisfying) life in opposition to it. Moreover, they imply that the individual has the right to make this choice. Thus they seem hardly compatible with a 'strong' holism – which conceives of 'wholes' as organisms in which the parts lack autonomy. They may fit in with a 'weak' holism which conceives of wholes as communities of autonomous but interdependent individuals (see Katz 1985).

In the second place, even without much research one can observe that human beings differ widely in psychological habits, needs, and so on. Hence it seems unlikely – though not impossible – that everyone will feel deeply satisfied with a *friluftsliv* or 'life in nature' as advocated by Naess and other deep ecologists. This point will be discussed further, however (see pp. 30–1).

A third type of argument in favour of holism is ecological in the strict sense. In essence, it implies prudential, if not instrumentalist, ethics: if we want to save our environment we should become holists. As long as we remain individualists, we will continue to drive cars, clear rain forests, reduce the ozone layer and exhaust energy supplies. In the long run, our individualistic

25

behaviour may hurt human interests; but in the long run, we are all dead anyway. If we do not have children, why worry about posterity? To the green theorists who use this kind of argument – Williams Ophuls (1976: 226), Mark Sagoff (1988: 169–70) or C. A. Hooker (1983), for example – one might object that they confuse individualism with (ethical) egoism. An ethical individualist should grant future individuals equal rights to energy supplies, rain forests, clean air and so forth.

But what about the last human being on earth? In this (hopefully) rather hypothetical case, the anthropocentric individualist might cut the last tree on earth for his pleasure. Robinson Crusoe could have set fire to his island before leaving it, as a farewell celebration – but somehow we all feel he should not, Mary Midgley (1983: 166–81) argues. Intuitively, Crusoe might have been a holist, because he left his island in peace. Alternatively, he might have been a biocentric individualist, an animal-rights individualist or an agnostic anthropocentrist. In other words, apart from ecological holism there are other ways of advocating non-interference for islands and other ecosystems: respect for animals and plants, or uncertainty about the (side) effects of interference on human interests. Even Callicott admits other (plausible) non-holistic arguments for the intrinsic value of non-human species (Callicott 1989: 129–55).

To conclude, ecological holism has been defended on ontological, psychological or ecological grounds. The arguments may not compel us to accept a strong form of holism, but at best a weak form. We may be convinced that we should try to preserve the integrity of the 'biotic community' to which we belong. Ecological ethics need not be holistic, however.

ECOLOGICAL INDIVIDUALISM

Ecological individualism may be a confusing label, as it does not refer to one particular school of thought but might include at least three: (a) anthropocentric ecologists; (b) animal rights theorists or 'extensionists', who want to extend (individual) human rights or utilitarian ethics from human beings to all sentient beings or at least to mammals; (c) biocentric ecologists such as Paul Taylor. As this chapter deals only with 'dark green' theories, that is, ecocentric and biocentric ecologism, (a) and (b) will be neglected here.

Taylor agrees with ecological holists that, 'like all other living things on our planet, one's very existence depends on the fundamental soundness and integrity of the biological system of nature' (Taylor 1986: 44). Yet he refuses to derive an Ought from this Is. Moreover, he asserts that 'a population has no good of its own', and 'the good of a biotic community can only be realized in the good lives of its individual members': it is merely meaningful as a statistical concept (Taylor 1986: 69–70). This is a classical criticism of any form of holism; but in my eyes not a very convincing one. If a human community – for example, a corporation – can grow, prosper and fail, why could it not have a good? Even as a statistical concept, the good of a community might be different from the sum of the good lives of its members. Derek Parfit – not necessarily a holist – makes this clear in his Repugnant Conclusion (Parfit 1984: 349–442). In scenario A the population of this planet grows in the near future to the upper limits of the carrying capacity of the biosphere, thus reducing the quality of each individual life to a bare minimum – people are not unhappy enough to commit suicide, but very close to it. In scenario B, the population is ten times smaller, but the quality of their lives five times higher (and the environment probably also in a better state, but Parfit remains anthropocentric here). For a strict individualist, especially an act-utilitarian, scenario A may be repugnant but rationally preferable to B, as the sum of happiness in A doubles that of B. Preference for B could be justified, it seems to me, only if we refrain from adding up individual happiness but define the good of human society as the average happiness of its members. Thus we define the good of a community in statistical terms, but accept the holistic principle that the whole (good/happiness) is more than the sum of its parts.[2]

Having rejected holism, Taylor then develops a biocentric ethics based on respect for every member of the Community of Life: 'each is a unique individual pursuing its own good in its own way', hence each creature has 'inherent worth' equal to others (Taylor 1986: 100). Diamonds and computers may be more useful to human beings than gnats or rats, but the latter are pursuing their own good whereas the former are not. If we are impartial, as any ethics requires, we have to accept that we are not inherently more worthy than other living beings. If our interests clash with those of other creatures we should have recourse to five priority principles: the right to self-defence; proportionality (vital needs or basic interests of one species take precedence over non-vital needs of other species, including human beings); distributive justice (equal shares for all, if basic interests compete); minimum wrong; restitutive justice (compensation of damage).

In theory, this list of principles seems sound and reasonable. In practice, I suspect it will not work. This harsh judgement requires empirical testing, of course, but even Taylor's efforts to operationalize his principles lead to ambiguities and inconsistencies. For example, he would allow the construction of a highway through a natural forest even if it does not serve vital human interests – as it rarely does: one can almost always drive around a forest using existing roads of poorer quality – and would destroy the lives of many plants and animals, obviously (Taylor 1986: 256–313). A strict interpretation of his principles may be too unpleasant for the human species. It may also imply absurd conclusions. For example, starving Indians or Brazilians might be allowed to cut the last trees in their country to grow food – thus ruining their own ecosystem – whereas wealthy Canadians would be forbidden to clear a small part of their immense forests to build summer cottages. And what about the vital needs of mosquitoes, rats, bacteria, cockroaches and other 'pests'? Am I allowed to swat a mosquito in my bedroom as a form of self-defence, even though a few mosquito bites will never kill me? It may be unfair to confront Taylor with all these practical questions which are difficult to answer for any ethical theorist, but I tend to agree with critics like Brennan, Johnson and Norton that there are too many unresolved questions here (Brennan 1988: 146, 188–91; Johnson 1984: 346–9; Norton 1987).

Taylor's theory might become more practical if he were to drop the axiom about equal inherent worth of all living things, or at least weaken it by adopting an agnostic view. At some point he comes close to this – for example, when he restates the axiom as 'humans are not inherently superior to other living things' (Taylor 1986: 100) – yet at other moments he claims 'we are ready to place the same value on their [other living beings] existence as we do on our own' (ibid. 1986: 128). His effort to distinguish between 'inherent worth' as a more or less objective or absolute quality on the one hand and intrinsic or inherent value as relative to subjective (human) experience and evaluation seems useful but not quite clear enough. It should be clarified what perspective is employed here: the 'objective' one of the spectator or the 'inter-subjective' one of the participant. As a spectator I can observe that all organisms pursue an 'inherent' purpose (not an extrinsic one, imposed from outside as in the case of machines) and I may interpret this as 'worthwhile' – for them, not necessarily for me. As a participant in a rational discussion, I could try to achieve consensus about the inherent value of each organism and the way conflicts between their purposes should be settled. This procedure has been advocated by Habermas (1982). One might object that Habermas is an anthropocentrist; how can we communicate with other participants in nature? At best, we could exchange growls and miaows with our pets – hardly a rational ethical discourse. Nevertheless, we could extend the notion of communication to include non-verbal expressions of sympathy, protest and resignation. We can observe, at least to some extent, that animals suffer. In some cases we communicate more easily with animals than with human beings – if the latter are unborn babies, completely paralysed patients, or speakers of a foreign language. Some (very dark) greens even communicate with trees – for example Roel van Duijn (1988: 50). This kind of communication will remain weak and often inconclusive; as a result our partners (babies as well as animals) will not enjoy equal rights, but at least some (minimal) rights.

This attitude seems incompatible with 'strong' individualism, which denies not only any ultimate values outside the individual but also any (inter)dependence of the individual on communication. Hence Habermas (1982: 141–7) rejects individualism, at least in its stronger forms. Weaker forms of individualism may be more in tune with respect for nature. One might think of Nancy Chodorow's 'relational individualism' (Chodorow 1986: 197–207) or alternatively of Parfit's radical reductionism.

Parfit questions the indivisibility of individuals on ontological as well as psychological grounds. 'A person is like a nation. . . . The existence of a person, during any period, just consists in the existence of his brain and body, and the thinking of his thoughts, and the doing of his deeds' (Parfit 1984: 275). Inspired by Buddhist ideas, Sigmund Kvaloy (1990: 1–25) makes a similar argument. From a biological viewpoint, too, individual organisms can be analysed as ecosystems, and the other way around – as Wouter Achterberg (1986: 182–8) points out. Therefore, the difference between holism and individualism – or better: 'dividualism' – may be relative rather than absolute.

Nevertheless, there are moral dilemmas where one has to choose between the two. The choice is especially difficult when communication between the concerned (in)dividuals is impossible – or when we have not yet learned how to communicate. Neither Taylor nor Habermas can help us to solve conflicts between our (non-vital) interests and vital interests of bacteria. In that case, ecological holism may be more helpful – by assessing the functions of both bacteria and human beings in the ecosystem, for instance. But what if the bacteria appear more useful to the system than the human beings? Can we avoid the dilemma?

BEYOND INDIVIDUALISM AND HOLISM?

Three ways have been suggested to avoid the dilemma of holism versus individualism: constructing a third position; negating the dilemma, opting for both; or negotiating a compromise between the two. All three routes have been taken by ecologists: the first one by the Routleys, the second one by Naess, the third one by Brennan.

Non-reductionism or *tertium datur*?

Val and Richard Routley reject both holism and individualism – which they call 'partism' (Routley and Routley 1980: 217–332). Both are forms of reductionism in their eyes: the former reduces all entities to wholes while the latter reduces wholes to parts. They associate 'partism' with empiricism but also with capitalism, whereas holism stands for collectivism or Marxism in the social and political sphere. Both tend to neglect the environment; the 'partists' lay all responsibility on the individual and castigate his selfishness, the holists rely only on the state. Both, however, strive for economic growth, large-scale organizations and mass consumption.

A third position is possible and desirable, the Routleys argue: nonreductionism. Individuals are real and autonomous but also social, environmental and interdependent beings. Internal relations between things cannot be observed empirically, yet are important – *vide* quantum theory and relativity theory. In the political and social sphere, anarchists like Kropotkin and Bakunin have developed an alternative to both capitalism and (state) socialism: a federal system of co-operating and self-managed collectives. Decentralization and social control would reduce waste and pollution. Production will be attuned to needs through consultation between producers and consumers. Exchange will be based on labour time, rather than on a market of supply and demand.

One difficulty with this ambitious package deal is, of course, that one cannot take one part of it and leave the rest. Yet parts of the project seem rather questionable. For one thing, the Routleys have attacked simplistic abstractions rather than real currents of thought. Their non-reductionist alternative looks realistic in comparison to these men of straw, but may obfuscate the real dilemma. Of course, individuals are social beings, as only libertarian diehards would deny; co-operation is as human as competition. Yet even social individuals may have to decide at some point between their individual good and the common good. When the chips are down, social anarchists should give priority to the common good, it seems to me. Without social control, anarchism or federalism will never work – even with social control it may not work all that well. If this interpretation is correct, the Routleys leave us with a fairly attractive sketch of Utopia, but not a way out of the holism/individualism dilemma.

In a similar vein, one could criticize Alan Carter's 'interrelationism', which is also presented as an alternative to both individualism and holism or collectivism (Carter 1990). In his view, a society consists of relations, rather than isolated individuals. Isolated individuals do not exist, nor do supra-individual institutions. A nation – and presumably also an ecosystem – is no more than a pattern of relations between individuals. This point of view seems quite sensible to me, but not substantially different from what I have already described as 'relational individualism' or 'weak individualism'.

Deep ecology and the ecological self

Arne Naess defines deep ecology as an approach 'characterized by our deep relationship with the environment and a joyful acceptance of this relationship. It is taken for granted that the self is basically ecological' (Naess 1990: 131). Bill Devall and George Sessions state that 'the foundations of deep ecology are the basic intuitions and experiencing of ourselves and Nature which comprise ecological consciousness' (Devall and Sessions 1985: 65).

If we identify with Nature to such a degree that we consider it part of our Self, protection of our natural environment coincides with our self-interest. (In fact, even the term 'environment' loses its meaning in that case.) Thus Devall concludes correctly:

> As we discover our ecological self we will joyfully defend and interact with that with which we identify; and instead of imposing environmental ethics on people, we will naturally respect, love, honor and protect that which is of our self.
>
> (Devall 1990: 43)

This would solve the fundamental moral question: why bother about the environment? Or to be more specific: why would rational individuals (without children) sacrifice the use of a car, a daily bath, meat, ski-ing in the Alps, colour television, aerosol and so many other polluting luxuries which they

PAUL LUCARDIE

enjoy? In most cases it is not in their own immediate interest to renounce these pleasures – except in return for praise of significant others, or to avoid unpleasant sanctions such as fines or additional (ecological) taxes. Hence their individual freedom would have to be restricted – whether by social control, ethical norms or environmental policies. Deep ecologists, however, need not restrict their individual freedom, as their individual identity has been broadened to incorporate the whole earth.

One might wonder what remains of individual identity, however, if the world is our body. Deep ecologists are aware of the problem. 'How can the individual self maintain and increase its uniqueness while also being an insep-arable aspect of the whole system wherein there are no sharp breaks between self and the other', Devall and Sessions (1985: 65) ask themselves. Arne Naess points out 'a difficult ridge to walk: to the left we have the ocean of organic and mystic views, to the right the abyss of atomic individualism' (Naess 1989: 165).

Perhaps Kvaloy's notion of 'multiple personalities' will help us to walk the ridge. The Ecological Self is one of many selves; Kvaloy admits he also has a different, urban and consumption-oriented personality (Kvaloy 1990: 19–22). In some individuals the Ecological Self may be conscious and strong, in others weak or non-existent. This notion of multiple selves chimes in with the 'dividualist' and reductionist critique of individualism discussed previously. If a person is like a nation, as Parfit argues, a nation or an ecosystem can be seen as a person. Hence holism and (in)dividualism are reconciled, being but different ways of looking at the same reality.

Though plausible, the conception of Kvaloy may weaken the coherence of deep ecology. If Devall and Sessions try to convince us 'that humans have a vital need to cultivate ecological consciousness and that this need is related to the needs of the planet' (Devall and Sessions 1985: 8), one could answer: 'I don't feel that need at all, let alone the needs of my planet.' In the end, deep ecologists rely – like other ecocentrists – on psychological arguments, as Warwick Fox (1990: 246–7) admits. Their perspective is neither objectivist nor intersubjectivist, but either subjectivist or transcendent – 'transpersonal', in Fox's terms. Rather than convince us through logic and morals, they try to convert us through their example and experience.

So deep ecology might be restricted to certain groups in society, more sensitive or saintly than others perhaps, who share the mystical experience of identification with Nature. Other people still need environmental ethics, if not ecological taxes and fines, to change their anthropocentric wasteful behaviour. If deep ecologists forget this, they might be tempted to force their self-realization on others and end up imposing an 'eco-Fascist' dictatorship on the less ecologically conscious masses. So far, however, most of them seem to be much too humane and non-violent to even consider this.

31

Towards a compromise? Brennan's 'ethical holism'

If there is no third way beyond individualism and holism and the two can be reconciled only sometimes by some people, one might look for a simple compromise between the two. Brennan's 'ecological humanism' or 'ethical holism' seems an interesting example of such a compromise (Brennan 1988).

In his eyes, all things can be described both as individual objects and as (functional) parts of a system or environment. Brennan distinguishes essential or basic properties and supervenient properties. The former are intrinsic to individuals, the latter depend on the environment. Populations have supervenient properties, too, within an ecosystem. Ecosystems may heighten the individuality of organisms, but they cannot be regarded as individuals as they lack a purpose or a good of their own. Yet our self reflects to some extent our environment and 'our alienation from nature is also a kind of alienation from ourselves, a failure to recognise ourselves in our real location in the world' (Brennan 1988: 195). Thus ecosystems – 'the home in which life is set' – deserve our respect, and so do individuals. Yet Brennan rejects ideas about inherent value or worth of non-human nature.

His arguments remain eclectic – as he admits – and lack a coherent framework; but this need not detract from their plausibility. Holism and individualism are ways to look at the world; they are ontological or methodological constructions, rather than metaphysical theories. Hence they do not necessarily exclude each other. However, ethical discourse requires (reasonable) choices, rather than constructions. When faced with the choice, Brennan takes up ethical holism – a form of 'weak holism', as previously discussed (see pp. 24–6). The justification of his preference remains a little weak too, perhaps – 'muddling through' according to Rolston (1989).[3] Ethical (intersubjectivist) and psychological (subjectivist) arguments are not always distinguished clearly.

CONCLUSIONS

The question of holism versus individualism in green political theory can be addressed from four different perspectives.

First, from a spectator's point of view, holism and individualism are two conceptual models or levels of explanation, both of which have heuristic value. Thus, even individuals can be described and explained as systems – 'dividuals', multiple personalities. In an ontological sense, both extreme individualism ('atomism') and extreme holism ('organicism') seem exaggerated simplifications, however. Individuals are social and environmental beings, interdependent and interrelated but relatively autonomous. Ecosystems can be seen as communities, but rarely as organisms. Excluding the simplified extremes, we are left with two viable options: 'weak holism' and relational or 'weak' individualism.

Second, the ontological argument has only limited relevance to the moral dilemma of the individual good versus the common good. An ecosystem may be more than the sum of its parts but need not be a moral community. In the course of history, our moral community has expanded from family or tribe to city-state and nation, from nation to 'united nations' and the human race. This process – analysed as 'moral development' at the individual level by psychologists such as Piaget and Kohlberg – is still unfinished at present (Lucardie 1990: 57–73). Racism, sexism and nationalism have not yet disappeared from the earth, as we all know. Hence it seems a little premature to expect the expansion of our moral community into the animal kingdom, let alone the whole planet, in the near future. Nevertheless, in the long run such an expansion seems possible as well as desirable, in my opinion. Even today, some people communicate more adequately with their pet animals than with their neighbours. Lacking a common language in the formal sense, one uses gestures and non-verbal sounds; perhaps even telepathy. With wild animals communication is more difficult, but not impossible either – otherwise they could not have been domesticated or tamed (see also Ted Benton's contribution to this volume). As Barbara Noske argues quite convincingly, we should approach the animal not as a machine nor as a disabled human being, but in the way anthropologists approach an alien tribe, learning its language rather than trying to impose ours (Noske 1992: 203–17). Human beings have been adopted by animals – apes, but also wolves and gazelle – and learned their language quite effectively. Particularly sensitive people claim to communicate even with plants. One day, therefore, we may become individual members of a moral Community of Life and treat all living beings with equal respect.

At present, however, we cannot grant equal rights to all living beings, it seems to me, but only (hardly, in fact!) to all human beings. Non-human beings should enjoy minimal rights, however, in so far as we can communicate with them (verbally or non-verbally). If communication fails, we have to adopt an objectivist approach and consider the functional value of a species in the ecosystem. In the end, we should preserve the integrity of our ecosystems if only for prudential ecological and anthropocentric reasons: we depend on them, as they depend on us (to some extent). Therefore, we end up with a pragmatic compromise between communicative (in)dividualism and prudential holism in our ethical discourse – not very different from what Callicott suggests in one of his more moderate essays (Callicott 1989: 45–59).

Third, from the subjectivist perspective, the question of holism versus individualism is contingent on the experience and mood of the individual at a particular moment. Hiking in the Rockies I might feel one with the mountains; back home in my urban apartment I might feel alienated again as an individualist. Holistic cosmological theories or beliefs may help me develop a more permanent ecological consciousness, as Warwick Fox (1990: 249–58) has argued. In the end, however, ecological consciousness requires a religious or (at least) a transpersonal perspective.

Finally, in transcendent or transpersonal experience, individualism gives way to holism, one might expect. In the *unio mystica*, however, the distinction between individual and whole disappears. Deep or transpersonal ecologists, who identify their Ecological Self with Gaia, the Community of Life, or at least their bioregion, follow the path of the mystics. For ecological as well as psychological reasons their example should be followed widely. Yet their moral arguments are weak, if not irrelevant; in principle, deep ecologists shun moral arguments altogether and refer only to the interest of the Ecological Self. In their case, egocentrists are by definition ecocentrists. For the egocentric agnostics and sceptics who have not yet attained this state of consciousness, however, ecocentrism is not a tautology but at best an evasive end of a long evolutionary process.

NOTES

1 Translated from the German: 'Wir Grünen erleben mitten durch uns hindurch, fast in jeder Versammlung, diese Zwickmühle: entweder mein Ich in der Selbstverwirklichung oder die anderen mit mir in der Gemeinschaft gleichberechtigt in einer Einheit ohne Schranken. Entweder das eine oder das andere. Wir aber möchten beides' (Manon Maren-Grisenbach 1982: 74).
2 As Parfit (1984) shows in Chapter 18 of his book, this Average Principle leads to absurd conclusions, too; here I am not trying to defend the principle itself, however, but only its logical possibility. For simplicity's sake, I also ignore here another problem pointed out by Parfit: the identity of future generations is affected by our choice; this makes individualistic approaches to environmental ethics impossible, according to Bryan Norton (1982).
3 Rolston (1989) characterizes Brennan's study as 'muddling through' and lacking conceptual clarity; see his review in *Environmental Ethics*, 11(3): 259–67.

BIBLIOGRAPHY

Achterberg, W. (1986) *Partners in de natuur: een onderzoek naar de aard en de fundamenten van een ecologische ethiek*, Utrecht: Van Arkel.
Brennan, A. (1988) *Thinking About Nature*, London: Routledge.
Callicott, J. B. (1989) *In Defense of the Land Ethic. Essays in Environmental Philosophy*, Albany: State University of New York Press.
Carter, A. (1990) 'On individualism, collectivism and interrelationism', *Heythrop Journal* 31: 23–38.
Chodorow, N. (1986) 'Toward a relational individualism: the mediation of Self through psychoanalysis', in Thomas Heller and David Wellbery (eds), *Reconstructing Individualism*, Stanford, Calif.: Stanford University Press.
Devall, B. (1990) *Simple in Means, Rich in Ends: Practising Deep Ecology*, London: Merlin Press.
—— and Sessions, G. (1985) *Deep Ecology*, Salt Lake City: Peregrine Smith.
Dumont, R. (1983) *Essais sur l'individualisme*, Paris: Seuil.
Fox, W. (1990) *Towards a Transpersonal Ecology. Developing New Foundations for Environmentalism*, Boston: Shambala.
Habermas, J. (1982) *Theorie des kommunikativen Handelns*, Frankfurt am Main: Suhrkamp.
Happold, F. C. (1964) *Mysticism. A Study and an Anthology*, Harmondsworth: Penguin.
Hooker, C. A. (1983) 'On deep versus shallow theories of environmental pollution', in

R. Elliott and A. Gare (eds), *Environmental Philosophy*, Milton Keynes: Open University Press.

Johnson, E. (1984) 'Treating the dirt: environmental ethics and moral theory', in T. Regan (ed.), *Earthbound: New Introductory Essays in Environmental Ethics*, Philadelphia: Temple University Press.

Katz, E. (1985) 'Organism, community, and the substitution problem', *Environmental Ethics* 7(3): 241–56.

Ketcham, R. (1987) *Individualism and Public Life*, Oxford: Basil Blackwell.

Kvaloy, S. (1990) 'Green philosophy', in J. Button (ed.), *The Green Fuse. The Schumacher Lectures 1983–8*, London: Quartet Books.

Lemaire, J. and Van de Meulebroeke, M. (1986) *Les individualismes*, Bruxelles: Editions de l'Université de Bruxelles.

Lucardie, P. (1990) 'A stage in moral development?', in L. Allison (ed.), *The Utilitarian Response*, London: Sage.

Maren-Grisenbach, M. (1982) *Philosophie der Grünen*, Munich: Olzog Verlag.

Midgley, M. (1983) 'Duties concerning islands', in R. Elliott and A. Gare (eds), *Environmental Philosophy*, Milton Keynes: Open University Press.

Naess, A. (1989) *Ecology, Community and Lifestyle: Outline of an Ecosophy* (translated and revised by David Rothenberg), Cambridge: Cambridge University Press.

—— (1990) 'The basics of deep ecology', in J. Button (ed.), *The Green Fuse. The Schumacher Lectures 1983–8*, London: Quartet.

Norton, B. (1982) 'Environmental ethics and the rights of future generations', *Environmental Ethics* 4(4): 319–37.

—— (1987) 'Book review', *Environmental Ethics* 9(3): 261–7.

Noske, B. (1992) *Huilen met de wolven. Een interdisciplinaire benadering van de mens-dier relatie*, Amsterdam: Van Gennep.

Ophuls, W. (1976) *Ecology and the Politics of Scarcity*, San Francisco: Freeman.

Parfit, D. (1984) *Reasons and Persons*, Oxford: Clarendon Press.

Rolston, H. (1986) *Philosophy Gone Wild. Essays in Environmental Ethics*, Buffalo: Prometheus.

—— (1989) 'Book review', *Environmental Ethics* 11(3): 259–67.

Routley, V. and Routley, R. (1990) 'Social theories, self-management, and environmental problems', in D. Mannison, M. McRobbie and R. Routley (eds), *Environmental Philosophy*, Canberra: Australian National University.

Sagoff, M. (1988) *The Economy of the Earth. Philosophy, Law and the Environment*, Cambridge: Cambridge University Press.

Seed, J. (1985) 'Anthropocentrism', in B. Devall and G. Sessions, *Deep Ecology*, Salt Lake City: Peregrine Smith.

Staal, F. (1975) *Exploring Mysticism*, Harmondsworth: Penguin.

Taylor, P. (1986) *Respect for Nature. A Theory of Environmental Ethics*, Princeton: Princeton University Press.

Van Duijn, R. (1984) *Voeten in de aarde*, Amsterdam: Meulenhoff.

—— (1988) 'God is niet zo'n vriendelijk ventje', in H. Oosterhuis (ed.), *Wat heet God. Gesprekken*, Amsterdam: Balans.

Voogd, E. (1990) 'Medestanders gezocht', *GRAS* 5(5): 6.

Zimmerman, M. E. (1988) 'Quantum theory, intrinsic value, and panentheism', *Environmental Ethics* 10(1): 3–30.

Part II

GREEN POLITICS: THE STATE AND DEMOCRACY

3

TOWARDS A GREEN POLITICAL THEORY[1]

Alan Carter

INTRODUCTION

Many of the values that radical Greens espouse – such as decentralization, participatory democracy, self-sufficiency (or, perhaps more realistically, self-reliance), egalitarianism, alternative technology, pacifism and inter-nationalism – have their sources in earlier political traditions. In particular, feminism, socialism and anarchism have each made a significant contribution to the development of green political thought.

Feminism has contributed much to green thinking, having exerted a particularly strong influence on Die Grünen, where policies designed to combat patriarchy were incorporated into their 1983 election manifesto (see Die Grünen 1983). One thing that feminists have argued for is more partici-patory and less hierarchical political structures.[2] They have stressed the need for a consensual rather than a conflictual approach to decision-making. And they have not only contributed a general critique of patriarchy (as well as of the domination of nature, which many ecofeminists tend to see as related to the domination of women), they have also been especially active in the peace movement, where they have stimulated a considerable rebirth of interest in pacifism. (Feminist opposition to nuclear weapons, for example, has taken a highly visible form at the women's peace camp at Greenham Common.) However, it should be noted that some feminists have been critical of certain tendencies within the green movement – in particular, criticisms have been levelled against those who are seen as coming from a 'macho' socialist back-ground and who are, therefore, insufficiently sensitive to a more consensual approach (see, for example, Spretnak and Capra 1985).

This notwithstanding, the socialist tradition has also contributed much to green thinking. The egalitarian stress on the need for redistribution in order to alleviate poverty and the demand for a global, internationalist perspective both have their roots in nineteenth-century socialism. However, some socialists, too, have expressed criticisms of the green movement. They have characterized it as, amongst other things, 'petit bourgeois radicalism' (for example, Eder 1985), concerned solely with middle-class issues that do not deal adequately with the problems faced by the proletariat.[3] For such socialists, Greens are regarded as being theoretically naïve, and the remedy is argued to be an injection of Marxist theory into the green movement.

Anarchism, too, has contributed a great deal to green thinking. The stress on self-sufficiency and the insistence on decentralization[4] both have their roots in the nineteenth-century anarchist movement. However, anarchists have been very critical of the parliamentary tactics adopted by sections of the green movement, being especially scathing in their denunciations of ' *"realos"*, who are trying to turn their movement into a completely reformist parliamentary party' (Bookchin 1989: 273),[5] and their willingness to cooperate with social democrats.

Undoubtedly, one reason for the existence of tensions within the green movement is that these contributory traditions have often been antagonistic towards one another. Marxists and anarchists, for example, have a long history of bitter disagreement,[6] and it is clear that such conflicting traditions cannot merely be combined without contradictions emerging. Any cogent green political theory would have to be extremely judicious in its selection of elements drawn from often competing traditions if it is to be at all consistent. One cannot just help oneself to parts of different political ideologies without running the very real risk of producing something that is incoherent. It is far too likely that such self-service, cafeteria politics would prove to be totally indigestible. What needs to be ascertained, then, is can such diverse elements as decentralization, participatory democracy, self-sufficiency, egalitarianism, alternative technology,[7] pacifism and internationalism actually form the basis of a coherent political theory? Can they be clearly and cogently related? Or is radical green thinking merely a random hotch-potch of inconsistent values? If we are to answer these questions, we need first to address what I take to be the most fundamental question in political theory: What is the role of the state?

THE ROLE OF THE STATE

Until recently, few theorists of the modern nation-state – with the notable exception of Machiavelli, who is 'often regarded as the first theorist of the modern state' (Held 1987: 43) – have regarded it as anything other than an instrument, in some sense or other, of civil society. This can be brought out by briefly considering the two opposing theories that have the widest support amongst political theorists today: pluralism and Marxism. According to pluralist theory,[8] the state serves to reconcile competing interests within civil society. According to traditional Marxist theory, the modern state serves to secure the interests of one particular class within civil society – the bourgeoisie.[9]

Unfortunately, neither theory provides a satisfactory account of why the state should be confined to whichever role it is supposedly allocated. Certainly, pluralists have argued that a political party seeking to attain or remain in office will have to satisfy as many interest groups as it can. But a government only need do that as long as it continues to offer itself for re-election. This is not something that all democratically elected governments have chosen to do. Hitler's didn't, to take one obvious example. In other words, merely claiming that an elected government has to reconcile conflicting interests in civil society begs the question of why it must do so.

Now, there are reasons why a democratically elected government might offer itself for re-election. But they do not necessarily show the state to be an instrument of civil society. One reason suggested by Anthony de Jasay is that a government might place constitutional limits on governmental activities, and abide by its own self-imposed limits, not because the state

> mistrusts *itself* and would rather not have levers or powerful tools lest it should misuse them. It knows that *it* could not possibly be tempted to misuse power. It is its rivals for state power who would, by the nature of their ambition, misuse it. . . . [Thus] fearing its capacity for wrong-doing in profane hands, the capitalist state is rational in adopting the contours of the minimal state.
>
> (de Jasay 1985: 31)

Moreover, should the government be defeated, an incoming government could reason in the same way and similarly choose to remain limited or to respect constitutional restrictions. So, as an example, governments could *choose* to have their power constrained by an 'independent' judiciary. And, as de Jasay remarks, 'The judiciary is definitely a safeguard against the executive as long as the executive lets it be' (de Jasay 1985: 68). The problem is that the judiciary 'has no powers to enforce its own independence' (de Jasay 1985: 68–9). In which case, governments would only be constrained as long as it suited them to be.

A more plausible reason for governments accepting constitutional limits, amongst which is the requirement of periodic elections, is that they allow the state to purchase consent rather than having to rely on force to secure its rule.

> Agreeing to constitutional guarantees, then, is an intelligent move, a gesture to reassure the minority that nothing really harsh is going to be done to them. As disarming the mistrust of the prospective minority is, so to speak, a condition for getting everybody's signature on the social contract, there may very well occur historical conjunctures where it is *rational for the state actually to suggest* limits to its own power if its purpose is to maximize it. It has long been known that it can be rational for the wolf to put on sheep's clothing and to refrain for a while from eating sheep.
>
> (de Jasay 1985: 191)

However, as this means that it is the state which binds itself with constitutional guarantees, it would always be up to the state as to whether or not it chose to remain bound (see de Jasay 1985: 192–3).

It would seem, though, that an even more plausible reason for governments agreeing to stand for re-election is that another part of the state (the civil service or the military, for example, on which the government depends for its continued rule) might insist that the government offer itself for re-election. De Jasay fails to consider this possibility because of his tendency to view the state as a single entity, rather than as a supra-institution comprising sometimes conflicting institutions (such as central government, local government, the police, the military, etc.). In any case, none of the reasons just proposed establish that the state is an instrument of civil society. What they all suggest is simply that the state rationally chooses to present itself as such.

Marxists, on the other hand, have usually accorded such explanatory primacy to economic factors that they have tended to take it for granted that the state will be a reflection of civil society and, in particular, of its class nature. Nevertheless, some Marxists have offered theories about the state having to secure bourgeois interests. For example, the state has been described as 'the factor of cohesion between the levels of a social formation' (Poulantzas 1973: 44). The state is where class struggle is condensed, and its function is to secure the interests of the bourgeoisie. But this is no explanation at all, for it is either a variety of functionalism that simply takes for granted the reproduction of the social and political order, or it takes seriously class struggle as a mechanism but fails to answer why it is that class struggle condensed at the level of the state will always result in the securing of bourgeois interests. This would only be the case while the bourgeoisie were, in some significant sense, the strongest political entity. But this rests on the highly implausible view that the state has no independent power. Only classes are deemed to have power.[10]

Other Marxists have assumed that the economic power of the bourgeoisie will inevitably constrain the state. But as with pluralist theory, this begs the question. The bourgeoisie might only be strong as a class and only able to use their economic power to constrain the state while the state lets them. Certainly, the bourgeoisie can harm the state by failing to invest. But they might only be able to do so as long as the state chooses not to appropriate bourgeois property. Alternatively, the bourgeoisie can harm the state by transferring their capital to another country. But again, they might only be able to do so as long as the state allows them to.

Why, then, should the state secure bourgeois interests and thereby constrain itself? One reason could be that doing so serves the interests of state actors. For example, as Dearlove and Saunders observe of Britain:

> the commitment of senior civil servants to the preservation of the established economic order is perhaps revealed in their spectacular migration to jobs in private industry which has gathered pace over the last two decades. . . . Most Senior Permanent Secretaries now expect a clutch of new jobs after they retire at 60 and this may well have implications for the way in which they choose to conduct official business.
>
> (Dearlove and Saunders 1984: 125)

If state actors, whether politicians or civil servants, can expect to benefit from a later move into the private sector, then it is rational for them to secure the capitalist order. But this doesn't necessarily make the state the instrument of a class in civil society. Instead, all it might mean is that there is a contingent correspondence between the interests of state actors and the interests of the bourgeoisie (see Carter 1992).

Hence, both pluralist and Marxist theories have an inadequate view of the state.[11] What is remarkable is that both theories, by failing to identify a plausible mechanism that reduces the state to an instrument of civil society or to a class within it, end up regarding state actors as if they were a different kind of species from the rest, who appear to be viewed as members of *homo oeconomus*. Those who are occupied in the economy are perceived, by and large, as rational actors pursuing their own self-interests. But state actors are supposed either to serve the public by reconciling conflicting interests in civil society or to serve a particular class. Neither theory takes sufficiently seriously the possibility that all humans belong to the same species, and that state actors are also pursuing their own rational self-interest. While we in civil society recognize ourselves to be self-serving, we assume state actors to be predisposed to serving others. Our masters appear to us as our servants. Clearly, whether or not we are all self-interested, the time has come for political theorists to start taking the state seriously.[12]

THE PRIMACY OF THE POLITICAL

How, then, might we begin to take the state seriously? If we are to take the state seriously, and if we are to describe its actual role, it might help if we were first to draw some distinctions. Let us therefore distinguish between the political and the economic instances, and between their forces and relations. This gives us a fourfold set of distinctions, as summarized in Table 3.1. Relations of political control are relations of control of the forces of 'defence' – usually coercive forces. Coercive forces comprise political labour-power (that capacity which the agents of coercion supply) and the means of coercion (for example, weapons). Relations of economic control, on the other hand, are relations of control of the forces of production. And the productive forces comprise economic labour-power (that capacity which the agents of production supply) and the means of production (for example, tools).

Having drawn these distinctions, we might now be in a better position to describe the actual role of the modern state. It can be argued (see Carter 1992) that those who enjoy a dominant position within the relations of political

Table 3.1 Political and economic forces and relations

	Relations	*Forces*
Political	Relations of political control	Forces of defence
Economic	Relations of economic control	Forces of production

control (ordinarily state actors) select or stabilize relations of economic control that are in their interests.[13] And of course, it is the control of coercive forces that would usually enable state actors to select or stabilize those economic relations that serve their purposes. In other words, if the state chooses to stabilize capitalist economic relations and thereby adopts the role of guarantor of bourgeois interests, it is not, on this view, because civil society has allocated to it such a role, nor because the bourgeoisie have so decided; rather, it is because it is in the interests of state actors to assume such a role. *Such a role is self-chosen by the state.* This would mean that those who enjoy a dominant position within the relations of economic control do so on the sufferance of state actors, for it is in the interests of the latter that the former retain economic control. And why might this be so? Because those who are allowed to retain economic control are well-suited to organizing the accumulation process that the state depends upon.

Such a consideration would become paramount were the modern state to find itself, as it ordinarily does, located within an international structure of competing states (see Skocpol 1979: 30–2).[14] In order to compete militarily and secure or further its interests, the state would need to develop the coercive forces. But this would only be possible if the productive forces were developed sufficiently to provide the surplus that the development of the coercive forces requires. Hence, it would be in the interests of state actors to select or stabilize economic relations that were especially conducive to developing the productive forces.[15] Thus, state actors would stabilize relations of economic

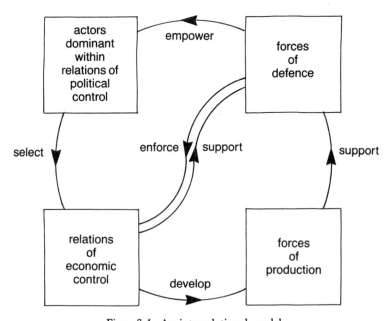

Figure 3.1 An interrelational model

control that benefit the bourgeoisie if, and so long as, those economic relations seem to be in the interest of the state. Although this has the appearance of the state being an instrument of a class, the state would, on this account, remain an autonomous agent. And of course, that is not to say that there would not be real economic constraints which the state would have to take into account. Nevertheless, it would be the political instance rather than the economic that had primacy.[16]

From this we could derive the following abstract dynamic. Those who enjoy a dominant position within the relations of political control select or stabilize relations of economic control that develop or sustain the forces of production, whose form and productivity support the forces of defence, which empower those who are politically dominant. And it is their control of the forces of defence that enables them to stabilize the economic relations, for it is precisely the various forces of defence that ultimately preserve and enforce the relations of economic control. Moreover, the relations of economic control that are selected or stabilized are those which are especially conducive to supporting the forces of defence – for example, by extracting the surplus upon which coercive forces depend. (See Figure 3.1.)

AN ENVIRONMENTALLY HAZARDOUS DYNAMIC

Let us now consider how this abstract dynamic can be seen to be exemplified in a capitalist social formation. A centralized, pseudo-representative, quasi-democratic[17] state stabilizes competitive, inegalitarian economic relations that develop 'non-convivial', environmentally damaging 'hard' technologies,[18] whose productivity supports the (nationalistic and militaristic) coercive forces that empower the state. Technologies that facilitate centralized, authoritarian control are preferred (such as nuclear power, which also provides plutonium for nuclear weapons). Such technologies serve the interests of state actors and those who benefit (the economically dominant class) from the economic relations the former choose to stabilize. Moreover, the competitive, inegalitarian economic relations that are stabilized maximize the surplus available to the state in order to finance its weapons research and to pay for its standing army and police (the coercive forces). And these coercive forces enable the state to preserve the inegalitarian relations of production it has chosen to stabilize. (See Figure 3.2.)

What should be clear is that this dynamic is environmentally hazardous in the extreme. Centralized states with sham representation and little real accountability support inegalitarian relations of production (that develop the productive forces) in order to enjoy the surplus and the environmentally harmful technology thereby produced, both of which are essential for the development of the forces of coercion, which must be developed to remain competitive within an arms race. Not only might such an arms race result in one state appearing to have developed a first-strike capability, which could force another state into launching a pre-emptive strike as its only 'defence',

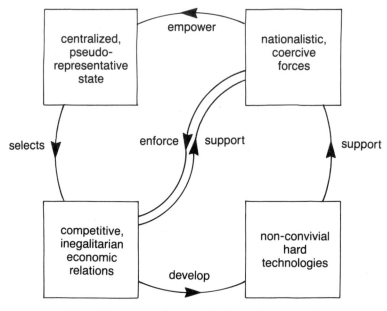

Figure 3.2 An environmentally hazardous dynamic

thereby precipitating a nuclear war – as environmentally catastrophic a scenario as can be imagined (see Schell 1982) – but this dynamic demands ever-increasing productivity, entailing a high consumption of resources and an equally high output of pollution. Those concerned about the environment therefore have no choice but to attempt to undermine this dynamic. And such a dynamic does not have to be driven by any state actually having imperialist designs on another state. The mere fact that some other militarily competing state can be feared to have imperialist designs is sufficient to drive this dynamic. In order to defend its territory against another state which it views as a potential aggressor, the state must remain militarily competitive.[19]

How, then, could such an environmentally hazardous dynamic be inhibited? Perhaps all that needs to be done is to replace the present government with a more genuinely environmentally aware one? But any state serving its own interests, and therefore having to remain within an arms race (given that the employment by the state of coercive methods of controlling its own population will inevitably pose a threat to other states), would find itself locked in this dynamic irrespective of its level of environmental concern – which is why authoritarian responses to the environmental crisis would remain part of the problem rather than providing a solution.[20]

How about the creation of an environmentally concerned, centralized, global state as a solution? But can one really imagine all nuclear powers agreeing either to one of them becoming such a super-state or to their joint

46

subordination to a state above them all? The history of the United Nations attests to the implausibility of the latter. Moreover, surely it is sufficient to recall that the major human, large-scale catastrophes, with their corresponding environmental damage, which relief organizations such as Oxfam have dealt with since the Second World War (Bangladesh, Biafra, Ethiopia), were all wars of secession. Such conflict would surely increase were a centralized, global super-state set up – and that would provide an internal drive for an environmentally hazardous dynamic.[21]

Well, perhaps it is sufficient to replace a sham representative state with a participatory democracy because the people would, possibly, have less of an interest in remaining within this dynamic? But would they, in fact, choose to leave it? Theorists of competitive elitism have argued that ordinary individuals are at the mercy of political persuasion. They are less rational in their choices of political policies than in their choices of consumables, for they do not suffer the direct consequences of their policy choices in the near future and therefore do not learn from their mistakes. They do not take the trouble to inform themselves, as they do when purchasing some expensive item. They live in a political fantasy world about what is desirable and possible, and degenerate to an irrational level where they act on the most basic emotions. They respond on the basis of prejudice and sheer impulse, rather than on considered and informed thought. In short, the general public are politically irresponsible, and it is fortunate, in the view of several theorists of competitive elitism, that they are politically apathetic. To quote the most influential of these theorists, Joseph Schumpeter:

> the typical citizen drops down to a lower level of mental performance as soon as he [sic] enters the political field. He argues and analyzes in a way which he would readily recognize as infantile within the sphere of his real interests. He becomes a primitive again.
>
> (Schumpeter 1987: 262)

However, theorists of participatory democracy have seen a route out of this problem. If the average citizen is a 'political primitive', it is as a result of being prevented from participating in political decision-making. So, although politically responsible behaviour has to be learnt, it can be. As Carole Pateman writes:

> The existence of representative institutions at national level is not sufficient for democracy; for maximum participation by all the people at that level socialisation, or 'social training', for democracy must take place in other spheres in order that the necessary individual attitudes and psychological qualities can be developed. This development takes place through the process of participation itself. The major function of participation in the theory of participatory democracy is therefore an educative one, educative in the very widest sense, including both the psychological aspect and the gaining of practice in democratic skills and procedures.

Thus there is no special problem about the stability of a participatory system; it is self-sustaining through the educative impact of the participatory process. Participation develops and fosters the very qualities necessary for it; the more individuals participate the better able they become to do so. Subsidiary hypotheses about participation are that it has an integrative effect and that it aids the acceptance of collective decisions.[22]

(Pateman 1970: 42–3)

Unfortunately, the theorists of participatory democracy are trapped in something of a vicious circle.[23] The problem is that though a participatory democracy, once established, could persist because it would have citizens with the right consciousness, it wouldn't arise without people of the right consciousness, and we do not have such people today. People today do not have a sufficient sense of community, or sufficient confidence in their ability to participate in decision-making, and so on. Where, then, could citizens obtain the necessary experience of participating in decision-making? Theorists of participatory democracy reply that the experience must be gained at the local level and in the workplace.

But if this is so, then one cannot merely introduce a participatory democracy at the political level. That, on its own, would be insufficient. One would also have to introduce more participatory and egalitarian economic relations. Well, if the introduction of more participatory and egalitarian relations of economic control could allow a more participatory political system, would introducing such economic relations suffice to inhibit the environmentally hazardous dynamic portrayed in Figure 3.2? Apparently not. Those who benefit from the existing inequality in society are not going to risk any genuine participation by the less privileged.[24] Were the latter granted such participation, then they might very well do something about the prevailing inequality. And it is the state itself that is one of the beneficiaries of inegalitarian economic relations, as they provide it with the surplus it requires. Is it likely that those who are at present benefiting from the relations of economic control would undermine their own privileged position by sanctioning developments that would lead to a more active and demanding citizenry? Of course not. Hence, it is highly implausible that a non-participatory state would endorse the introduction of significantly participatory or egalitarian relations of economic control. Moreover, centralized states are presently taking away the very local control that would be necessary to make participation in local decision-making meaningful. But what is most worrying is that if egalitarian and participatory workplaces arose on a significant scale, then the state might very well impose inegalitarian economic relations upon the workers[25] because if they were in control of their workplaces, they might choose to work less hard and make less surplus available to the state.

A further problem is that non-convivial, hard technologies are not suited to a more democratic workplace (see Braverman 1974 and Marglin 1982; also see Elliott and Elliott 1976). Well, then, is the introduction of alternative

48

technologies[26] –'convivial', 'soft' technologies – an effective answer to the environmentally hazardous dynamic? Again, the answer must be 'no'. How are such technologies to be developed and implemented? Alternative technologies would not support the coercive forces required by the state (they would make everyone more independent, thereby undermining central control and offering the state less surplus), and so neither research into them nor their implementation on a major scale would be enthusiastically promoted by the state. And, to the extent that such technologies undermined the existing relations of economic control, they would not be funded by those who presently benefit from those relations and who own the private capital which would be needed for the development and production of convivial technologies if the state had no interest in them.

This leaves us with the final element of the environmentally hazardous dynamic: the militaristic coercive forces. Were their development to be replaced by a widespread commitment to pacifism and the widescale adoption of non-violent direct action (NVDA) against any potential aggressor, would this not fundamentally inhibit the dynamic? This seems the most promising suggestion so far. But how would NVDA be promoted on a wide scale? If the population were highly trained in non-violent resistance and non-cooperation with an aggressor, then such a population would be ungovernable. However, that would apply not only to an external aggressor but also to the present state. Consequently, it is highly improbable that proof of NVDA working effectively as an alternative defence strategy would be forthcoming, for as Richard Routley acutely observes:

> Nonviolent resistance is . . . unlikely to be put to the test in any adequate way in present state-determined circumstances. No state would be prepared to risk training its populace in full nonviolent action techniques (civil defence is different). It would then be all too easy for them to 'rout' the police: civil obedience, for example, could no longer be ensured by customary violent means.[27]
>
> (Routley 1984: 132)

Moreover, unless there is a greater sense of community and trust amongst the population, then any attempted use of collective NVDA would be severely inhibited. But a general feeling of community and shared trust is unlikely to arise in a hierarchical or an inegalitarian society, with its tremendous social divides (see Baker 1987: Ch. 4). Hence, pacifism on its own does not, prima facie, appear to be a completely satisfactory response to the environmentally hazardous dynamic. If all this is so, and if our very survival as a species depends upon stopping such a dynamic, what is to be done?

AN ENVIRONMENTALLY BENIGN DYNAMIC?

The answer, it would appear, is not to regard each of the proposed solutions as sufficient to inhibit the environmentally hazardous dynamic but to see them as necessary conditions which might be jointly sufficient, for it is the absence of the other conditions being met that renders each condition insufficient. In other words, it would not do to negate a centralized, pseudo-representative state or inegalitarian economic relations or non-convivial, hard technologies or nationalistic and militaristic coercive forces without also negating the other elements of the environmentally hazardous dynamic. And interestingly, when all of these elements are simultaneously negated, a different dynamic could be produced – one that is environmentally benign.

The negation of the first element – a centralized, pseudo-representative state – is a decentralized, participatory democracy. For the people to remain in political control, they would have to ensure the perpetuation of the egalitarian relations of production that are one of its preconditions (if the theorists of participatory democracy are right). But it is at least plausible that a population of equals[28] participating in a participatory democracy would be more politically informed and would want to retain their egalitarian economic relations both for their own sake and because they were understood to be a precondition for the continuance of their participatory democracy. Moreover, a more consensual democracy would mean that those who would lose out from inegalitarian economic relations would be able to veto their introduction. In short, whereas a centralized, authoritarian state chooses to preserve inegalitarian economic relations because they are functional for it, egalitarian economic relations are functional for a participatory democracy, which might, therefore, be expected to choose to preserve them.

However, inegalitarian economic relations could only be avoided if local economic control were retained (as economic control from afar would certainly end up being exploitative), and that would require each locality to be as self-sufficient as possible. But it is also plausible that this is what the mass of people (being more informed as a result of equal economic control) would insist on, given that they would, in all likelihood, wish to remain in control of the productive forces. And more self-sufficient, egalitarian economic relations are, of course, the negation of the second element – inegalitarian, competitive economic relations.

But egalitarian relations could only be preserved if the workers employed a convivial technology. And it seems not unlikely that the majority of informed workers situated in egalitarian economic relations that they controlled would insist on technologies that facilitated equal control rather than technologies that made a few workers privileged and the rest subservient. It is those who have enjoyed dominant positions within the relations of economic control who have introduced non-convivial technologies (see Braverman 1974; also see Marglin 1982). And convivial technologies are, of course, the negation of this third element of the environmentally hazardous dynamic – non-convivial technologies.

Now, convivial technologies, in being incompatible with authoritarian, central control and in offering less surplus to fuel any potential development of militaristic coercive forces, would not be conducive to an arms race and could thereby inhibit its re-emergence. What is more, that would make the society less of a threat to its neighbours, which might reduce the need to participate in an arms race and, alongside that, reduce the need to develop technologies that support an arms race. Thus, a participatory democracy could feel that it had an interest in using convivial technologies and, unlike a coercive, centralized state, it could regard itself as being in a position to be able to afford to do without less convivial ones (which a coercive state requires in order to retain power) because in a participatory democracy the citizens would exercise control over themselves. Moreover, the sharing and trust that convivial working arrangements would most probably foster is a condition for pacifist defence and non-violent social control. To the extent that this would be less confrontational and conflictual, it could facilitate the development of a less nationalistic perspective – something which an awareness of the global nature of the environmental crisis also promotes. Furthermore, the less it was confined to a single nation, the more effective would a pacifist approach be. Hence, there are good reasons for such a society wishing to promote pacifism internationally. And a population with a more global, international outlook prepared and able to employ pacifist methods is the negation of the fourth element – nationalistic and militarist coercive forces.

Finally, a widespread ability to engage in collective NVDA would empower a participatory democracy and enable it to preserve egalitarian economic relations. In addition, if the citizens of a participatory democracy wished to enjoy their own produce rather than supporting expensive coercive forces, then they would have good reason to develop cheaper, non-violent methods of defence (methods that are unavailable to authoritarian states, as we have noted). And a less inegalitarian society would most likely have less need of coercive forces as there would be fewer inequalities needing to be protected. Furthermore, an egalitarian, non-violent democracy would be unable to force exploitative relations onto other (for example, poorer) countries, thereby playing its part in a more egalitarian world. This means that it would have to be more self-sufficient. And were there greater self-sufficiency, less international competition and exploitation, and consequently no need to remain within an arms race, there would be no seemingly inescapable dynamic forcing the squandering of resources, the unhindered pollution of the environment, or the headlong rush into nuclear holocaust.

In which case, were such an alternative dynamic (as represented in Figure 3.3) to be realized, it would be environmentally benign, unlike the dynamic that has taken us to the brink of ecological catastrophe (represented in Figure 3.2). Thus, the environmentally benign dynamic commends itself to those who are concerned about the environmental crisis we currently face. And as all the elements of this benign dynamic are so interrelated, as are those of the hazardous dynamic, then an appropriate political strategy would be to oppose the latter on all fronts – in fact, as I have been arguing, if it were not opposed on all fronts, then it would simply re-emerge.[29]

But the state would surely resist any attempt to oppose the environmentally

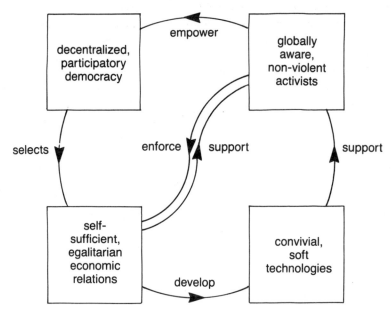

Figure 3.3 An environmentally benign dynamic

hazardous dynamic on all fronts, as that dynamic is intimately related to the serving of its interests. How, then, could this dynamic be effectively opposed? How can we move from the hazardous to the benign? How can we even begin to get a foot in the door? One possible answer would arise if it were in fact the case that the coercive forces were insufficient to preserve state power on their own and the state were partly empowered by the compliance of its people. Just as it appears rational for the state to back economic relations which develop the productive forces that provide the surplus it requires, and just as it appears rational for members of the dominant economic class to support the state in so far as it stabilizes the economic relations they benefit from, it also appears rational for subordinate economic classes to back the state in defending their nation from being subjugated by another, for such subjugation would lead to greater toil being imposed upon them. It is not surprising, therefore, that nationals comply with their state and, perhaps, thereby empower it.

However, if this support for the state results in an environmentally hazardous dynamic posing an even greater threat than that posed by imperialist aggressors (real or imagined), then it is no longer rational to continue backing the state.[30] Hence, if the state is empowered not only by its coercive forces but also by the compliance of its people (who have hitherto considered it rational to support the state in their own defence), then widespread, individual non-cooperation with the state (in response to the growing need to take action against the increasingly threatening environmental crisis the state is implicated in) could disempower it. In other words, the extent of the environmental problems that we face could provide the rationale and motivation for the disempowering of the state through non-cooperation that could begin to undermine the environmentally hazardous dynamic. In which case, the disempowerment of the state by non-violent civil disobedience,[31] and the correlative empowerment of those practising it,[32] would be the most promising place to start undermining the environmentally hazardous dynamic. And the recent history of Eastern Europe certainly suggests that widespread non-cooperation with the state can be an effective strategy for radical transformation.[33]

But, to deal with one possible worry about any pacifist response, wouldn't the rejection of violence, and with it the coercive state, imply that justice could no longer be carried out effectively?[34] This does not, in fact, follow. It only implies that justice would have to be carried out by non-violent means. It is, therefore, worth stressing some of the problems that result from viewing violence 'as the ultimate instrument of justice'. As H. J. N. Horsburgh points out:

First, the financial costs are huge. Billions of dollars are thrown away on arms and armed forces that might have been directly applied to the relief of suffering and the remedying of injustice. Secondly, these preparations are constantly aggravating and multiplying disputes, partly through deepening fear and suspicion, and partly through causing crises, shortages and revised priorities. Thus, it is violence and preparations for violence as much as anything else which produce the situations in which violence is said to be necessary. Thirdly, preparing for violence has harmed the environment in innumerable ways, including the testing of nuclear weaponry, the appropriation and spoliation of large tracts of beautiful country, and the world-wide industrial expansion which it has necessitated or promoted. Finally, the quest for new and superior weaponry and counter-weaponry has acted as a lopsided spur to the development of science and technology, setting us mounting problems that we are less and less able to meet.

(Horsburgh 1981: 66–7)

In short, we have diverted vast resources to the development of nuclear weapons and seriously threatened the environment in the process because military goals which serve the state's purposes have taken priority.[35]

To conclude, then, *what links together theoretically the various aspects of radical green political theory* – decentralization, participatory democracy, self-sufficiency, egalitarianism, alternative technology, pacifism and internationalism – *is the need to inhibit the environmentally hazardous dynamic that we are presently imprisoned within.* Hence, *the various elements of radical green political thought consist in the systematic negation of every element of this dynamic.* The negation of the need to develop militaristic forces of coercion requires either pacifism or the 'defensive defence' proposed by Johan Galtung.[36] It also requires a more internationalist approach. The negation of the technology appropriate to supporting the arms race (such as a civil nuclear power programme) is convivial, soft technology. The negation of competitive and inegalitarian relations of production which offer a surplus to the state is their replacement by egalitarian relations of production and greater self-sufficiency (also a feature of 'defensive defence'). And finally, the negation of an unrepresentative, centralized state is a decentralized participatory democracy.[37] What is more, it is the urgent need to inhibit the environmentally hazardous dynamic that provides the most compelling of motivations for embracing decentralization, participatory democracy, self-sufficiency, egalitarianism, alternative technology, pacifism and internationalism. So, it seems to me, this isn't, after all, a fast-food, cafeteria political ideology, grabbing from here and there without any rhyme or reason; instead, it seems well-balanced and wholesome. And it's top of today's menu.

NOTES

1 An earlier draft of this chapter received a wide circulation and was read by numerous people, but I would especially like to thank the following for their comments, criticism or encouragement: Robin Attfield, Brian Barry, Andrew Brennan, Jerry Cohen, Teddy Goldsmith, David Miller, Tim O'Riordan, David Pepper, Jonathon Porritt, Richard Sylvan, and those who participated in the Green Political Theory Workshop at Malvern, Worcestershire in December 1989. A later draft was presented at the workshop on 'Green Political Theory' at the European Consortium for Political Research Joint Sessions at Essex University in March 1991, and I am grateful to those who participated – in particular, Wouter Achterberg, Ted Benton, Andrew Dobson, Bob Goodin, Keekok Lee and Paul Lucardie. I would also like to thank my colleagues at London University who have made valuable comments on various drafts of this chapter.

2 It is not surprising that it was a feminist who wrote the seminal book arguing for participatory democracy – namely, Pateman (1970).

3 This criticism was most famously expressed in Enzensberger (1974).

4 For a comprehensive defence of decentralization, see Sale (1980).

5 Bookchin is without doubt the leading eco-anarchist, and many of the central features of radical green thinking can be traced to his 1965 essay 'Ecology and revolutionary thought', reprinted in Bookchin (1974).

6 The difference between Marxist and anarchist political strategies parallels the division in the environmental movement between 'technocentric' and 'ecocentric' modes of thinking. Ecocentrism 'argues for low impact technology (but is not anti-technological); it decries bigness and impersonality in all forms (but especially in the city); and demands a code of behaviour that seeks permanence and stability based upon ecological principles of diversity and homeostasis'. In contrast, technocentrism 'is almost arrogant in its assumption that [humanity] is supremely able to understand and control events to suit [its] purposes' (O'Riordan 1981: 1). For an example of the latter, see Grundmann (1991).

7 The need for an alternative technology has been argued for by certain feminists, socialists and anarchists, though their visions of an alternative technology have not always been identical. See, for example, Thomas (1983), Morris (1970), and Kropotkin (1974).

8 The most influential account is that presented in Dahl (1956).

9 As Marx and Engels (1970: 37) write in the 'Manifesto of the Communist Party': 'the executive of the modern State is but a committee for managing the common

affairs of the whole bourgeoisie'. However, although most pluralists and Marxists have employed a 'cipher image' of the state, not all have done so. For an overview of the various standpoints that have been taken, see Dunleavy and O'Leary (1987).

10 For a critique of this view (and for a general green critique of Marxist theory), see Carter (1988: 203–4).

11 As de Jasay (1985: 34) observes: 'Neither provides any good ground for supposing that the state, once it has the monopoly of force will not, at times or forever, use it *against* those *from* whom it received it. Neither is a theory of the state in the proper sense, i.e. neither really explains why the state will do one thing rather than another.'

12 Whereas neo-pluralists have come to take economic relations more seriously than pluralists did (see Dunleavy and O'Leary 1987: 293–7 and Held 1987: 203–4), there has been a growing awareness on the Left of the need to accord greater independence to the state. Much of the initial impetus has come from Claus Offe, who has recognized that 'Since the state *depends* on a process of accumulation which is beyond its power to *organize*, every occupant of state power is basically interested in promoting those conditions most conducive to accumulation' (Offe and Ronge 1982: 250). Thus the state is not allied to the bourgeoisie, nor is it subject to the political power of the capitalist class. Instead the state has 'an institutional self-interest . . . in guaranteeing and safeguarding a "healthy" accumulation process upon which it depends' (Offe and Ronge 1982: 250). Nevertheless, despite this theoretical advance, Offe still regards the state as basically 'reactive' (see Held 1987: 212). For example, he claims that 'the state is *denied* the power to control the flow of those resources which are indispensable for the *use* of state power' (Offe and Ronge 1982: 250). But this fails to realize that the state might not be denied control of accumulation. It may well deny itself that control.

A further theoretical advance is made in Block (1980), where the state is granted even more of an active role. Block acknowledges that 'state managers collectively are self-interested maximisers, interested in maximising their power, prestige, and wealth' (Block 1980: 229). Moreover, Block argues that at certain historical conjunctures, states have greater freedom in relation to the dominant economic class. Hitler, for example, took 'advantage of the dynamics of an exceptional period to free [himself] of constraints imposed by the capitalists' (Block 1980: 233). However, Block fails to realize the extent to which Hitler could have created such an exceptional period.

Yet more autonomy is granted the state, though from opposing theoretical standpoints, in the work of Theda Skocpol and, more recently, that of Michael Taylor (see Skocpol 1979; also see, for example, Taylor 1988). The state is taken most seriously as an independent actor in de Jasay (1985) and, from a diametrically opposite political standpoint, in Carter (1988). Whereas the former takes private property for granted, the latter is concerned not only about the power of the state, but also about the problems posed by inegalitarian economic relations. For a critique of propertarian views (the holding of which distinguishes the libertarian Right from the libertarian Left), see Carter (1989).

13 For an account of state actors selecting new relations of economic control in France from the fifteenth century see Taylor (1989: 124–6) and in Russia from the eighteenth century (see ibid. 128–32).

14 Weber, of course, saw the state as being in competing military relations with other states and in terms of coercion, defining the state as 'a human community that (successfully) claims the *monopoly of the legitimate use of physical force* within a given territory' (Weber 1970: 78).

15 Of course, states are not always successful at stabilizing the prevailing order. For an

illuminating account of when they are likely to be successful and when they are not, see Goodwin and Skocpol (1989).

16 In Marxist theory, with respect to the prediction of an egalitarian, post-capitalist society (which is the principal purpose of Marx's theory of history), the productive forces are deemed to have explanatory primacy (see Cohen 1978). However, were the post-capitalist state to impose inegalitarian economic relations rather than withering away, then the productive forces would no longer have explanatory primacy. Instead, the state would have explanatory primacy to the extent that it selected economic relations that were perceived to be functional for it. It is for this reason that I refer to this generalized account as 'the State-Primacy Model' (see Carter 1992). Such an account employs a purposive variety of functional explanation without it being functionalist. Also on the explanatory primacy of the state, see Carter (1988: section 6.3, especially 258–9).

17 For an account of how elitists have usurped the term 'democracy', which previously referred to what is now called 'direct democracy', see Arblaster (1987).

18 The application to technology of the term 'convivial' derives from Illich (1975: 12): '[A] society, in which modern technologies serve politically interrelated individuals rather than managers, I will call "convivial". . . . I have chosen "convivial" as a technical term to designate a modern society of responsibly limited tools.' The distinction between 'hard' and 'soft' technologies derives from Lovins (1979: 38): 'There exists today a body of energy technologies that have certain specific features in common and that offer great technical, economic, and political attractions, yet for which there is no generic term. For lack of a more satisfactory term, I shall call them "soft" technologies: a textual description, intended to mean not vague, mushy, speculative, or ephemeral, but rather flexible, resilient, sustainable, and benign.'

19 It might be objected that recent developments in superpower relations vitiate this analysis. But consider the following: What if two militarily competing states select different relations of economic control and one set of relations is more productive than the other? The state with the less productive economic relations, if it is to remain militarily competitive, will have to select more efficient economic relations or it will have to attempt to decelerate the arms race. The Soviet Union seems to have attempted to pursue both courses simultaneously, which is perfectly consistent with theoretical expectations as informed by the State-Primacy Model. Moreover, although the United States seems to have won the arms race because of its more powerful economy, the cost has been an unsustainable burden on that economy. Between 1980 and 1985 the United States' national debt doubled, and this was 'due more to the growth in military expenditures than to any other factor' (Waring 1989: 169). It is not surprising, therefore, that the United States should entertain a new détente.

Nevertheless, this has not meant an abandonment of weapons research, and annual global military expenditure remains in excess of $1,000 billion, with more being spent per capita on armaments than 'on food, water, shelter, health, education, or ecosystem protection' (Waring 1989: 167). A temporary halt to arms build-up while superpower economies recover provides no evidence for the cessation of the environmentally hazardous dynamic. What is more, it remains a distinct possibility that the Russian military might reject perestroika and stage a coup d'état. Alternatively, in order to remain in power, the future Russian leadership might transform their policies into those more in line with the military's liking. Either possibility could result in an unprecedented escalation of the arms race. It is not surprising, therefore, that faced with this possibility, some western states (most notably Britain, with its insistence on going ahead with Trident) should refuse to partake in any serious disarmament and thereby continue to fuel the dynamic.

56

20 It should also be noted that were an elected Green government to try to disarm, the rest of the state would hardly be enthusiastic about aiding it in what would appear to be the undermining of state power. (State institutions have, for example, obstructed British Labour governments whose policies were far less radical than those which committed Greens would attempt to enact.) Hence, the election of a Green government would certainly be insufficient for bringing about a green society. One conceivable response to the election of such a government is a military coup, as the military is unlikely to accept quietly a Green government slashing its budget and dispensing with its traditional role.

21 This is why, even if the 'Russian threat' were to disappear completely, the United States could fuel an environmentally hazardous dynamic by offering itself as the (Nozickian) global protection agency, for such a 'mercenary state' (to use Noam Chomsky's perceptive phrase) could be expected to demand payment from all beneficiaries of its services. We have seen the US make such demands over the Gulf War, and (trumped-up) threats, for example, of 'upstart' Third World states or Islamic fundamentalism, would provide the apparent need for its continued services. This would be especially attractive to the US state for it would enable it to expand beyond what its own ailing economy could support.

22 In other words: 'The advocates of the contemporary theory argue that certain personality traits (the "authoritarian" or "non-democratic" character) have to be taken as given – the active participation of such individuals would be dangerous for the democratic political system. The participatory theory, on the other hand, argues that the experience of participation itself will develop and foster the "democratic" personality, i.e. qualities needed for the successful operation of the democratic system, and will do so for all individuals' (Pateman 1970: 64).

23 C. B. Macpherson argues that a change in consciousness and a reduction in social inequality are both prerequisites for participatory democracy. 'Hence the vicious circle: we cannot achieve more democratic participation without a prior change in social inequality and in consciousness, but we cannot achieve the changes in social inequality and consciousness without a prior change in democratic participation' (Macpherson 1977: 100).

However, Macpherson does think that there are some loopholes that allow the possibility of society escaping from this apparently vicious circle. The first is that the environmental costs incurred by our society are making some people question the consumer mentality. Environmental problems arising from our worship of consumption draw attention to the need for some notion of public interest. And it is clear that the public interest is not adequately served by consumers merely pursuing their own private interests irrespective of others. The very serious ecological costs of the consumer mentality can thus lead more and more people to reject that mentality. The second loophole is that the costs of apathy are becoming more obvious. There is a price to be paid for remaining apathetic – for example, being dominated by massive corporations. Hence the demand for workers' control. And workers' control can lead to demands for greater participation elsewhere. People are also dominated by large-scale corporations at the level of the neighbourhood. Hence the demand for greater local control, whether it be regarding the dumping of nuclear waste, the siting of factories or airports, or whatever. The third loophole is the inability of the capitalist system to meet consumer expectations. The present system cannot continually deliver the consumer goods that its consumer mentality requires in ever-greater abundance. And it certainly cannot deliver them to everyone who wants them. The system will either break down or there will be growing demands for a more equal distribution of goods. And this will lead, Macpherson thinks, to workers demanding greater participation in political affairs.

24 This is why a reduction in social inequality is one of the prerequisites for participatory democracy.

25 The Bolshevik state did precisely this within a year of Lenin coming to power (see Carter 1992).

26 For a brief discussion of alternative technology, see Clarke (1975). For more comprehensive accounts, see Boyle and Harper (1976) and Dickson (1974).

27 Routley's observation suggests that if the widespread adoption of pacifist techniques would not be either promoted or even sanctioned by the state (because they might undermine its power over its own population), and if their adoption is one of the things that is required to avoid being embroiled in an arms race – a precondition for inhibiting the environmentally hazardous dynamic – then it would also be necessary to oppose the state as an institution. In other words, the full ramifications of pacifism might be a lot more radical than is usually assumed – certainly much more radical than that of mere passivity. On the distinctions between pacificity and passivity, and between acting forcefully and acting violently, see Routley (1984).

28 For an appropriate conception of 'equality', see Baker (1987).

29 This is not to say that *only* a sudden revolution would provide a solution. A transition could be gradual, but all elements of the environmentally hazardous dynamic would have to be transformed in tandem. Moreover, the environmentally hazardous dynamic and the environmentally benign dynamic are 'ideal types'. Societies will, clearly, fall between the two types: some will be more environmentally hazardous, some more benign. And interestingly, those societies that are more benign – for example, Denmark – not only have more soft technologies, they also have more political participation, are less militaristic and are more egalitarian. What is needed, generally, is a move further from the hazardous and much more towards the benign.

All this does, however, raise an important philosophical point: certain phenomena that might appear problematic for the analysis presented here are not necessarily evidence for the environmentally hazardous dynamic being other than described, but, arguably, instances of an environmentally benign dynamic. In other words, although the analysis is based on contrary ideal types, it is not as straightforwardly simple to refute as might be assumed because apparently disconfirmatory evidence with respect to the nature of the hazardous will often tend to be corroborative evidence for the plausibility of the benign. See, for example, note 33 below.

30 As Jonathon Porritt (1984: 217) writes: 'Everything that once served to enhance both individual and collective security now serves to undermine it: larger defense budget, more sophisticated weaponry, the maximization of production and consumption, higher productivity, increased GNP, the industrialization of the Third World, expanded world trade, the comprehensive exploitation of the Earth's resources, an emphasis on individualism, the triumph of materialism, the sovereignty of the nation-state, uncontrolled technological development – these were once the hallmarks of success, the guarantors of security. Collectively they now threaten our very survival.' And this threat to our survival is now recognized by the United Nations in the authoritative study undertaken on its behalf by the World Commission on Environment and Development (see Brundtland *et al.* 1987).

31 Civil disobedience on environmental grounds, even towards a state claiming to be democratic, is ably defended in Singer (1973). For less extensive justifications of civil disobedience, see Rawls (1971) and Dworkin (1971).

32 Thus NVDA can provide an alternative support for participatory democracy, for as Bookchin (1982: 339) argues: 'direct action is literally a form of ethical character-building in the most important social role that the individual can undertake: active citizenship. . . . Direct action is at once the reclamation of the public sphere by

the ego, its development toward self-empowerment, and its culmination as an active participant in society.'

33 Whereas the changes in Eastern Europe might be thought to show that states are capable of more radical transformation than this analysis suggests, in so far as the changes were brought about by the undermining of state power by a disaffected citizenry, they are, instead, evidence for the possibility of a move towards a more benign dynamic. Unfortunately, to the extent that the peoples of Eastern Europe look towards western political and economic models, unless they soon see the environmental costs of adopting them, the future looks bleak. Clearly, what is appealing to many in Eastern Europe is the level of affluence enjoyed in the west.

This raises an interesting issue. States can remain in power not just by the threat of force, but also by appearing to be able to offer the material goods. Materialism can seduce the people to such an extent that the need for change is deflected. This means that there could be an internal drive to the environmentally hazardous dynamic even without any military threat. If materialist values prevail, then in order to retain power, states would have to sustain the material productivity necessary to keep its people seduced, and thus introduce or preserve those economic relations most conducive to sustaining it. And to the extent that this is successful, states have an interest in maintaining materialist values.

However, such materialism could be challenged by demonstrating that its environmental costs make it counter-productive to pursue it – a task made easier the more those costs become apparent. This is one possible explanation for the rise of post-materialist values, whereas the standard explanation sees post-materialist values as arising once affluence has been enjoyed (see Inglehart 1981; also see Elgin 1981). If either explanation is correct, then values which would undermine the environmentally hazardous dynamic might be expected to spread and deepen as it progresses. In this chapter I have relied solely on rational choice explanations because they predominate in current political theory. The introduction of ideological values greatly complicates the issue. On the one hand, ideological inertia makes change more difficult. On the other hand, the costs of materialism are becoming ever-more apparent, dissatisfaction with materialism has emerged in the latter half of the twentieth century, and the subsequent growth of post-materialist values can provide a motive for radical transformation.

It will no doubt be claimed that rational choice assumptions entail a centralized solution to environmental problems. This claim is cogently rebutted in Taylor (1976). On some of the limits of rational choice theory, see Taylor (1982).

34 For such an objection, see Narveson (1971). A cogent reply is contained in Routley (1984). We might include within our idea of 'justice' the prevention of, and compensation for the effects of, environmentally damaging behaviour in so far as it causes harm to others. On the increasingly apparent limitations of tort law with respect to environmental 'accidents', see Gaskins (1989).

35 And as Horsburgh (1981: 67) asks: 'Is it not possible – even likely – that the acceleration of nuclear conflict may prove fatal to our species?' In which case, the value of non-violence becomes obvious, for 'only the non-violent can inherit the earth: the violent can only deny them a world to inherit' (Horsburgh 1981: 73). For the fullest discussion of pacifist methods, successes and theory, see Sharp (1973).

36 Galtung (1984) sees four dimensions to a genuine security. The first is '*the extent to which the country has a credible non-provocative defense*, and not an offensive military capacity'. The second is 'non-alignment, *the degree of decoupling from the superpowers*'. The third is '*the extent to which the country itself has inner strength*, by being reasonably self-reliant in essentials (food, energy, health, defense); not being too centralised; having some reservoir of intermediate technology to fall back on; not being too easily fragmented by class, ethnic and other conflicts; above all by being

autonomous'. The fourth, and most problematic, is *'the extent to which the country is useful to others* if left in peace, so that belligerents prefer to leave it intact' (Galtung 1984: 12–13).

37 One possible objection to the decentralist solution defended here is that it appears to be incompatible with egalitarian demands. As there are different levels of resources in different parts of the world, wouldn't a centralized, global super-state be necessary to redistribute from the rich to the poor? And doesn't this show decentralization, self-sufficiency and egalitarianism to be incompatible? In response: first, the most effective organizations with respect to environmentally benign development (albeit on far too small a scale) are non-governmental organizations such as Oxfam, which help the poor to help themselves; and second, the *major* problem is surely not a lack of redistribution, but the redistribution currently practised – namely, from the poor to the rich. Merely ending international exploitation would not, of course, provide global equality, but it may be the best practicable, widespread approach, given that terminating underdevelopment or environmentally hazardous, dependent development would be far more egalitarian and less problematic than allowing a global super-state to redistribute resources, when a significant proportion would inevitably be redistributed in its own direction in the process. And to the extent that egalitarians are most concerned to reduce the inequalities arising from exploitation, then self-sufficiency and de-linking from the world economy as an answer to underdevelopment or dependent development would be egalitarian. On how the State-Primacy approach adopted in this analysis is not incompatible with a theory of underdevelopment, as might at first be assumed, see Carter (forthcoming).

Of course, there are independent environmental reasons for preferring decentralization, self-sufficiency, egalitarianism, alternative technology, pacifism and internationalism. Decentralized, small-scale, self-sufficient communities have a far lower environmental impact (see Goldsmith *et al.* 1972: 50–3). Only greater equality can prevent the poor (never mind the excessively affluent) from destroying the environment – for example, by being driven onto marginal land that cannot sustain them (see Brundtland *et al.* 1987). Only alternative technology allows an environmentally sustainable economy. Unlike dropping Agent Orange on complex ecosystems or exploding nuclear devices, NVDA is environmentally harmless. And although decentralized, small-scale, self-sufficient communities would have to act locally, they would have to take into account the global implications of their actions. However, here I have been concerned solely with the political interrelationships between the various elements of radical green thinking. And as they have been demonstrated to be linked together systematically through an analysis of contemporary society that takes into account both political and economic inequalities, then green political theory does not have to be Marxist for it to avoid being theoretically unsophisticated or inherently biased toward the middle class. For the theoretical underpinnings of the analysis presented here, see Carter (1992).

REFERENCES

Arblaster, A. (1987) *Democracy*, Milton Keynes: Open University Press.

Baker, J. (1987) *Arguing for Equality*, London: Verso.

Block, F. (1980) 'Beyond relative autonomy: state managers as historical subjects', in R. Miliband and J. Saville (eds), *The Socialist Register 1980*, London: Merlin Press.

Bookchin, M. (1974) *Post-Scarcity Anarchism*, London: Wildwood House.

—— (1982) *The Ecology of Freedom: The Emergence and Dissolution of Hierarchy*, Palo Alto: Cheshire Books.

—— (1989) 'New social movements: the anarchic dimension', in D. Goodway (ed.), *For Anarchism: History, Theory, and Practice*, London: Routledge.

Boyle, G. and Harper, P. (eds) (1976) *Radical Technology*, London: Wildwood House.

Braverman, H. (1974) *Labor and Monopoly Capital: The Degradation of Work in the Twentieth Century*, New York: Monthly Review Press.

Brundtland, G. H. *et al.* (1987) *Our Common Future*, Oxford: Oxford University Press.

Carter, A. (1988) *Marx: A Radical Critique*, Brighton: Wheatsheaf Books.

—— (1989) *The Philosophical Foundations of Property Rights*, Hemel Hempstead: Harvester–Wheatsheaf.

—— (1992) 'Functional explanation and the state', in P. Wetherly (ed.), *Marx's Theory of History: The Contemporary Debate*, Aldershot: Avebury.

—— (forthcoming) 'The nation-state and underdevelopment'.

Clarke, R. (1975) 'Technology for an alternative society', in R. Clarke (ed.), *Notes for the Future: An Alternative History of the Past Decade*, London: Thames & Hudson.

Cohen, G. A. (1978) *Karl Marx's Theory of History: A Defence*, Oxford: Clarendon Press.

Dahl, R. A. (1956) *A Preface to Democratic Theory*, London: University of Chicago Press.

Dearlove, J. and Saunders, P. (1984) *Introduction to British Politics: Analysing a Capitalist Democracy*, Cambridge: Polity Press.

de Jasay, A. (1985) *The State*, Oxford: Basil Blackwell.

Dickson, D. (1974) *Alternative Technology and the Politics of Technical Change*, London: Fontana.

Die Grünen (1983) *Programme of the German Green Party*, London: Heretic Books.

Dunleavy, P. and O'Leary, B. (1987) *Theories of the State: The Politics of Liberal Democracy*, London: Macmillan.

Dworkin, R. M. (1971) 'Law and civil disobedience', in J. Rachels (ed.), *Moral Problems: A Collection of Philosophical Essays*, New York: Harper & Row.

Eder, K. (1985) 'The "new social movements": moral crusades, political pressure groups, or social movements?', *Social Research* 52(4): 869–90.

Elgin, D. (1981) *Voluntary Simplicity*, New York: William Morrow.

Elliott, D. and Elliott, R. (1976) *The Control of Technology*, London: Wykeham Publications.

Enzensberger, H. M. (1974) 'A critique of political ecology', *New Left Review*, no. 84: 3–31.

Galtung, J. (1984) *There Are Alternatives! Four Roads to Peace and Security*, Nottingham: Spokesman.

Gaskins, R. H. (1989) *Environmental Accidents: Personal Injury and Public Responsibility*, Philadelphia: Temple University Press.

Goldsmith, E., Allen, R., Allaby, M., Davoli, J. and Lawrence, S. (1972) *A Blueprint for Survival*, Harmondsworth: Penguin.

Goodwin, J. and Skocpol, T. (1989) 'Explaining revolutions in the contemporary Third World', *Politics and Society* 12(4): 489–508.

Grundmann, R. (1991) *Marxism and Ecology*, Oxford: Clarendon Press.

Held, D. (1987) *Models of Democracy*, Cambridge: Polity Press.

Horsburgh, H. J. N. (1981) 'Reply to Kai Nielsen', *Inquiry* 24: 59–73.

Illich, I. (1975) *Tools for Conviviality*, London: Fontana.

Inglehart, R. (1981) 'Post-materialism in an environment of insecurity', *The American Political Science Review* 75: 880–900.

Kropotkin, P. (1974) *Fields, Factories and Workshops Tomorrow*, C. Ward (ed.), London: George Allen & Unwin.

Lovins, A. B. (1979) *Soft Energy Paths: Toward a Durable Peace*, New York: Harper & Row.

Macpherson, C. B. (1977) *The Life and Times of Liberal Democracy*, Oxford: Oxford University Press.

Marglin, S. A. (1982) 'What do the bosses do? The origins and functions of hierarchy in capitalist production', in A. Giddens and D. Held (eds), *Classes, Power, and Conflict: Classical and Contemporary Debates*, London: Macmillan.

Marx, K. and Engels, F. (1970) *Selected Works in One Volume*, London: Lawrence & Wishart.

Morris, W. (1970) *News from Nowhere*, London: Routledge & Kegan Paul.

Narveson, J. (1971) 'Pacifism: a philosophical analysis', in J. Rachels (ed.), *Moral Problems: A Collection of Philosophical Essays*, New York: Harper & Row.

Offe, C. and Ronge, V. (1982) 'Theses on the theory of the state', in A. Giddens and D. Held (eds), *Classes, Power, and Conflict: Classical and Contemporary Debates*, London: Macmillan.

O'Riordan, T. (1981) *Environmentalism*, London: Pion.

Pateman, C. (1970) *Participation and Democratic Theory*, Cambridge: Cambridge University Press.

Porritt, J. (1984) *Seeing Green: The Politics of Ecology Explained*, Oxford: Basil Blackwell.

Poulantzas, N. (1973) *Political Power and Social Classes*, London: New Left Books.

Rawls, J. (1971) 'The justification of civil disobedience', in J. Rachels (ed.), *Moral Problems: A Collection of Philosophical Essays*, New York: Harper & Row.

Routley, R. (1984) 'On the alleged inconsistency, moral insensitivity and fanaticism of pacifism', *Inquiry* 27: 117–36.

Sale, K. (1980) *Human Scale*, London: Secker & Warburg.

Schell, J. A. (1982) *The Fate of the Earth*, London: Picador.

Schumpeter, J. A. (1987) *Capitalism, Socialism and Democracy*, London: Unwin.

Sharp, G. (1973) *The Politics of Nonviolent Action* (3 vols), Massachusetts: Porter Sargent.

Singer, P. (1973) *Democracy and Disobedience*, Oxford: Oxford University Press.

Skocpol, T. (1979) *States and Social Revolutions: A Comparative Analysis of France, Russia, and China*, Cambridge: Cambridge University Press.

Spretnak, C. and Capra, F. (1985) *Green Politics*, London: Paladin.

Taylor, M. (1976) *Anarchy and Cooperation*, London: John Wiley.

—— (1982) *Community, Anarchy and Liberty*, Cambridge: Cambridge University Press.

—— (1988) 'Rationality and revolutionary collective action', in M. Taylor (ed.), *Rationality and Revolution*, Cambridge: Cambridge University Press.

—— (1989) 'Structure, culture and action in the explanation of social change', *Politics and Society* 17(1): 115–60.

Thomas, C. (1983) 'Alternative technology: a feminist technology?', in L. Caldecott and S. Leland (eds), *Reclaim the Earth: Women Speak out for Life on Earth*, London: The Women's Press.

Waring, M. (1989) *If Women Counted: A New Feminist Economics*, London: Macmillan.

Weber, M. (1970) 'Politics as a vocation', in H. H. Gerth and C. Wright Mills (eds), *From Max Weber*, London: Routledge & Kegan Paul.

4

GREEN DEMOCRACY?

Michael Saward

Between a great people and the earth springs a passionate attachment, lifelong – and the earth loves indeed her children, broad-breasted, broad-bowed, and talks with them night and day, storm and sunshine, summer and winter alike. . . . Owners and occupiers then fall into their places; the trees wave proud and free upon the headlands; the little brooks run with a wonderful new music under the brambles and the grass. . . . Government and law and police then fall into their places – the earth gives her own laws; Democracy just begins to open her eyes and peep! and the rabble of unfaithful bishops, priests, generals, landlords, capitalists, lawyers, Kings, Queens, patronisers and polite idlers goes scuttling down into general oblivion, faithfulness emerges, self-reliance, self-help, passionate comradeship.

Edward Carpenter, *Towards Democracy*

The style is different, but the sentiments of nineteenth-century English anarchist Edward Carpenter could express the hopes of a range of contemporary Greens.[1] Not least of the many threads from communitarian anarchism present in 'dark green' utopian visions of a sustainable society is that it will be more democratic than our present societies (Dobson 1990: 3–4). Commonly, the hope and the belief is that truly ecological societies will be small, decentralized communities with decision-making procedures based on 'direct' rather than 'representative' democracy. This, however, is by no means the whole picture. As Bramwell writes, '[p]olitical ecology . . . started as a progressive, science-based, anti-democratic movement' (Bramwell 1989: 7). Contemporary media images of the Greens have raised the spectre of 'the Stalins of greenery' – the title used by Richard Davy when he wrote 'it is difficult to see how many of [the Greens'] central propositions can be translated into politics without very authoritarian methods' – and have pointed to the 'dogmatic' analyses, 'authoritarian' policies and 'messianic' messages on 'the dark side of the Greens', in Andrew McHallam's terms.[2] Are Greens undemocratic? If so, how? And what can they do about it?

A key premise of this chapter is that all political ideologies (especially party ideologies) tend to use the term 'democracy' for legitimation of positions rather than illumination. The Greens are no exception to the rule, just different in the way they do it. Democracy is a word whose meaning is unfixed, perhaps 'essentially contestable' (Connolly 1983). We can, and should, get behind the rhetoric and explore the substance of ideological invocations of 'democracy'.[3]

The discussion proceeds as follows: first, the relationship between green values and democracy is explored; second, the vision(s) of democracy set out by various green political writers will be discussed; third, alternative or modified visions of democracy which may be less incompatible with green values will be suggested; and finally, the question of political culture and green strategies will be explored in the light of the tensions in green positions outlined previously. The overall aim is to clarify, criticize and suggest revisions to the green invocation of democracy.

GREEN VALUES AND DEMOCRACY

The main point of this section is that there is a strong potential contradiction between green policy values and the styles of democracy which are (a) generally included as a part of those values, or (b) posited alongside them as an additional green 'good'. In other words, ecological value-sets often contain a considerable tension between advocating certain essential policy outcomes and valuing (direct) democratic procedures. To show this, we need to look at the nature of green ideas on value, value-sets and hierarchies of values.

It is often claimed that society as we know it will crumble without acceptance of ecological principles such as the need to create a sustainable society.[4] Such principles are often put forward in the context of two opposing 'worldviews', between which there is little or no intermediate ground. O'Riordan has referred to this as the 'simple binary choice' that environmental philosophers tend to offer (O'Riordan 1981: 300). Kvaloy contrasts the 'Industrial Growth Society (IGS)' with the 'Life Necessities Society (LNS)' (Kvaloy 1990). Sale contrasts 'Bioregional' and 'Industrio-Scientific' paradigms (Sale 1985: 50). Clearly, the language is such that our choice is no choice – survival or self-administered destruction. For some writers, values or principles become imperatives. From Ophuls's point of view, for example, 'liberal democracy as we know it . . . is doomed by ecological scarcity; we need a completely new political philosophy and set of institutions' (Ophuls 1977a: 3). Incremental tinkering is part of the problem and cannot be, or give rise to, a solution (Ophuls 1977b: 160).

To the extent that the realization of certain green principles – like dealing urgently with over-population – is seen as essential, we are dealing with an imperative that has a no-real-choice quality. The particular intellectual strategy involved is to (a) define the existing state of affairs in terms of single imperatives (growth, 'progress'); (b) set up an opposing, green, imperative; and (c) the force of the expressed necessity of getting from the eco-bad to the eco-good society is present by the choice being restricted to two alternatives, one of which is rationally unchoosable. As Porritt writes, the 'ecological imperative' reminds us 'that the protection of the Earth's natural systems is something we *all* depend on' (Porritt 1984: 98).

There is no doubt, then, that we are in many cases dealing with an imperative. It usually contains a number of elements, variously economic, political, social, geographical, religious, and so on. Its force comes partly from the holism it embodies, and partly from its basis in the idea of the 'intrinsic value' of nature. Holism implies that the various elements which make up the imperative are compatible – or, that taken singly they are necessary but insufficient conditions for an 'environmentally benign dynamic' (see Carter, Ch. 3 this volume). The elements of the imperative gain their importance, and their links with each other, by being referable back to a common, intrinsic value of nature. It is at this point that we can pick up the position of democracy or 'direct democracy' in lists of basic values set out by Greens.

Lists of principles or values abound in green writing. In the present context, the important point is that democracy, in one or other of its forms (often direct or participatory[5]), is included in the lists. I will cite three examples.

Paehlke lists thirteen 'central value assertions' or 'value priorities' of environmentalism. These include the need for a global perspective, human humility, heightened respect for all life, sustainability, simplicity and decentralization. The thirteenth value assertion is a commitment to democracy. This one, though, has a distinct status in his list. It 'can be seen as the most acceptable and practical means to achieving the previous twelve' (Paehlke 1989: 145). It is not a value in quite the same sense as his other twelve. The other values are important because they have intrinsic merit, once a certain view of life is adopted. The value of democracy, however, is of a different order, more instrumental and pragmatic. The justification for its being in the list at all rests on different grounds from the other twelve priorities, and these grounds are apparently not moral ones, aside from a vague notion of 'acceptability'.

Porritt offers an impressive list of twenty-nine characteristics of the 'politics of ecology' paradigm (as opposed to the 'politics of industrialism' paradigm). One item contrasts ecological politics' 'direct democracy' with the 'representative democracy' of industrial politics (Porritt 1984: 216–17). The question is, is direct democracy – which I understand to be a decision-making procedure by which a specified group of people themselves make binding collective decisions without intermediaries or representatives – something that can fit comfortably with the other elements of the overall imperative on such a list? A small excursion to look at democracy will help us here.

In its more pure or direct forms, democracy is a method of decision-making where decisions are made *by* the people and not in any sense *for* them. This is the line taken by May, for example, in his attempt to offer a more-or-less neutral definition of the term. May defines democracy as 'responsive rule': 'necessary correspondence between acts of government and the wishes with respect to those acts of the persons who are affected' (May 1978: 1). In other words, the outcomes that the majority want are the ones that they get, barring constitutional limitations. Clearly, much depends upon what constitutional limitations ought to be placed on outcomes. The most logical answer for a democrat is along the lines 'only those limits which are logically necessary for the persistence of responsive rule'. This is close to the notion of democracy as being 'self-binding': it restricts itself, or proscribes certain types of outcome, in order to preserve itself (Salecl 1991). Such general terms set the framework, though just what are the logically necessary conditions for democracy is another (long and probably inconclusive) story, for which there is insufficient space here.

The terms by which democracy self-binds can by no means encompass the range of outcomes or desirable characteristics of the 'politics of ecology' which Porritt sets out. Is a direct democratic procedure compatible with imperative goals like 'local production for local need', 'low consumption', 'labour-intensive production', and 'voluntary simplicity' (other items from Porritt's list)?

In the same way we can account for the logical tensions in the programme of the German Green Party. 'Grassroots democracy' is one of the four 'basic principles' of the party's 'global conception' (*Programme of the German Green Party* 1983: 7–9). Another is the 'ecological': 'Proceeding from the laws of nature, and especially from the knowledge that unlimited growth is impossible in a limited system, an ecological policy means understanding ourselves and our environment as part of nature' (*Programme of the German Green Party* 1983: 7). In effect, this means that certain outcomes are proscribed from decision-making procedures. Such proscribed outcomes must surely go well beyond any plausible list of outcomes which must be proscribed in the interests of defending a direct democratic decision procedure. Therefore, there is a clear tension between elements of the value-set, whereas given the holism the green imperative is based on we would have the right to expect these goals and values to be thoroughly compatible.

The ambiguous position of democracy in Paehlke's list of 'value assertions' is an unspoken product of this kind of tension. Democracy, especially direct democracy, is just not something that sits comfortably in such a list. Paehlke puts himself in a contradictory position by citing democracy as a central value while providing a distinct, and distinctly instrumental, justification for its being on the list at all.

The idea that nature has 'intrinsic value' adds to the problem. Something of intrinsic value has, in the first instance at least, more value than something valued for contingent reasons. Such values cannot be overridden by something for which only instrumental justifications can be offered. The notion of intrinsic value, or intrinsic merit, is present in much of the green writing[6]: note for example the 'law of nature' approach in the German Greens' *Programme*. And as Bramwell writes: 'The ecologist believes that nature embodies eternal reality. . . . There is a scepticism about "traditional" science, but no rejection of objectivity' (Bramwell 1989: 18). On ecologism's own bases, democracy's membership of the family of green values seems shaky indeed.

This dilemma is recognized in some green writing. Stillman recognizes it in terms of consent for government:

> ecologically sound policies by an effective and strong government would limit freedom as currently defined [and] the scope of democratic decision-making and political compromise . . . [to do so] is to limit major factors that produce consent among citizens of this country [the US] and thus produce legitimacy for the government.
>
> (Stillman 1974: 56)

Commenting on a similar line of thought, Boris Frankel accuses Rudolf Bahro of an 'anti-democratic' vision of an ecological society, given that politics as conflict will have no place in a sea of 'givens' (Frankel 1987: 230). Frankel sees the dilemma as being similar to that of socialists – deeming certain things to be desirable in an ultimate sense, but proclaiming attachment to democracy and the respect for a diversity of values which it implies (Frankel 1987: 158). Ophuls has stated the matter especially clearly. The basic question about politics, he writes, is 'Is the way we organize our communal life and rule ourselves compatible with ecological imperatives and other natural laws? . . . how we run our lives will be increasingly determined by ecological imperatives' (Ophuls 1977a: 7–8).

However, this tension arises with *lists* of green principles. The lists discussed briefly here do not set out which of the values included are to have priority.[7] Would establishing a hierarchy of values lessen the logical tensions outlined? Here, we need to consider ways in which values might, in a certain context, be traded off against each other without any one value being traded right off the board. Barry has suggested that trade-offs can operate according to a principle of consistency. That is, so long as one trade-off and the next accord to some common criteria of relative merit, trade-offs can be formulated at a given time according to the yardstick of precedent (Barry 1965). This does not help us, however. Consistency has no moral content in and of itself. To be consistent may be to be consistently wrong. Goodin and Wilenski suggest that trade-offs between principles operating at the same level can be made by appeals to higher-level principles (Goodin and Wilenski 1984). But in our case, the higher-level principles can only be akin to 'laws of nature', against which democratic procedures must also inevitably be traded off the board.

So, while having a hierarchy of values might provide some criteria by which trade-offs can be made, direct democracy as a value cannot even remain in the new, ordered value-list. Democracy will not be even be retained as a mechanism to decide trade-offs, since the 'laws of nature', which by virtue of being intrinsic ought always to govern our actions in a way that more contingent values do not, will themselves do this job (which is to say that someone interpreting the laws will do it). Having a hierarchy of values does not get us around the basic problem. Kraft thinks he sees a way around:

> Although no-one is quite sure what an ecological politics might look like, a reasonable definition might suggest a polity in which individual behaviour and government policy making are fundamentally consistent with ecological principles. The various elements in such a system would have to be based on a similar set of values and would have to interlock more or less harmoniously. Within those parameters, the extensive political possibilities are still to be explored. There are surely many options beyond the rather grim authoritarian systems foreseen by some.
>
> (Kraft 1977: 179–80)

It seems to me that Kraft is expressing a hope rather than presenting a well-grounded argument. On his own terms, even if issues with little scope, or no far-reaching implications, can be treated democratically in a sustainable society, this is a rather paltry democracy which could not be worthy of the name by any reasonable criteria. Dobson recognizes the problem, basing his discussion on Sale's 'bioregional' account of ecological society (Dobson 1990: 123–9). The logic of problems with highly decentralized communal life leads him to see a number of dilemmas confronting Greens who argue for an egalitarian and democratic sustainable society. Following this logic, he sees that more authoritarian conclusions are difficult to avoid. However, he writes, 'if this is the case, then we are no longer talking about Green politics' (Dobson 1990: 129). This is a curious statement, given what came before it. Dobson implies that green politics can only be a highly democratic politics but his pessimism about the realization of a green democracy is considerable.

The important conclusions to this section are: that at best direct democracy can only be at or near the bottom of value-lists of Greens. A commitment to democracy must clash with core green values which, if taken on board, limit the range of acceptable policy outcomes beyond those self-binding constraints that democracy logically requires.

Before moving to the next section, two further points require consideration. First, it is not rare for democracy to be subsumed under other, perhaps incompatible, values. For example, many prominent democratic theorists agree that liberal democracy is, historically and theoretically, much more liberal than democratic (Macpherson 1977). Indeed, the 'founding father' of liberal democracy, Locke, put natural laws centring on property at the core of his political theory, which attenuated liberal variants of democracy from the start.[8]

Green democracy is perhaps little different from liberal democracy in this respect. Each just interprets the logically necessary conditions of democracy in different ways – liberalism in terms of freedoms that cannot be overridden, and Greens in terms of similarly sacrosanct ecological imperatives. The difference, however, is that liberalism, in theory at least, leaves the conception of the good pursued by individuals up to those individuals, while green theory seeks to define and enact a broad conception of the good to which individuals must conform. If democracy is understood as responsive rule (see pp. 65–6), meaning that rulers are responsive to the felt wishes of (a majority of) citizens, then there is a natural compatibility between liberalism and democracy which does not obtain between ecologism and democracy. Now, given the green-house effect and the depletion of the ozone layer, it *may* be desirable that we move more towards full realization of green imperatives and (if need be) reduce our adherence to both liberalism and democracy. That, however, is a different argument. What is at stake here is the coherence of the claims that many Greens make about democracy within their political ideas.

Second, there is a fall-back green position not dealt with above: the argument that democracy can be derived from principles of nature. If this argument were convincing, then a good deal of the critique above would be turned upside down. Dobson summarises the arguments of various green writers as follows:

> The principal features of the natural world and the political and social prescriptions or conclusions that can be drawn from them are:
> diversity   – toleration, stability and democracy
> interdependence   – equality
> longevity   – tradition
> nature as 'female' – a particular conception of feminism
>
> (Dobson 1990: 24)

Note the variety of good things in the right column which can allegedly be derived from nature. A number of points need to be made about this. First, some of these implications for people are radically underspecified. 'Equality' for example is one of the slipperiest terms in the political vocabulary. This is why Rae, for example, talks about 'equal*ities*' (Rae 1981). On its own the word specifies nothing useful or illuminating. Second, there are major tensions between these goods. Take stability and democracy. Dahl's classic account from the 1950s sees the two as compatible: his vision of pluralist democracy allowed for competition between interest groups in the context of accepted norms internalized by 'social training' (Dahl 1956). But he and Almond and Verba, for instance, have been among a range of writers on democracy who have been accused convincingly of granting greater priority to stability than democracy (Almond and Verba 1989, Pateman 1970). Can democracy also be applauded for flexibility and dynamism? Can *they* not be derived from nature also? Further, is stability necessarily good in itself? And just what kind of 'stability' is being applauded here? Romania was a rather stable polity up to Christmas 1989. 'Tradition' is another difficult concept. Did not Burke oppose republicanism, and the rights of the working class and agricultural labourers to express their concerns themselves without their 'betters' doing it for them, in the name of tradition (Burke 1986)? How, then, does tradition sit with democracy – or equality? In short, the vagueness and incompatibilities in the table render it next to meaningless. This is quite apart from the fact that, without too strenuous an effort, just about any prescription could surely be found a basis in 'nature'. Try it with 'freedom' or 'autonomy'. Or perhaps the 'war of all against all'.[9]

There may, to be sure, be more convincing ways of 'deriving' democracy from 'nature' than those presented here. Any such argument, however, will rely on metaphor for its power. Arguments based on metaphor require that the person on the receiving end of the argument must actively participate in perceiving the truth being claimed, much more so than in other forms of argument. As Combs-Schilling writes:

> Metaphor places no restrictions on the equivalence it asserts. It boldly states that one is the same as the other without specifying what the equivalence involves, thereby demanding that the reader/observer actively use his or her imagination to resolve wherein the likeness lies, what qualities the two subjects hold in common. The reader/observer must, so to speak, fill in the blanks.
>
> (Combs-Schilling 1989: 245–6)

Any asserted metaphorical equivalence of nature and democracy, however brilliant, will always be limited by the possibilities inherent in metaphorical argument.

The next section explores more closely what some prominent Greens say about democracy, especially direct democracy. We can then move on to examine how the position established so far need not lead us to bleak conclusions.

WHAT GREEN DEMOCRACY?

If Greens claimed that the rather attenuated form of democracy that our contemporary liberal democracies display were the basis for their vision of democracy, then the above tensions would be lessened. They would be lessened at the expense of greater democracy, and in favour of greater bureaucracy; less government by the people, more government for the people. In other words, when they talk about democracy the Greens could just say that they would run the present, highly indirect, 'democratic' systems in a slightly different way than other parties. Some basic tensions would remain, as suggested by the brief discussion of visions of 'the good' above, but large doses of scepticism about green claims regarding democracy would be less founded. However, by and large this is not the position of 'dark Greens' at least. In the work of Porritt, Naess, Bahro, Bookchin and others (and see Carter, Ch. 3 in this volume), the radical green aim is to deepen democracy, to institute direct democracy in decentralized units far from the impersonal and distant institutions of state characteristic of modern liberal democracies. In other words, many Greens seek to bring about direct democracy in forms other than those with which most of us are reasonably familiar, such as the referendum and the initiative. We have seen that democracy can only be subordinate in a green hierarchy of values. This is underlined when radical forms of direct democracy are what is being advocated. Advocates of direct democracy reject 'government for the people' – which implies representatives activating some notion of people's 'best interests' possibly against their immediate felt interests[10] – in favour of 'government by the people', where only subjective interests are taken into account.[11] We need now to be more specific about just what green visions of democracy entail, in order to see if there is something in them which unnecessarily inflames the basic tension between central green values and the green advocacy of democracy.

There is no unified vision of green democracy. We need to be careful not to impose an artificial unity where none exists (Frankel 1987: 248). Ophuls warns about specifying too much since we cannot be sure what shape a truly sustainable society might take (Ophuls 1977a: 222). Nevertheless, we can set out two sorts of vision, the authoritarian (which fits with central green values) and communitarian direct democracy (which does not).

The most outrageous authoritarianism comes from extremist groups like the American *Earth First!* Scott worries about 'brown spots' in the greenery (Scott 1990: 100). Beyond these extremes, the work of Ophuls – who deals explicitly and at length with ecological political theory – can be taken as a clear example of authoritarian tendencies.[12] He has suggested that with the return to scarcity we must 'question whether democracy as we know it can survive' (Ophuls 1974). He suggests a return to 'competence', or what Dahl calls 'guardian-ship' (Dahl 1989), and calls on a metaphor as old as western political theory:

> the closer you are to the situation of a vessel embarked on a dangerous voyage, the greater the rationale for the rule of the competent few. But, as the earth and its various territories approach more and more closely to a realization of the spaceship metaphor with each step toward the ultimate ecological limits, the highest degree of competence will become indis-pensable for effective rule, and even a democratic theorist might have to begin to echo Plato's *Republic*: The polity is a ship of state that must be commanded by the best pilots, or it will founder.
>
> (Ophuls 1974: 40)

The 'best pilots' will be those who have, more than anything else, wholly accepted the strong priority of central green values. We ought on this account to revive Plato on competence and Burke on strong trusteeship. Ophuls sees a return to the nondemocratic 'classic polity' (Ophuls 1974: 42) – which leaves one wondering where the Athenian democracy might fit into his picture. On the whole, Ophuls represents the clearest credible example of the authoritarian tendency in green political theory.

Most visions of green democracy are, however, variants on a model of direct democracy in small, often rural, face-to-face communities, charac-terized by labour-intensive production, self-reliance if not self-sufficiency, a related minimization of trade and travel between communities, and decision-making by face-to-face assemblies along the lines of the Athenian assembly. For Bookchin, the emphasis is on public talk and public spaces in the decentralized communities, breaking down distinctions between politics and administration, and the need for 'reempowerment' of people through 'participation, involvement, and a sense of citizenship that stresses activity, not on the delegation of power and spectatorial politics' (Bookchin 1982: 335-6). The German Greens emphasize direct democracy at the base of their party structure. The central importance of direct democracy in decentralized communities is emphasized in a variety of accounts of green politics.[13] Accounts vary, of course. Sale gives priority to 'bioregional' organization of communities over direct or other forms of democracy; Bookchin gives a higher priority to direct democracy. Nevertheless, this is a strong and persistent thread in green writing.

Is the green vision of direct democracy *desirable*? We can explore this briefly through the elements of the green vision: the stress on small decentralized communities, face-to-face assemblies and proximate forms of participation and accountability, rotation of representatives and a strong emphasis on equality of input from all community members. Face-to-face participation arguably gives rise to greater opportunities for manipulation of the assembly (Frankel 1987: 175-6). The German Greens have had to face up to presentational and other problems associated with the rotation of leaders, admittedly in the context of a representative system (Spretnak and Capra 1985: 38-9). Breaking down politics/administration distinctions may open up sensitive posts and jobs to inexpertness and incompetence. Proximity does not guarantee genuine access and, in particular, the power of ordinary assembly members to influence the shape of the assembly agenda. Not having a structure of representation in any consistent respect opens up the possibility that informal leaders will be able to impose themselves rather than be proposed by the subject population. Equality *between* communities – for example, in terms of health care and education – is a persistent problem; indeed, the broader question of links between decentralized communities, and the extent to which extensive links might undermine the autonomy and scope of decision-making in individual community assemblies, is a persistent theme in the critical literature (Dobson 1990: 124). Potentially undermining all aspects of a commune-based direct democracy is the problem which Gorz raises:

> the more self-sufficient and numerically limited a community is, the smaller the range of activities and choices it can offer to its members. If it has no opening to an area of exogenous activity, knowledge and production, the community becomes a prison.
>
> (Dobson 1990: 124)

In sum, first, there is no need to doubt the sincerity of various green visions of radical direct democracy. It is rather the basis on which such visions are put forward, and the doubtful desirability of direct democracy *in this form*, which is questionable.

ELEMENTS OF AN ALTERNATIVE VISION

We can set out in general terms the elements of a semi-direct democracy which is arguably (a) more likely to enhance citizen participation and influence, (b) more feasible, and (c) possibly even more in line with central green values. There are five key areas of revision: the possibility of 'teledemocracy'; the environmental advantage of urban living; breaking down rigid divisions between direct and representative forms of democracy; the ready acceptance of confederal (and perhaps supranational) institutions; and philosophical pragmatism.

The idea that developments in communications technologies could usher in radically new forms of direct political participation is an old one. Recent commentators have explored the possibilities of interactive communication technologies for voting, consultation, conferencing, and so on.[14] Less sober accounts see direct voting via television referenda as completely cutting out intermediaries and giving power back to the people: Toffler's view was that 'Public opinion will become the law of the land' (Arterton 1987: 18). More sober accounts stress a variety of 'teledemocracy' schemes and a number of problems, such as access, agenda-setting and citizen apathy, associated differentially with each of them (Arterton 1987). Logical problems with voting procedures which neither people nor computers can solve are stressed by McLean in his account of new technology and democracy (McLean 1986). There is far from being a single, unified account of the extent of the promise of teledemocracy or the forms it might take.

A number of real teledemocracy projects, though, have shown some of the things that discussions and voting using new interactive technologies can achieve – or at least can add to representative structures. Largely, the achievements can be seen as being in the area of the direction of communications in democracies. New technologies can add a stronger 'bottom-up' dimension to communications between leaders and led, and slightly differently to more 'horizontal' communications between citizens which would overcome their individual isolation (von Alemann and Tonnesmann 1990). Arterton's study shows the promise (as well as the many problems) of some ways of using technology to stimulate and enhance the impact and quality of citizen participation in politics in the US, almost exclusively at the local level (Arterton 1987). Barber is perhaps the most prominent example of a democratic theorist putting great faith in teledemocracy to revitalize local participation and local political power in his vision of 'strong democracy'. As one of a range of far-reaching reforms, including the establishment of 'neighbourhood assemblies', he advocates 'a national civic communications cooperative to regulate and oversee the civic use of new communications technology and to supervise debate and discussion of referendum issues' (Barber 1984: 307).

While the forms of teledemocracy are many and various, and such concrete evidence as exists suggests that not much more than rather modest applications on a local level can seriously be contemplated, there is food for thought here for Greens who worry about democracy. There is often a strong ambivalence about the role of technology in a sustainable society. As Bramwell writes: 'Technophiles and technophobes have always warred within ecologism' (Bramwell 1989: 7). Bookchin wants just face-to-face communication: 'we could expect that . . . members of the communities would be disposed to deal with one another in face-to-face relationships rather than by electronic means' (Bookchin 1982: 345). Others stress the dangers of taking the technological road for a variety of reasons (Ophuls 1974: 41). Of course, there are technophiles as well.[15] The point is that accepting some new communications technologies might help to enhance and make more realistic the radical green vision of direct democracy. For one thing, the need for and dangers of face-to-face proximity in decision-making assemblies can be partially avoided – by 'virtual proximity' as it were. Frankel discusses the work of Feenberg in this context: 'According to Feenberg, teleconferencing liberates participants from the usual constraints of face-to-face communication – physical and mental intimidation, emotional outbursts, gender discrimination and wasted energy' (Frankel 1987: 176).

The second revision of the green vision of direct democracy would be to accept the ecological and political advantages of urban living. Hostility to cities is a persistent theme in green writing. Sale has written that: 'The contemporary high rise city . . . is an ecological parasite as it extracts its lifeblood from elsewhere and an ecological pathogen as it sends back its wastes' (Sale 1985: 65). Communities will be 'rooted in the land' and cities will 'shrink', on Ophuls's account (Ophuls 1977a: 241). Paehlke, however, offers a sober and telling antidote to such views, setting out nine 'principal environmental advantages of high-density urban living' (Paehlke 1989: 247–50):

1 city homes are closer together and use less energy as a result;
2 birth-rates in cities are lower;
3 there is a greater use of energy-efficient public transport;
4 distances travelled are less;
5 carless cities can be designed;
6 recycling, re-use and repair are less costly;
7 some major ecological problems – acid rain, the greenhouse effect – have little to do with getting back to the countryside;
8 hazardous waste treatment facilities with greater coverage can be used;
9 urban living protects land and agriculture.

This is a convincing list, to which we could add the qualities of a diversity of activities and contact with more people. Further, the chances of using tele-democratic mechanisms are in some respects greater in urban concentrations than elsewhere. The MINERVA project involving large multi-occupancy buildings discussed by Arterton is a case in point (Arterton 1987: 82ff).

The third suggested revision is that green theorists ought not to see direct and representative democracy as mutually exclusive categories, as Weale (1983) and Bobbio (1987) suggest. Most accounts of direct democracy which call on existing or feasible examples cite democracy as a complement to, and a deepening of, representative democracy. Some of the more promising results of Arterton's teledemocracy study come from projects where direct grilling of local representatives via interactive cable television enhanced the capacity and the confidence of local citizens in voicing their concerns and getting them followed up (Arterton 1987: 97ff). And while public inquiries, such as those in Britain in recent years into new civil nuclear installations, have had a strongly tokenistic, co-optive flavour (Saward 1992), the basic format can be seen as promising in terms of enhancing genuine participation of groups and people who might otherwise be marginalized from political decision-making procedures.

The fourth revision involves Greens accepting confederal and perhaps supranational political structures. A prominent green slogan is 'think globally, act locally'. Sometimes thinking globally must involve acting globally as well – or at least acting more than just locally, and therefore by implication differently in different localities/communities. Green attitudes in this area do vary a good deal. Some, like Sale, are very wary of the dangers of confederation (Sale 1985: 96). Dobson, commenting generally on green ideas in this area, sees the apparent inevitability of supracommunal structures but draws no clear conclusions regarding the implications of this for democratic practice (Dobson 1990: 122). It is better to bite the bullet here and see the positive side of supracommunal structures in democratic terms. As Frankel argues:

> a new democratic public sphere of empowered, decentralized and diverse local communities needs a set of national and regional state structures to facilitate legal, economic, educational and cultural values and practices, to support those local citizens lacking in material and cultural resources, and to settle the many disputes and conflicts which will continue to be a part of any foreseeable social formation. A combination of local, direct democracy and new semi-direct democratic structures at the national level will make life for traditional political parties very difficult if not impossible. This development is to be applauded because too many citizens in contemporary societies have an impoverished notion of the possibilities of democratic participation and often equate democracy with voting rituals.
>
> (Frankel 1987: 230–1)

These four revisions are basically institutional ones. The final, and most important, revision is a philosophical one. If convincing, it suggests that Greens should not think in terms of overriding principles or imperatives. Indeed, it suggests that to think in terms of imperatives based on arguments about intrinsic merit is unjustifiable.

We can start with the justification of democracy itself. Most classic accounts do not see democracy as a value in itself, justifying it (or a version of it) rather as a means to some separate, valued end. Locke justified the ultimate accountability of government to citizens in terms of natural laws which owed nothing to the value of democratic procedures – the attachment was instrumental (Locke 1924). Bentham and James Mill were heavily critical of contractarian arguments based on natural law fictions, but justified their advocacy of (representative) democracy in terms of another reductive assumption that the common good was the greatest happiness of the greatest number (Mill 1978). This, too, was an instrumental justification. Schumpeter was a reluctant democrat whose justification of his 'economic' model of democracy was that it might avoid Fascist tyranny (Schumpeter 1976).

The efforts of Thorson have signalled a different approach. He argues that 'we are never justified in refusing to consider the possibility that we might be wrong' (Thorson 1962). It is on the basis of such pragmatism, the acceptance that we can never be certain, that he finds a justification for democracy that does not rest on some assumption about nature or human nature. 'Do not block the way of inquiry', as he quotes Pierce (Thorson 1962: 120). His bottom-line idea is that a lack of proof cannot cancel the possibility of rational justification. On this view, democracy can be justified rationally precisely because of the impossibility of incontrovertible proof of anything. Further, it can be justified in terms of both representative and direct democracy, so long as correspondence between policies and citizen preferences is attained to some minimally acceptable degree.

Pragmatism forms the basis for Barber's critique of liberal democracy, which he likens to 'politics as zookeeping' in so far as liberalism conceives of individuals as isolated units of wants rather than as social beings (Barber 1984: 3ff). Rather than find foundations in nature, or in human nature, for democracy, he argues for a conception of 'politics as epistemology', where the 'quest for certainty' has been abandoned and participatory democracy becomes the basis for discovering practical and fulfilling actions in human communities. Crucially, in the light of the above discussion, Barber writes: 'Truth in politics seems, as William James said of truth in general, to be something which is "made in the course of experience" rather than something discovered or disclosed and then acted upon' (Barber 1984: 65).

The suggestion here is that green imperatives, like liberal assumptions about nature and human nature, put democracy in a strait-jacket in that they are based on notions of intrinsic value and holism. At the same time, there is no strong justification for Greens advocating democracy. This is why Paehlke, for example, has to fall back upon different, and thoroughly instrumental, grounds to justify his inclusion of democracy in his list of 'central value assertions' of environmentalism. Arguments about 'intrinsic merit', of course, can be enormously intricate (Dobson 1990: 51ff). They are, in the end, an unnecessary hindrance to green thought. Action need not be based on ultimate givens or certainties. Ophuls is wrong to claim that: 'however difficult and controversial the task, we have no choice but to search for some ultimate values by which to construct a post-modern civilization' (Ophuls 1977a: 237). On any account, to equate 'ultimate values' and 'post-modernity' is eccentric.

PRAGMATISM AND POLITICAL CULTURE

It seems that we have a complete opposition between green imperatives and an acceptable justification of democracy. But this is not necessarily the case. Politics without certainty – indeed, politics as a substitute for certainty – has strong echoes in green political thinking. Let us cite two brief examples. Ophuls cites Burke on respecting tradition in the face of apparent certainties which would demand that the world be turned upside down (Ophuls 1974: 42–3). Barber, too, cites Burke approvingly as no respecter of claims to ultimate values (Barber 1984: 130–1, 165). Bookchin writes about the ecological society in terms of public space, public talk, and a conception of direct democracy as encompassing action (Bookchin 1982: 335–6). This has many resonances with Barber's account of 'the particular political functions of talk' in his pragmatic strong democracy (Barber 1984: 176–7). The details have much in common; the bases, though, are radically different, between imperatives based on intrinsic merit on one side and 'politics as epistemology' on the other. On the one side, democracy has no moral justification; on the other, it has.

Our final task is to see if there is a way around this dilemma. Our attention has to move away from political mechanisms and their justification to political culture. There needs, from a green perspective, to be a change in political culture such that it will be compatible with sustainability. This, of course, is a familiar theme from green writing (Ophuls 1977a: 222, Dobson 1990: 13, 59). How does one go about changing attitudes? How to do this, especially, if the 'quest for certainty' is abandoned and we are prepared to suspend full belief in the truth of our own claims?

Green principles expressed as imperatives leave open authoritarian solutions in part by having a highly instrumental attachment to democracy. A revision of the green approach to knowledge, and to democracy, has one very important implication. It strongly underlines the need to embrace uncertainty and therefore the need for constant self-interrogation on what people are being asked to accept and believe. In other words, it suggests that Greens abandon imperatives and accept that persuasion from a flexible position based on uncertainty can be their only legitimate political strategy. This is not to say anything especially new. It can only be the case that 'political change will only occur once people think differently or, more particularly, that sustainable living must be prefaced by sustainable thinking' (Dobson 1990: 140). By abandoning foundationalist myths of intrinsic merit, Greens abandon the implicit arrogance that has made democracy such a tenuous part of green political theory. This does not mean anyone has to stop believing in the need for a radically changed society. It does suggest that the grounds on which someone might seek to bring such a society about will not include the claim to have access to some immutable laws of nature, or of human nature. Therein lies respect for the nonbeliever, and a reconciliation between green principles and democracy.

NOTES

1 In addition to the EPCR workshop participants, the author would like to thank Greg Claeys and John Mattausch for their comments on an earlier draft of this chapter.

2 Davy's views were expressed in *The Independent*, 4 August 1990. McHallam's views were expressed in *The Guardian*, 26 November 1991. The latter article, an extract from an Institute for European Defence and Strategic Studies pamphlet, prompted responses from (among others) Jonathon Porritt (see *The Guardian*, 29 November 1991 and 3 December 1991).

3 We are dealing with 'deep ecology' accounts here for the most part (see Naess 1990).

4 See Bahro's views cited in Scott (1990), chapter 4.

5 'Direct' and 'participatory' democracy are not necessarily the same thing. Direct democracy is about people making decisions directly. Participative democracy may be just about increasing the forms and extent of participation in politics (see Sartori 1987).

6 Bunyard and Morgan-Grenville write: 'We need an ethic that recognises the intrinsic value of all aspects of the nonhuman world' (quoted in Dobson 1990: 51).

7 See Carter (Ch. 3, this volume) for an assertion that *all* elements of an 'environmentally hazardous dynamic' equally must go if we are to achieve an 'environmentally benign dynamic'. My problems with this view stem from its all or nothing approach, especially where democracy is concerned. Carter simply calls liberal democratic states 'centralized, pseudo-representative states', ignoring their benefits, and believes (hopes) simply that a 'decentralized, participatory democracy' will be thoroughly compatible with (for example) an attachment to 'soft technologies' and 'self-sufficient, egalitarian economic relations'.

8 I would argue that what we could call 'nation-ism' – the belief that the nation-state is somehow the basic unit of political organization – has also been granted priority over democracy since roughly the time of Hobbes. Greens at least aim to 'rescue' democracy from the nation-state. But this does not help to ease the basic tensions outlined.

9 Dobson is himself sceptical about many of these values. He writes: 'ecologism encounters a similar problem to that found in the liberal tradition from which it draws: how to have a conception of the Good Society that requires people behaving in a certain way, and yet advertize [sic] for diverse forms of behaviour' (Dobson 1990: 25).

10 Government 'for' the people is prominent, for example, in J. S. Mill's 'Representative government' (Mill 1975), where elite control of policy is advocated in a context of controlled increases in citizen participation in politics.

11 May's 'responsive rule' definition of democracy rules out 'beneficient' rule (see May 1978).

12 O'Riordan (1981: 305ff) briefly discusses other authoritarian writers.

13 See, for example, Spretnak and Capra (1985: 219ff), Porritt (1984), Sale (1985: 62), and Naess (1989: 135, 144).

14 On 'teledemocracy' see Arterton (1987), Barber (1984), McLean (1986), and von Alemann and Tonnesmann (1990).

15 Paehlke (1989: 198–9) cites Leiss: 'The objective of an alternative social policy would not be to return a larger portion of the population to the harshness of circumstances which have in the past often characterized life in the hinterland, but to disperse the advantages of modern technology – deliberately sacrificing some of the dubious ''efficiency'' of centralized production – over a wider variety of situations.'

MICHAEL SAWARD

BIBLIOGRAPHY

Alemann, U. von and Tonnesmann, W. (1990) 'Democracy and new information and communication technologies', Paper presented to the workshop of the same title, ECPR Joint Sessions.
Almond, G. and Verba, S. (1989) *The Civic Culture*, London: Sage.
Arterton, F. C. (1987) *Teledemocracy*, Beverly Hills: Sage.
Barber, B. (1984) *Strong Democracy*, Berkeley: University of California Press.
Barry, B. (1965) *Political Argument*, London and Henley: Routledge & Kegan Paul.
Bobbio, N. (1987) *The Future of Democracy*, Cambridge: Polity.
Bookchin, M. (1982) *The Ecology of Freedom*, Palo Alto: Cheshire Books.
Bramwell, A. (1989) *Ecology in the Twentieth Century*, New Haven and London: Yale University Press.
Burke, E. (1986) *Reflections on the Revolution in France*, London: Penguin.
Burnheim, J. (1985) *Is Democracy Possible?*, Cambridge: Polity.
Combs-Schilling, M. E. (1989) *Sacred Performances*, New York: Columbia University Press.
Connolly, W. (1983) *The Terms of Political Discourse*, Oxford: Martin Robertson.
Dahl, R. A. (1956) *A Preface to Democratic Theory*, Chicago: University of Chicago Press.
—— (1989) *Democracy and its Critics*, New Haven and London: Yale University Press.
Dobson, A. (1990) *Green Political Thought*, London: Unwin Hyman.
Frankel, B. (1987) *The Post-Industrial Utopians*, Oxford: Blackwell.
Goodin, R. and Wilenski, P. (1982) 'Beyond efficiency', *Public Administration Review*, November–December, 512–17.
Kraft, M. (1977) 'Political change and the sustainable society', in D. Pirages (ed.), *The Sustainable Society*, New York: Praeger.
Kvaloy, S. (1990) 'Green philosophy', in J. Button (ed.), *The Green Fuse*, London and New York: Quartet.
Locke, J. (1924) *Two Treatises of Government*, London: Everyman.
McLean, I. (1986) 'Mechanisms for democracy', in D. Held and C. Pollitt (eds), *New Forms of Democracy*, London: Sage.
Macpherson, C. B. (1977) *The Life and Times of Liberal Democracy*, Oxford: Oxford University Press.
May, J. D. (1978) 'Defining democracy', *Political Studies* 26(1): 1–14.
Mill, James (1978) 'Essay on government', in J. Lively and J. Rees (ed), *Utilitarian Logic and Politics*, Oxford: Clarendon.
Mill, John Stuart (1975) 'Representative government', in J. S. Mill, *Three Essays*, Oxford: Oxford University Press.
Naess, A. (1989) *Ecology, Community and Lifestyle*, Cambridge: Cambridge University Press.
—— (1990) 'The basics of deep ecology', in J. Button (ed.), *The Green Fuse*, London and New York: Quartet.
Ophuls, W. (1974) 'Reversal is the Law of Tao', in S. S. Nagel (ed.), *Environmental Politics*, New York: Praeger.
—— (1977a) *Ecology and the Politics of Scarcity*, San Francisco: W. H. Freeman & Co.
—— (1977b) 'The politics of the sustainable society', in D. Pirages (ed.), *The Sustainable Society*, New York: Praeger.
O'Riordan, T. (1981) *Environmentalism*, London: Pion.
Paehlke, R. (1989) *Environmentalism and the Future of Progressive Politics*, New Haven and London: Yale University Press.
Pateman, C. (1970) *Participation and Democratic Theory*, Cambridge: Cambridge University Press.
Porritt, J. (1984) *Seeing Green*, Oxford: Blackwell.
Programme of the German Green Party (1983) London: Heretic.

Rae, D. (1981) *Equalities*, Cambridge, Mass.: Harvard University Press.
Sale, K. (1985) *Dwellers in the Land*, San Francisco: Sierra Club.
Salecl, R. (1991) 'Democracy and violence', *New Foundations*, no. 14: 17–25.
Sartori, G. (1987) *The Theory of Democracy Revisited* (vol. 1), New Jersey: Chatham House.
Saward, M. (1992) *Co-optive Politics and State Legitimacy*, Aldershot: Dartmouth.
Schumpeter, J. (1976) *Capitalism, Socialism and Democracy* (5th edn), London: Allen & Unwin.
Scott, A. (1990) *Ideology and the New Social Movements*, London: Unwin Hyman.
Spretnak, C. and Capra, F. (1985) *Green Politics*, London: Paladin.
Stillman, P. (1974) 'Ecological problems, political theory, and public policy', in S. S. Nagel (ed.), *Environmental Politics*, New York: Praeger.
Thorson, T. (1962) *The Logic of Democracy*, New York: Holt, Rinehart & Winston.
Weale, A. (1983) *Political Theory and Social Policy*, London and Basingstoke: Macmillan.

5

CAN LIBERAL DEMOCRACY SURVIVE THE ENVIRONMENTAL CRISIS?

Sustainability, liberal neutrality and overlapping consensus

Wouter Achterberg

This chapter deals with the problem of legitimacy which, in liberal democracies, results from the pursuit of sustainability or sustainable development as an effort to find a structural solution to the environmental crisis. After giving a rough outline of the political context in which this problem develops, I will discuss the concept of sustainable development as well as some attempts to elaborate it into guidelines for the structural solution or control of environmental problems; I will also give some examples of structural changes in the organization of society which could be the result of the implementation of these guidelines. Thus, the necessity of the legitimacy of a consistent environmental policy, directed at sustainability, becomes clear in a concrete manner. Subsequently, the liberal ideals of political legitimacy and neutrality, and especially Rawls's idea of an overlapping consensus as a theoretical elaboration of these ideals, will be dealt with. Finally, I will explore whether and to what extent Rawls's idea is useful, or can be made useful by alteration and supplementation, to the justification of a structural environmental policy which derives from sustainability as a norm. Special attention will be paid to the situation in The Netherlands.

INTRODUCTION

It seems that a serious environmental policy has not yet got off the ground in liberal-democratic countries, or at least not fast or radically enough. By 'serious environmental and nature policy', I mean a policy that aims at structural changes within society in order to achieve an enduring solution to environmental problems, or at least to create a situation in which they can be controlled. Such a policy is not only directed at maintaining nature as a basis of our social activities for generations to come (sustainability of our use of the environment), but also at protecting, maintaining and developing nature for its own sake (sustainability of nature) (Achterberg 1990).

Probably, radical changes in our system of producing and consuming will be necessary – that is to say, changes in the nature of our (social market-) economy, industry, traffic and agriculture; in short, our entire way of life. Opposition to these changes is likely to be considerable for some time. This is hardly surprising: acquired rights, established interests and deep-rooted life-styles threaten to be infringed.

Therefore, a necessary condition for a structural solution to the environmental crisis is that it is permanently supported by as many people involved (citizens) as is possible. Participation in the decisions which affect one's own life is a central political value of democracy anyhow; but, for strategic reasons also, a structural solution to environmental problems can only be a democratic one: the required sacrifices and the changes of lifestyle connected with it can never be lasting if they are imposed in an authoritarian way. These sacrifices and changes demand voluntariness, understanding and the (conditional) preparedness of all people involved.

Nevertheless, liberal democracies appear to have a hard time as far as a structural solution to environmental problems is concerned. How hard can be illustrated as follows. The government is inclined either to take too little action or no action at all because it is permanently paralysed by continuously changing majorities against every proposed serious regulation or policy – which is certainly partly due to the short-term vision of both politicians and voters – or to impose more or less radical measures, which might be defended as serving the general interest but have no (or insufficient) public support. Both horns of this 'dilemma' are unattractive, to say the least. Either way nothing is really solved, and this is morally unacceptable. The second horn in particular merits some attention.

The imposition, or in any case the selective encouragement, by public policy, of one or more of a set of closely connected conceptions of the good (life) which give pride of place to sustainability but on which there is no consensus in a pluralistic society like ours, is, in general, morally doubtful, since this clashes, for instance, with the basic intuition of liberal (political) morality. According to that intuition the government should be neutral or impartial towards various conceptions of the good life. Since neutrality is an important element of the liberal-democratic conception of the function of government, a plausible justification of its (seeming) loss of neutrality is necessary. The starting points of such a justification must be public as well as generally accepted. Where and how do we find these starting points?

Further, authoritarian impositions are prima facie reprehensible because they require coercion and force, and they are risky too as they are most probably ineffective: every government has only limited means to control and enforce compliance of the great many environmental measures that would be necessary, whereas to refrain from enforcement would affect the legitimacy of the environmental policy and, in the long run, even of public policy in general.

How can one explain the predicament of liberal democracy noted above? It seems to be rooted in structural shortcomings of the democratic political system, particularly in so far as it has taken shape as a pluralism of competing interest groups, which has been called 'polyarchy' by Robert Dahl. Polyarchy can be conceived as the embodiment of interest group liberalism.

> Interest group liberalism is really a formula for a politics of incrementalism and compromise between *organized* interests. In such a system the less organized and the unorganized lose ground, particularly in hard economic times. The elderly, the poor, the unemployed, and the ill are grossly underrepresented. So too, of course, are future generations and other species. Furthermore, . . . interest group liberalism does not allow for moral arguments. Decisions are quantified, disagreements resolved by splitting the difference. Policies favor the most organized groups, whose members tend to be wealthy and tend to seek concrete, economically self-interested, and immediate gains.
>
> (Paehlke 1989: 200)

In such a system only moderate solutions are sought. 'Moderate solutions are piecemeal, partial and technical. They rarely address the need for fundamental changes in our production, consumption and "disposal" habits' (Paehlke 1989: 211). The difficulties of democracy, conceived as the embodiment of interest group liberalism, with the solution of environmental problems can be made clear on the basis of this description of its core.

There seems, however, to be a way out. Its general nature is suggested by Barbour:

> Democracy does . . . face serious challenges in times of social conflict. The answer, I suggest, lies in the development of *common social purposes*, not in the reduction of participation or increased reliance on authority and technical expertise. Only when there are common loyalties to more inclusive goals are people willing to compromise private ends in the public interest, as occurs during time of war or threats to the nation.
>
> (Barbour 1980: 124)

Assuming that we are in the comfortable position of having time to wait for this development to happen, the remedy is, then, the forming of a (new) consensus on a broadened conception of the general interest or the common good. An example of such a conception, which is also non-anthropocentric, is presented by the Dutch environmental economist Hans Opschoor:

> The environment has to be recognized as an essential, fundamental part of the *infrastructure* of social activities and processes . . . the government should realise that it has the task of guaranteeing the continuity of this infrastructure, and not just for the present generation, and not just for human beings . . . even if this is to be at the expense of the present generation's economic interests.
>
> (Opschoor 1989: 184–5)

Dryzek takes a somewhat stronger position here. He suggests that a pre-requisite for the effective solving of environmental problems is 'a consensus about the primacy of ecological values' in society (Dryzek 1987: 130). He deems this difficult because liberal democracy:

> cannot be driven by a single goal. Therefore the fate of ecological values in a polyarchy is to be severely compromised by other values. . . . The paradox is that, unless the members of polyarchy accept a common ecological purpose, then all other human purposes are endangered.
>
> (Dryzek 1987: 130)

We see, then, the possibility of a 'third way', however paradoxical, past the dilemma noted above. Perhaps 'primacy' is too strong. But at the very least the fundamental importance of ecological values for the public realm should be generally acknowledged. And they should be off the political agenda, in the sense that they should not be subjected to the calculus of the benefits and burdens of social co-operation. This implies, as we will shortly see, that the consensus about them has to be overlapping in Rawls's sense. Also the paradox is less marked than Dryzek suggests: the background consensus about the institutional core of liberal democracy can, in the light of the urgency of the environmental crisis, be reactivated and, perhaps, extended to the normative principle of sustainability without jeopardizing the liberal ideal of neutrality. Precisely, Rawls's view about an overlapping consensus is very useful for this purpose.

Before coming back to Rawls I will first examine what the outlines of the structural changes resulting from a serious environmental policy – that is, a policy aiming at sustainability – could be like. Finally, the relationship between overlapping consensus and sustainable development will be discussed.

SUSTAINABILITY

In the literature concerning the environmental crisis and the ecological move-ment, two visions of the nature and solution of environmental problems are traditionally distinguished. First, there is a 'superficial' or reformist vision ('environmentalism'). According to this vision, environmental problems are mainly management problems, soluble within the context of the dominant political and economic system, and without any rigorous change in our values and culture.

Second, there is a profounder vision, aiming at more structural change ('ecologism': for example, 'deep ecology'), according to which a radical change in our attitude towards nature, and therefore also in our political and social system, is necessary (see, for example, Dobson 1990: 13, 33).

To be distinguished from the classical conservationist vision, both visions should be considered the extremes of a continuum representing all the possible visions, from superficial to radical, on the nature of and solution to the environ-mental crisis and, in connection with it, on the relationship between man and nature. The value perspective of environmentalism is anthropocentric, that of ecologism is fully ecocentric. Ecocentric in this sense does not mean subordination of human values to (those of) nature, but complete recognition of non-human nature's intrinsic value. I will not concern myself with the classification of all sorts of positions on this scale, but only with the vision that derives from sustainability or sustainable development as the right path towards the solution of environmental problems. This view can be elaborated in such a way that it tends towards environmentalism, and can be extended as well, as previously suggested, to include proposals that recognize nature's intrinsic value.

The concept of sustainable development has become widely known, in particular through the report *Our Common Future* (1987) from the United Nations' World Commission on Environment and Development (WCED; also known as the Brundtland Commission, after its president). Sustainable development had been recommended as a strategy before – for example, in the *World Conservation Strategy* (International Union for Conservation of Nature and Natural Resources (IUCN) *et al.* 1980), although in this report the emphasis was on living resource conservation. In the Dutch *National Environmental Policy Plan* and *Nature Policy Plan* it has also been adopted as a central guiding notion (see pp. 86–8).

What does 'sustainable' mean? An activity, structure or process is sustainable, if 'for all practical purposes it can continue forever' (IUCN *et al.* 1991: 10). The WCED discusses sustainable development and describes it as follows:

> Sustainable development is a process of change in which the exploitation of resources, the direction of investments, the orientation of technological development and institutional change are all in harmony and enhance both current and future potential to meet human needs and aspirations.
> (WCED 1987: 9, 46)

The WCED does not pretend that this process will be easy or straightforward: 'Painful choices have to be made. Thus, in the final analysis, sustainable development must rest on political will' (WCED 1987: 9; see also xiv).

Elsewhere, the WCED describes sustainable development more concisely: 'sustainable development is development that meets the needs of the present generation without compromising the ability of future generations to meet their own needs' (WCED 1987: 43).

The guideline or criterion for sustainable development that the Commission applies is the next generation's prospect of disposing of a stock resource that is at least as large as the one inherited by the present generation. The capital to be left behind not only comprises goods and the like, produced by man, but also natural resources or the total of these: the 'natural capital' (WCED 1987: 52ff, 57ff; and Annexe 1 under 2). Apparently, the WCED regards capital produced by man and natural capital as interchangeable, and to be valued in the same terms – namely, in terms of their usefulness to the quality of human life. This is a disputable perspective, quite apart from the extremely anthropocentric attitude which is expressed by such a view. This anthropocentrism, incidentally, is frankly expressed by president Gro Harlem Brundtland in the preface: 'Our message', she says, 'is, above all, directed towards people, whose well-being is the ultimate goal of all environment and development policies' (WCED 1987: xiv). But the report also strikes different, non-anthropocentric notes. For example: 'the case for the conservation of nature should not rest only with development goals. It is part of our moral obligation to other living beings and future generations' (WCED 1987: 57; see also 13, 65, 147, 155). The emphasis, however, is on the resource perspective, apparently 'for those who demand an accounting' (WCED 1987: 155).

In this report, a comprehensive programme, inspired by much hope and great optimism, has been proposed. As a matter of fact, it is as much concerned with the First as with the Third World, with the environment as with the economy, and with the present (particularly with securing and improving the life chances of people in the poor countries) as with future generations. It is not surprising, then, that an unambiguous explanation of the term 'sustainable development' is hard to come by:

> The term has been criticized as ambiguous and open to a wide range of interpretations, many of which are contradictory. The confusion has been caused because 'sustainable development', 'sustainable growth' and 'sustainable use' have been used interchangeably, as if their meanings are the same. They are not. 'Sustainable growth' is a contradiction in terms; nothing physical can grow indefinitely. 'Sustainable use' is applicable only to renewable resources: it means using them at rates within their capacity for renewal.
>
> (IUCN *et al.* 1991: 10)

The authors of this report, *Caring for the Earth*, then suggest 'sustainable development' to mean: 'improving the quality of human life within the carrying capacity of supporting ecosystems' (IUCN *et al.* 1991: 10). So much for terminological clarity.

It may be interesting to consider the situation in The Netherlands, where the perspective of sustainable development has been adopted for environmental policy. The discussion about starting points of environmental and nature policies and their elaboration resulted in a number of important policy documents, including the *National Environmental Policy Plan* (NEPP, as well as the updated version NEPP Plus) and the *Nature Policy Plan* (NPP), both accepted in the Parliament (2nd Chamber) by a very large majority in, respectively, September and November 1990. In this context, both policy plans deserve our attention.

The NEPP has adopted the starting point of sustainable development from the report *Our Common Future* (WCED 1987). Sustainable development has to satisfy the needs of the present generation, without endangering the possibilities of future generations for satisfying their needs.

The main objective of environmental management is to maintain the environment's carrying capacity on behalf of sustainable development. The carrying capacity of the environment is damaged if environmental quality can lead to irreversible effects within a generation, such as mortality or morbidity among people, severe nuisance and damage to well-being, the extinction of plant or animal species, the deterioration of ecosystems, damage to water supplies, soil fertility or cultural heritage and impediments to physical and economic development. The environment's carrying capacity is, of course, not exceeded if one single effect occurs, such as, for instance, the extinction of a species. But it is exceeded if these effects occur on a large scale as is currently the case. . . . Sustainable development involves finding a balance between environment and development.

(NEPP 1989: 92)

The NEPP makes it a long-term policy objective to solve or gain control of environmental problems within the time-scale of one generation. The general criteria that are applied are: closing substance cycles, less intensive use of energy resources, and furthering the quality of products instead of their quantity. Unfortunately, these criteria are only elaborated in a technical-scientific way.

So far, the NEPP seems to breathe an enlightened anthropocentric spirit. This is largely true. The NEPP contains a non-anthropocentric objective too, however, although it is hardly reflected in the measures proposed: 'For environmental policy it is important that sustainable development implies a level of environmental quality which does justice to the values of public health and well-being and to the intrinsic values of plants, animals and ecosystems' (NEPP 1989: 42).

The non-anthropocentric side of the policy is stated more emphatically in the NNP. In this document, the principal objective of the government's nature management policy is formulated thus: 'sustainable maintenance, restoration and development of the values of nature and landscape' (NPP 1990: 36). This objective is to be:

pursued in view of the meaning of nature and landscape for humans as well as out of respect for the values attributed to nature on its own. . . . Policy efforts should not only be directed at the protection of values such as public health and well-being, but also at the intrinsic values of plants, animals and ecosystems.

(NPP 1990: 36)

The basic idea of the NPP is directed at the realization of a physically stable 'ecological main structure' within a period of thirty years. This consists of core areas (highly valued nature reserves, including ancient rural landscapes), nature development areas and connecting zones. This main goal is complemented with a 'buffer policy', which has to guarantee the quality of the environment within the main structure, as well as with a policy directed at the protection of species in the areas outside the main structure.

In this connection, it may be interesting to note that article 21 of the Dutch Constitution says: 'the government's concern is aimed at the quality of life of the nation and the protection and improvement of the environment'. Although article 21 deals with a basic social right of Dutch citizens, which involves a duty of the state to guarantee the welfare of these citizens in this respect, it does not imply – if we take it literally – that this is a duty exclusively towards humans, *in casu* the citizens of The Netherlands. Be that as it may, the authors of the NEPP and the NPP appear to interpret this duty in a broad, non-anthropocentric sense!

If we may conceive the broad parliamentary support of the NEPP and the NPP as more than merely pragmatic and *ad hoc*, and if, as a consequence, the NEPP and the NPP not only have just a symbolic meaning, then we may speak of (the beginning of) a consensus of the type that could play the desired legitimating role (this is discussed further on pp. 95–8).

Taking sustainability and sustainable development seriously implies accepting limitations and sacrifices on the part of the citizens. In the prosperous part of the world this will mean a cutdown in consumption (and in this sense an 'economy of enough'), a change of lifestyle, and radical structural changes. To illustrate how far the changes can go, I will give some examples which at the same time draw more attention to the political-philosophical implications of a serious environmental policy.

The problem of *(auto)*mobility. Many people agree that the use of auto-mobiles must be reduced, in favour of other means of (personal) transport which require less energy and raw materials, cause less pollution and other nuisances, and take up less space. Financial incentives (fuel price and tax increases for example – that is, measures that only make driving a car more expensive), will not be enough according to traffic experts, particularly if we also have to take population growth into account. A volume-oriented policy is necessary therefore, even if this means nothing except a sharp decrease in parking facilities. The question is, however, whether this will be enough in the long run. It is likely that there can only be a real prospect of an enduring result if the need for transportation is affected (CREN 1990: 30). This need does not stand on its own, however, but is incorporated in a pattern of producing and consuming, of working and spending leisure time; moreover, it has become closely connected with relation patterns in the private sphere. Reduction of the need for transportation therefore necessarily requires alteration of life patterns and different patterns of physical planning. Thus, the CREN report remarks that

> if the distances between the locations where people live, work and spend their leisure time are minimized . . . then the use of cars can be diminished and substituted by non-motorized transport. *More compact* cities can

constitute an answer to the demand for reducing the need to move. This requires a more stringent policy regarding physical planning.

(CREN 1990: 30)

The implications go even further, as can be seen from the following remarks from Hans Alders, the Dutch Minister of Housing, Physical Planning and Environment, quoted in the Dutch newspaper *NRC-Handelsblad*:

> For years, nearly all political parties, including my own, have been pursuing a policy of social individualization. What has the result been? That in many families nowadays both partners have a job. But not always in the same place, which increases the need for transportation facilities. Therefore we have adjusted the physical planning. But now, we, from Physical Planning, have begun to ask ourselves, very tentatively, whether we have been wise to do this; whether we should not have dealt with the consequences of individualization in a different way. But this doubt from our side does not alter the cultural processes.
>
> (*NRC-Handelsblad*: 8 September 1990)

This example mentioned by Hans Alders makes it clear that cultural changes are necessary for solving environmental problems.

Furthermore, cars have a psychological, or rather a symbolic function. This can become clear when we consider the nature and the normative backgrounds of (auto)mobility. Our western societies are built upon and permeated by mobility. Walzer (1990: 11–12) distinguishes four 'mobilities':

1 geographic mobility;
2 social mobility (going up and down the social ladder, in one's life or in relation to one's parents or children, but also mobility as a result of emancipation and individualization processes);
3 marital mobility (broken marriages, broken families, etc.);
4 political mobility (floating voters etc.).

The cultural processes mentioned above by Alders mainly refer to 1 and 2, and also, but to a lesser degree, to 3.

The four mobilities mentioned by Walzer are deeply rooted in the liberal ethos; they are, for instance, a 'triumphant' (Walzer 1990: 17) manifestation of individual rights and civil liberties.

> In the liberal view . . . the Four Mobilities represent the enactment of liberty, and the pursuit of (private or personal) happiness. And it has to be said that, conceived in this way, liberalism is a genuinely popular creed. Any effort to curtail mobility in the four areas . . . would require a massive and harsh application of state power.
>
> (Walzer 1990: 12)

The conclusion must be that the serious application of even the most modest criteria of sustainable development can lead to explosive situations.

Our society is not only based upon and permeated by mobility, but also based upon and permeated by *growth* and development, in the field of economics as well as that of science and technology, which mutually reinforce each other again. From the view of sustainable development, economic growth has to be limited at least selectively. What is the cause of this urge for growth? According to Opschoor, our society is characterized by an inherent urge for growth at every level (Opschoor 1989: 92–3, 138ff). Most people in our society behave as if the rule 'rather more than less, particularly for myself' is their leading norm. This often results in myopic egoism and consumerism. Individual companies maintain their market position by trying to beat their competitors. As a consequence, they have to keep up or increase their market share and feel compelled to innovate and to pursue profit. The government also applauds economic growth, if only to be able to control the tensions flowing from social inequality.

In all this, a central role is played by the decentralized market which through the price mechanism co-ordinates the separate decisions of consumers and producers (individual companies), whereas the government watches and, if necessary, restores the efficiency of the market process or carries out compensatory actions from considerations of justice. The functioning of the market mechanism severely contributes to the presence and continuation of environmental problems. The imperfections include negative external effects (transfer of costs), time preference, subordination of weak interests that cannot be expressed in terms of money and, finally, the failing supply of collective goods, including a healthy and safe environment. The government is the institution *par excellence* to repair these imperfections by furthering or making a start with the supply of collective goods by way of regulations, levies and subsidies, and by volume-reducing measures; in general, by incorporating more 'planning elements' (Opschoor 1989: 152) into its public bodies. Opschoor summarizes as follows:

> the market economy is no longer allowed to dictate the direction in which society develops. Economic processes should be subordinated again to socially relevant criteria. This makes demands as to the political controllability of these processes, on a national and an international level.
>
> (Opschoor 1989: 128)

This subordination does not only imply changes in the rights and duties of individuals and enterprises, particularly in property rights, but also a far-reaching channelling or correction of the market mechanism – more far-reaching than we have been used to and than is considered desirable these days by, particularly, the many adherents of 'deregulation', a 'withdrawing' government operating 'according to market mechanisms' (all the more so since the democratic revolutions in Eastern Europe). It is true that we should not take an increase in the canalization and correction of the market mechanism too lightly, even though in our mixed economy the first steps in that direction were made a long time ago. Why should we not take them lightly?

First, because the market offers great advantages, such as the stimulation of efficiency and inventiveness. Second, because the market in a liberal democracy, in any case, counts as one of the central institutions of society, and is as much a triumphant expression of individual rights and civil liberties as the above-mentioned mobilities and as representative democracy itself. In the political philosophy of liberalism, redistributions are accepted to compensate for undesired inequalities caused or reinforced by the market, which implies in principle the acceptance of a mixed – that is, a social market – economy (see, for example, Dworkin 1978: 129–34). However, it is not clear or self-evident that the much more rigorous cuts and corrections, necessary because of a serious environmental policy, can be defended on the basis of the same philosophy. A strong opposition against the limitation of market processes is to be expected and therefore there is an urgent necessity for a shared public basis on which to ground the *legitimacy* of restrictions and corrections. This would be true *a fortiori* when the more controversial aspects of the pursuit of sustainable development, such as control of the population growth (or even reduction of the population) and (giving high priority to) the maintenance of the diversity and integrity of nature as an end in itself, will need to be realized.

The insight that the perspective of sustainable development is connected with the normative-political principles which could justify liberal democracy may be important in view of the legitimation of serious environmental policies. The path towards this insight leads via the liberal idea of neutrality and Rawls's idea of an overlapping consensus. This is what the next section is about.

LIBERAL NEUTRALITY AND OVERLAPPING CONSENSUS

First of all, I want to give a general outline of the relationship between political legitimation, liberalism and neutrality. A central element of liberalism as a political philosophy, is the idea of legitimacy. This means that the social and political order must be generally acceptable, that is to say, justifiable, towards all people on whom this order – perhaps even coercively – has been imposed.

Furthermore, common consent to the fundamental organization of society should at least be conceived as a necessary condition of its political legitimacy (Waldron 1987: 140). General consent does not only serve the aim of political stability. Some attach an independent moral value to the possibility of justifying the social and political system towards as many participants as possible (Nagel 1987: 219).

There is a difference of opinion within the liberal tradition about the nature of this common consent; some say it should be actual (whether or not tacit), while others begin from hypothetical consent. I assume that the idea of hypothetical general consent is the most plausible one, because it is the least problematic.

Hypothetical general consent implies that the political and social order must be acceptable for all people as reasonable beings. More precise: all people involved *would* give their consent to normative principles of the organization of society because (and as far as) they confine themselves to reasonable (rational) grounds. What sort of principles are, in this connection, likely to meet with common consent?

Principles that can be justified in terms of 'common ground' (Rawls) among reasonable people who otherwise have different interests, values, life-styles and ideas of the good (life). This 'common ground' comprises the principles that can be shared and recognized as such by people with divergent points of view – principles concerning fundamental interests and values. We can call these interests and values 'neutral' because, in the eyes of reasonable persons who may all have different conceptions of the good, they can serve as a common basis for the justification of the moral principles which have to determine the basic organization of society.

The principle of neutrality, introduced in this way, mainly refers to justi-fication. Thus, some authors speak of 'justificatory neutrality' (Kymlicka 1989: 884) or 'neutrality of grounds', described by de Marneffe as the idea that:

> the principles of justice that regulate basic social and political institutions must be justifiable in terms of moral and political values that any reason-able person would accept as the basis of moral claims regardless of his or her particular conception of the good.
>
> (de Marneffe 1990: 253)

He distinguishes 'neutrality of grounds' from 'concrete neutrality', which he conceives as 'the principles that the state may not limit individual liberties in ways that advance one particular conception of the good' (de Marneffe 1990: 253).

These are the outlines of a theoretical programme for liberal political philosophy. Rawls and Dworkin especially, have greatly contributed to its development. I will chiefly confine myself to Rawls, and in particular to his development of the concept of neutrality into the idea of an overlapping consensus.

During the last few years, Rawls has reinterpreted and elaborated his famous theory of justice (1971) in such a way that he now finds himself among the adherents of some form of justificatory neutrality (called 'procedural neutrality' by Rawls). The essence of his views on this point is shown by the following quotation.

> If we apply to it [the conception of 'justice as fairness'] the idea of procedural neutrality, we must do so in virtue of its being a political conception that aims to be the focus of an overlapping consensus. That is, the view as a whole hopes to articulate a public basis of justification for the basic structure of a constitutional regime working from fundamental intuitive ideas implicit in the public political culture and abstracting from comprehensive religious, philosophical and moral doctrines. It seeks

common ground – or if one prefers, neutral ground – given the fact of pluralism. This common, or neutral, ground is the political conception itself as the focus of an overlapping consensus.

(Rawls 1988: 261–2)

Naturally enough, Rawls hopes as well that 'justice as fairness' as a political conception meets the requirement of neutrality of aim: the basic structure, for example, is at any rate not designed to favour particular comprehensive visions. He considers neutrality of effect or result – for example, the government is not allowed to do anything which in fact results in unequal treatment of different parties – to be impossible in practice (Rawls 1988: 26). Now I will comment on the quotation.

Rawls's conception of justice, 'justice as fairness', is his answer to the fundamental problem of political justice: What is the most appropriate conception of political justice which can determine the conditions under which social co-operation is rationally and morally acceptable between citizens who are considered free and equal individuals who live and work together throughout their life? (Rawls 1985: 234). In the history of democratic thought, a range of divergent answers have been given to this question.

The conditions of social co-operation should be 'fair', and what this exactly means is explained in the famous principles of justice, which, in Rawls's latest version, run as follows:

1 Each person has an equal right to a fully adequate scheme of equal basic liberties, which is compatible with a similar scheme of liberties for all.
2 Social and economic inequalities are to satisfy two conditions: (a) They must be attached to offices and positions open to all under conditions of fair equality of opportunity; (b) They must be to the greatest benefit of the least advantaged members of society.

(Rawls 1982a: 5)

Under normal circumstances, the first principle has priority over the second one, while 2(a) prevails over 2(b).

The principles regulate the basic structure of society – that is, the principal political, social and economic institutions and their mutual relationships, which determine the fundamental organization of society (with a view to the realization of the values of liberty and equality). The main institutions referred to here are the Constitution, the market, property and family. Rawls's conception of justice chiefly concerns the basic structure of a modern constitutional democracy. 'Justice as fairness' is a *political* conception, partly because it only refers to the basic structure and partly because it articulates and orders fundamental intuitive ideas (about liberty, equality, fair conditions for co-operation), much alive in the democratic tradition and embodied in the political institutions of a constitutional democracy. It is obvious that 'justice as fairness' is also a *liberal* conception of justice (Rawls 1987: 18 and n. 27).

Rawls tries to make clear that 'justice as fairness' is the most appropriate conception of political justice by reformulating the idea of a social contract and the accompanying state of nature in terms of a hypothetical general agreement that is reached in an original position from behind a veil of ignorance. This means that the idea of concluding a social contract is considered by Rawls a 'device of representation' (Rawls 1985: 236), a dramatic staging of an imaginary bargaining situation in which all parties who are to come to an agreement about the principles of the fundamental organization of society are rational, free and equal indeed, but have to deliberate without all kinds of information on their particular endowment, social position, conception of the good (life), etc. The impartiality thus embodied in the bargaining situation excludes bargaining advantages, and guarantees, according to Rawls, a generally accepted agreement on the principles of justice. The justifying power of this construction reaches as far as the incorporated normative notions (rationality, liberty, equality, impartiality, 'sense of justice') carry. I will not go into the much-discussed problems of this derivation here.

The political and non-metaphysical character of Rawls's conception of justice has already been pointed out above. In his later works, he stresses this political character more and more. This is mainly due to the growing insight that modern democratic regimes, in the field of world views, religions, philosophical and moral attitudes, are characterized by pluralism. This is an enduring pluralism that cannot be suppressed by the government except by forceful means. Pluralism, in this context, implies clashing and often incomparable conceptions of the good (life). (These are conceptions about the meaning, value and purpose of life, says Rawls 1987: 4.) Therefore, an agreement about the fundamental organization of society is only possible as an 'overlapping consensus'. This is a consensus about a political conception of justice, a consensus 'in which it is affirmed by the opposing religious, philosophical and moral doctrines likely to thrive over generations in a more or less just constitutional democracy, where the criterion of justice is that political conception itself' (Rawls 1987: 1).

The political conception of justice is intellectually accessible and acceptable proceeding from the above-mentioned comprehensive doctrines (Rawls mentions a religious doctrine encompassing the principle of tolerance, and metaphysical liberalisms such as Kant's and Mill's, in which autonomy is the highest value in personal as well as political life), but can also be rationally acceptable in itself. Loyalty to the conception will, therefore, be able to survive a shift in the balance of power between the adherents of the comprehensive visions of the good. This is also why Rawls speaks about a consensus rather than a 'mere modus vivendi' in the sense of a compromise between individuals or interest groups, the stability of which lasts only as long as the balance of power in the underlying constellation of interests endures.

The political conception of justice has the extremely important function of ensuring in a pluralistic democracy (as previously described) a minimal but stable social unity over generations (an element of sustainability is, as it were, incorporated in the notion of an overlapping consensus, which considerably enhances its usefulness for our purpose!). Just because the shared values embodied in this conception probably ensure the existence of different visions of the good (life) from one generation to the next (this means that they will be able to find support again and again), it is unlikely, Rawls hopes, that they will be easily substituted by different, more specific values which belong to the individual conceptions of the good. There is one restriction, however: the political conception of justice is only neutral towards admissible visions on the good, the visions that are compatible with the political conception itself.

OVERLAPPING CONSENSUS AND SUSTAINABLE DEVELOPMENT

'The aims of political philosophy depend on the society it addresses' Rawls writes (Rawls 1987: 1). Due to the environmental crisis which threatens human existence and nature in general, our society finds itself at a turning point of its development. It would be appropriate, then, if political philosophy also concerned itself with the viability of a society embodying the fundamental arrangement of a liberal democracy which finds itself at this turning point. To me, Rawls's idea of an overlapping consensus, and the way he shapes it, seems to be useful in developing an idea about this. It is possible that Rawls's conception of justice, as he has elaborated it so far, has to be supplemented or modified on various points which do not directly concern the environmental crisis. Several proposals for such an adjustment have already been made; Rawls himself has put forward an extension of the range of application of his conception to the international order (Rawls 1989: 251, n. 46), an extension which is inevitable anyhow (Pogge 1989) if we take sustainable development seriously. I mainly use his conception here as a plausible and adequate core or basis: it is the focus of an overlapping consensus which is already working, while it can be extended and modified in the light of the environmental crisis and the perspective of sustainable development.

The term 'turning point' has come up. This is no coincidence. It is not only the seriousness of the environmental crisis that suggests this term – there is something else as well. Rawls often talks about the existence of 'reasonably favourable conditions (administrative, economic, technological and the like) which make democracy possible' (Rawls 1987: 4, 7; 1982a: 11). One of these conditions is 'the fact of moderate scarcity' (Rawls 1987: 22; in Rawls 1971 this was already an important objective 'condition of justice': 126–7). If there were only one thing we could learn from the environmental crisis it is that it is doubtful whether scarcity is that moderate, particularly in the long run, and certainly, if, in spite of population growth, a fair international distribution of wealth or resources is pursued. There is reason enough, then, from the perspective of Rawls's own conception, to consider how the overlapping consensus can be supplemented with new elements in order to enlarge the durability of this consensus itself and thus of liberal democracy as well.

The new elements have to be determined from the perspective that, in the end, it will only be possible to overcome scarcity through a different way of life (apart from technical miracles etc.). At least, this different way of life will have to be oriented towards sustainable development, with the emphasis on 'sustainable'. We have already seen that, in the Dutch context, there is a consensus about sustainable development. The conception of sustainable development has to be worked out more specifically, and this will probably give rise to many disagreements. It is not impossible that such elaboration will involve changes in and adjustments to basic institutions. I will give some examples (which have already been mentioned on pp. 88–91).

In the field of fundamental rights and liberties, a conflict might arise between the protection of the (mainly physical) integrity of the individual and freedom of movement (which Rawls also considers a part of the complex 'freedom and integrity of the individual'; for example, see Rawls 1982a: 50) or a conflict between the right to personal property (Rawls 1982a: 12) and the freedom and integrity of the individual. Hopefully, these conflicts will not immediately lead to restrictions on these liberties. According to Rawls, such restrictions are acceptable for the sake of other liberties which would come off badly otherwise; the purpose of these restrictions has to be the development of an adequate system of basic rights and liberties for individuals, and I add to this: with an eye to those of future generations! The conflicts should at least result in a more detailed regulation of rights and liberties, whereby, unlike restriction, their 'central range of application' remains unaffected (Rawls 1982a: 9–10).

Increased channelling of the market is another point on the agenda. This can imply, for example, a regulation of the right to own means of production and natural resources (according to Rawls 1982a: 12, the right to own means of production does not belong in the list of basic rights). It will probably also imply regulation and the introduction of (more) planning elements. This is a restriction of the market mechanism, since it is not a matter of correcting undesired market effects afterwards.

The *justification* of these and other restrictions and adjustments, at the level of the basic structure as well as at a less basic level, demands that both of Rawls's principles of justification (in an extended form, therefore also applied internationally) are supplemented with a third principle which corrects the effects of the other two in such a way that the basic possibility of sustainable development is secured. This means that the application of the two principles of justification depends on the condition that the third principle can be complied with. At least, this is the case in normal circumstances; the intention is not, for example, to sacrifice the present generation for the sake of future generations.

This third principle is not an 'alien' supplement because sustainable development itself is connected with the intuitive idea of justice, for example, between the generations. The third principle, a *transmission* principle, says (in the words of Richard and Val Routley, whom I do not follow, incidentally, either in their explanation or in their justification of it): 'We should not hand the world that we have used and exploited on to our successors in a substantially worse shape than we "received" it' (Routley and Routley 1982: 123).

As a justification of this principle, two arguments can be put forward. The *first* reason why we are not allowed to hand the world on to our successors in a worse shape is that this violates the principle of equal opportunities, applied to the relationship between generations. This is an anthropocentric argument.

An intergenerational principle of equal opportunities is defended by authors such as Barry, Page and Richards (see their articles in MacLean and Brown 1983, Barry 1989: 185–203; see also Achterberg 1989). Barry and Richards only refer to the Kantian element of justice as impartiality, which, incidentally, is also accepted by Rawls (represented in the original position by the 'veil of ignorance'). Of course, we can, in this intergenerational context, no longer speak of justice in a sense that implies reciprocity, which is a central element in Rawls, connected with the derivation from the original position, conceived as a bargaining situation, albeit a hypothetical one. Nevertheless, this is not just an arbitrary or *ad hoc* interference in Rawls's argumentation. Precisely because one or more (in this case objective) circumstances of justice are dropped, there is a reason to eliminate the emphasis on reciprocity from the argumentation. I have little to add to the arguments of, particularly, Barry and Richards on this point, although the discussion could do with a more serious account of Parfit's paradoxes and problems (Achterberg 1989). I do not know whether Rawls himself could agree with this modification and with the intergenerational application of the principle of equal opportunities.

Moreover, the modification concerns the weight of legislation and policy aimed at solving or controlling the environmental crisis. Rawls does not seem to consider them important enough to incorporate their normative starting points in a political conception of justice (Rawls 1990, first lecture: 7). Justifiably, the Dutch Constitution says something different (see p. 88). A good reason for this can be found in the quotation from Opschoor (see p. 83).

The *second* reason why we are not allowed to transfer our world to our successors in a considerably worse condition is that nature as well, in the world that we have received and used, must have the opportunities to survive (integrity) in the diversity which is characteristic of the biosphere. This is a non-anthropocentric argument. Nature *deserves* these opportunities when its 'self-standingness' and its own or intrinsic value have been recogized (see p. 87).

The notion of justice in a sense that implies reciprocity is irrelevant here: the intuitive idea of justice here means that justice is done to nature by giving or leaving it the opportunities to an independent existence and a development of its own, just like we appropriately do justice to other entities, having recognized their intrinsic (or inherent) worth (for example, humans or animals, who are sentient beings). A comprehensive theory of justice, which offers scope for direct moral concern for natural entities other than sentient animals, is presented by Wenz (1988).

The second reason requires that Rawls's frame of argumentation itself is supplemented, since the element which is introduced can only be justified by abandoning this frame, particularly regarding the restriction to 'the thin theory of the good' (the good or goods about which all who know themselves to belong to the same generation can be expected to come to an agreement on grounds of rationality). In fact, this is important to the first reason also. After all, in as much as the pursuit of sustainability is a morally relevant pursuit that goes further than mere survival, it must be connected with ideas – our ideas, of course: that is our responsibility for the future generations! – of the good: in human life, in human culture, and in nature. An environmental policy aiming at sustainability must help to secure favourable conditions for the protection, maintenance and development of this good (Achterberg 1990).

If we conceive the transmission principle in such a way that it also implicitly refers to the intrinsic value of natural entities, a non-neutral element (that is, one that cannot be neutrally justified) is introduced into the conception of political justice. This may not be harmful if in the context concerned (such as the Dutch) there appears to be the (beginning of a) consensus about that element. I take it for granted that the notion of an overlapping consensus about a political conception of justice is a useful concept, even if this conception has a partly different content than in Rawls and the justification of the conception itself is also different in Rawls.

Finally, we may apply the results of the previous section to the consensus in The Netherlands about sustainable development, *assuming* that we can conceive this consensus as more than just pragmatic or *ad hoc*. This consensus may be considered as an overlapping consensus (in the making), and not just because Rawls's overlapping consensus is part of it – I start from the plausible assumption that the overlapping consensus described by Rawls himself also applies to liberal democracy, as is found in The Netherlands. The consensus about sustainable development is also overlapping because it is a consensus: (a) about a political conception of justice towards future generations (and towards nature, too, if our moral sense is in any way fit to be incorporated in a *political* conception of *justice*), and (b) which is the object of an agreement, in Dutch society, between adherents of divergent comprehensive conceptions of the good (life) and is, or seems to be, rationally accessible and acceptable proceeding from these conceptions.

Its principles are in reflective equilibrium with our 'considered judgements' – that is, with judgements about the starting point or main objective of an environmental, or nature, policy, which are laid down by the government in the NEPP and the NPP, undoubtedly after ample consideration, and subsequently accepted in Parliament.

Further, the conception articulates and arranges intuitive ideas (about opportunities for posterity, future generations and nature) which are rather new, but have already become current in public culture (religious and secular conceptions of stewardship, the idea of integrity or 'wholeness of creation'; basically, the popularized views from the Brundtland Report and the earlier *World Conservation Strategy* (IUCN *et al.* 1980) also belong to these ideas).

If (a) and (b) are right, we may also assume of the conception of sustainable development, conceived as a political conception, that it is able to fulfil the function which Rawls ascribes to a political conception of justice: the enhancement of social unity and the stability of pluralistic society over generations.

The political conception of sustainable development is largely based upon central elements in the political philosophy of liberalism. Therefore, it can play a legitimizing role within a liberal democracy, which is necessary in view of the radical changes connected with the solution to or control of the environmental crisis.

CONCLUSIONS

The results of this chapter, which aims to be a contribution to the development of normative 'green' political theory – a significant and urgent task for political philosophers, as, I hope, will have become clear in the meantime – can be summarized as follows.

The idea of an overlapping consensus, as elaborated by Rawls, seems useful for two reasons:

1 It can be used to explain and analyse the problem of legitimacy which confronts liberal democracy if it decides to follow a radical environmental policy aimed at sustainable development.
2 If we look at what Rawls considers to be the focal point of this overlapping consensus – the political conception of justice – and at his arguments for it, then we discover the possibility of an important theoretical, albeit partial, contribution to the solution of the problem of legitimacy.

The political conception of justice is broadened with the introduction of a third principle – the transmission principle. The justification of that principle is partly formed by a controlled modification of Rawls's argumentation for his two principles. In so far as this principle is taken in a non-anthropocentric sense, Rawls's argumentation is at least heuristically useful. For it points to the direction in which the justification can be found – namely, by developing the 'thin theory of the good' into a conception of a more broadly conceived (non-moral) good, which comprises human society, culture and nature. In fact, an overlapping consensus about elements of such extended conception of the good at least seems possible.

BIBLIOGRAPHY

Achterberg, W. (1989) 'Identiteit en Toekomstige Generaties', *Algemeen Nederlands Tijdschrift voor Wijsbegeerte* 81: 102–18.
—— (1990) 'Ethiek en Duurzame Ontwikkeling', in CREN (RMNO), *Duurzame Ontwikkeling*, Rijswijk, Report no. 40, 39–47.
—— (1992) 'Environmental ethics and liberal morality', in A. W. Musschenga, A. Soeteman and B. Voorzanger (eds), *Morality, Worldview and Law*, Assen: Van Gorcum.

Barbour, I. G. (1980) *Technology, Environment and Human Values*, New York: Praeger.

Barry, B. (1989) *Theories of Justice*, London: Harvester–Wheatsheaf.

Council for Research into the Environment and Nature (CREN) = Raad voor het Milieu- en Natuuronderzoek (RMNO) (1990) *Duurzame Ontwikkeling*, Report no. 49, RMNO: Rijswijk.

Dobson, A. (1990) *Green Political Thought*, London: Unwin Hyman.

Dryzek, J. S. (1987) *Rational Ecology*, Oxford: Blackwell.

Dworkin, R. (1978) 'Liberalism', in S. Hampshire (ed.), *Public and Private Morality*, Princeton: Princeton University Press.

IUCN, UNEP, WWF (1980) *World Conservation Strategy*, Gland: Switzerland.

—— (1991) *Caring for the Earth. A Strategy for Sustainability*, Gland: Switzerland.

Kymlicka, W. (1989) 'Liberal individualism and liberal neutrality', *Ethics* 99: 883–905.

MacLean, D. and Brown, P. G. (eds) (1983) *Energy and The Future*, Totowa: N. J. Rowman & Littlefield.

Marneffe, P. de (1990) 'Liberalism, liberty and neutrality', *Philosophy and Public Affairs* 19: 253–74.

Naess, A. (1989) *Ecology, Community and Lifestyle*, Cambridge: Cambridge University Press.

Nagel, T. (1987) 'Moral conflict and political legitimacy', *Philosophy and Public Affairs* 16: 215–40.

NEPP (Ministry of Housing, Physical Planning and Environment) (1989) *National Environmental Policy Plan*, The Hague: SDU.

NPP (Ministry of Agriculture, Nature Management and Fisheries) (1990) *Nature Policy Plan*, The Hague: SDU.

Opschoor, H. (1989) *Na ons geen zondvloed*, Kampen: Kok Agora.

Paehlke, R. C. (1989) *Environmentalism and the Future of Progressive Politics*, New Haven: Yale University Press.

Pogge, T. (1989) *Realizing Rawls*, Ithaca: Cornell University Press.

Rawls, J. (1971) *A Theory of Justice*, Cambridge, Mass.: Harvard University Press.

—— (1978) 'The basic structure as subject', in A. I. Goldman and J. Kim (eds), *Values and Morals*, Dordrecht: Reidel.

—— (1982a) 'The basic liberties and their priority', in S. M. McMurrin (ed.), *Liberty, Equality and Law*, Cambridge: Cambridge University Press.

—— (1982b) 'Social unity and primary goods', in A. Sen and B. Williams (eds), *Utilitarianism and Beyond*, Cambridge: Cambridge University Press.

—— (1985) 'Justice as fairness: political not metaphysical', *Philosophy and Public Affairs* 14: 223–51.

—— (1987) 'The idea of an overlapping consensus', *Oxford Journal of Legal Studies* 7: 1–25.

—— (1988) 'The priority of right and ideas of the good', *Philosophy and Public Affairs* 17: 251–76.

—— (1989) 'The domain of the political and overlapping consensus', *New York University Law Review* 64: 233–55.

—— (1990) 'The idea of free public reason', Two Lectures, Irvine: University of California.

Routley, R. and Routley, V. (1982) 'Nuclear power – some ethical and social dimensions', in T. Regan and D. VanDeVeer (eds), *And Justice for All*, Totowa: N. J. Rowman & Littlefield.

Sagoff, M. (1988) *The Economy of the Earth*, Cambridge: Cambridge University Press.

Waldron, J. (1987) 'Theoretical foundations of liberalism', *Philosophical Quarterly* 37: 127–50.

Walzer, M. (1990) 'The communitarian critique of liberalism', *Political Theory*, 18: 6–23.

Wenz, P. (1988) *Environmental Justice*, Albany: State University of New York Press.
The World Commission on Environment and Development (WCED) (1987) *Our Common Future*, Oxford: Oxford University Press.

Part III

GREEN SOCIETY: ECONOMICS AND WELFARE

6

TO DE-INDUSTRIALIZE – IS IT SO IRRATIONAL?

Keekok Lee

Before one can answer the question raised in the title meaningfully, one must first examine the notion of industrialization itself to see what it stands for. This may be grasped via the standard account given of a mature economy by economists – namely, it is one with a long-term rise in capacity to supply increasingly diverse economic goods and services to the population at large. This growing capacity is based on advancing technology and the institutional and ideological adjustments it demands.[1] It refers to at least the following cluster of components[2] which are of direct relevance to the question in hand:

1 The industrial mode of production.
2 High universal consumption.
3 Indefinite exponential economic growth.
4 The first component above, historically, has involved at least two kinds of techniques (of mass production) to increase productivity and efficiency to propel growth (in bourgeois economies with the aim of maximizing profits) – namely the division of labour which leads to the fragmentation and simplification of the production processes, and the use of machines (and techniques) provided by science and technology. However, the simplification of the production processes will sooner or later be superseded under the most recent phase in the development of the industrial mode of production based on electronics and computerization. Robots (or computerized machines in general) will take over the routine tasks and, indeed, much more. The labour force will be a slimline one whose job it is to design, plan, oversee and operate these machines. It will be highly skilled, working flexibly as a team.
5 Productivity and efficiency are normally understood in terms of the lowering of the unit cost (in money terms) of production (or of the formula – same input, greater output). At least three things could be involved. First, labour could be displaced by fragmenting the production processes or using machines, or both (in the case of the latter, efficient machines displace inefficient humans and more efficient machines replace less efficient ones). Second, existential scarcity could be overcome – for instance, the production processes could be turned into a 24 hours, 365 days non-stop

105

operation through the simple device of shift work. Science and technology may be relied on to hasten the process of maturation of certain products, like cheese, beer, trees, etc. Technological improvements may improve thermodynamic efficiency so that from the same input one would get a greater output of energy or matter – for instance, more heat may be got from burning a given amount of coal, or quantity of oil.

This chapter will assume without further argument that the components outlined above constitute a self-reinforcing cluster (with one exception which will be discussed) so that to question one of them will involve questioning the rest. In other words, to argue for de-industrialization is to query them all. However, the practical implications of the critique can take one of two forms – the more radical form of outright rejection and replacement by their opposites (for instance, no power except human and animal, consumption at just above the level of subsistence, no growth beyond the level of extremely frugal consumption, etc.), the less extreme which argues for less consumption, less production, more labour-intensive rather than capital intensive modes of production but assisted by an ecologically sensitive technology which at the same time brings out the creative potential of humans instead of destroying it or lowering it to the capability of the machines themselves, etc. The critique itself may support either of these prescriptions although it will not be explicitly concerned to provide the additional arguments to settle the choice between them.[3]

The sense of thermodynamic efficiency mentioned above differs profoundly from economic efficiency in the sense of lowering the unit cost of production. The latter is merely monetary and no more, but the former is about Second Law efficiency. However, given its nature, this sense of efficiency has its limits which cannot be overcome by technological fixes. Enthusiasts of industrialization overlook this fundamental character of the workings of processes in the natural world and co-opt it as a prop of industrialization. But to strive to improve efficiency in this sense, while recognizing its limits, is perfectly consistent with a critique of industrialization. (There are similar limitations to certain attempts to overcome existential scarcity. For instance, science and technology may enable one to shorten the maturation processes in certain cases, but no matter how foreshortened, growth and maturation cannot be simultaneous.)

This chapter will set forth four main groups of reasons to show why it may not be irrational to de-industrialize:

1 The degradation of nature (ecological bankruptcy or exploitation of nature – that is, of non-human things).[4]
2 The exploitation of humans in terms of structural unemployment, the concentration of power in the hands of a few and the impossibility of the entire world becoming industrialized.
3 The exploitation of humans and non-humans in terms of the mode of industrial production focusing on manufacture and of a supply-led mode of production.

4 The impoverishment of human nature in terms of deskilling at the level both of (paid) work and basic skills of existence.

DEGRADATION OF NATURE

The argument stemming from the degradation of nature need not detain one for too long as it is becoming more and more obvious. Three strands of the argument may be briefly raised. First, an efficient technique of production, as characterized earlier, also usually involves an ecologically insensitive technology (EST for short) – for instance, in agricultural production pesticides and herbicides have not only replaced weeding but are also indiscriminately and liberally applied by helicopter spraying, thereby killing more life than that really intended and polluting the air, water and soil over extensive areas. Second, (indefinite) exponential growth has already exhausted quite a few of the non-renewable resources and is on course to exhaust many more. Renewable forms of energy which are ecologically sensitive – such as wind – are unlikely to be able to sustain the kind of industrial growth and intensity we know today. A form of renewable energy, such as the grandiose vision of capturing solar power through space mirrors and satellites will no doubt be able to support indefinite growth but it is not ecologically sensitive. (See the next point for an elaboration of this.) Indeed, a seemingly limitless supply of energy which can be used to transform matter in the pursuit of indefinite exponential growth would bring about the worst sort of ecological nightmare – life on earth, as we know it today, may no longer be possible. Third, EST, in conjunction with indefinite exponential growth (although the latter on its own is quite capable of producing similar results), runs up against that ultimate form of absolute scarcity as ecological scarcity – namely, the limited capacity of ecosystems, the biosphere in general, to act as a sink, to absorb waste, including heat. No technological ingenuity appears to be able to overcome this type of scarcity.

Productivity and efficiency have been achieved in the modern era largely, if not solely, at the expense of nature. However, this despoliation has never been officially acknowledged by standard theorizing in economics and related subjects. The spoils are to be divided between capital and labour – either more to the one and less to the other or vice versa. Indeed, nature is regarded as fair game to be exploited by human beings whether as capitalists or workers.

This argument assumes that the ecological integrity of nature is a good which in turn may be justified in at least two ways:

1 Instrumentally and anthropocentrically – namely, that the indiscriminate destruction of nature is a destruction of resources for future human production and consumption. This may be called resourcism.
2 It is not only human life that has value, all life on the planet has value. Hence one must not destroy other life forms indiscriminately. But as life can only exist if the biophysical systems which support it remain more or less

intact, it follows that one must not also ruin with no further ado the biosphere itself which sustains all life.

However, this is not the place to argue for either or both of these justifications.

EXPLOITATION OF HUMANS

Unemployment

Efficiency is also referred to as the productivity of labour. However, the productivity of labour turns out on examination to be a euphemism for the displacement of labour. In plain speech, it means unemployment. The demand of progress in the name of efficiency entails what economists call structural unemployment. In other words to have progress one must make some people unemployed. But economists have argued that any unemployment generated is short-term, because economic growth in that and other sectors will eventually absorb the (temporarily) unemployed.

Historically, in the mature industrialized economies, productivity in the agricultural sector led to the redundancy of farm labourers who then migrated to the expanding manufacturing sector in the growing cities. Efficiency in the manufacturing sector leads in turn to redundancy of labour which then goes into the service sector. Efficiency in the service sector will similarly generate redundancy, but it is not obvious where the redundant labour will turn to at this stage of development except to permanent unemployment. These mature economies are at the moment entering such a critical stage of development.[5]

Is there any satisfactory solution in sight to this pending crisis, of the euphemistically so-called post-industrial era? Some theorists have suggested a statutory universal minimum income. Those who wish to work may then add extra to that income; it is up to the individual to choose either less income but more leisure or more income but less leisure. But this may not be a satisfactory solution for it ignores the crucial feature which generates the problem in the first place – namely, that it is in the nature of industrialization (as characterized earlier) to produce on the one hand a smaller and smaller pool of the employed who would be highly paid and, on the other, a larger and larger pool of the unemployed who would be excluded by and large from the fruits of greater productivity. (That is why it is misleading to call it the 'post-industrial' era. There is nothing post-industrial about it. On the contrary, it is precisely the ultimate outcome of the industrial mode of production which is at its heart and sustains it. Less misleading, it may be called the era of mass permanent unemployment.) The unemployed must bear the burden of the cost of greater efficiency and progress. They are its victims who will then be labelled and stigmatized as parasites, scroungers. It is not a question of choosing to work more or to work less, to have more leisure or less leisure. The goal of the system is precisely to create leisure. (The word 'leisure' is used here as the equivalent of 'time, apart from sleeping, etc., not spent in gainful employment'.)

Stigmatization and poverty are bound to haunt those who are thus excluded from the sphere of production. To remedy this, one must argue for the right to participate in the productive process. A more labour-intensive technology rather than a more capital-intensive one would give at least greater scope to employment.

Concentration of power in the hands of the few

If the means of production are capital-intensive, then they are likely to be concentrated in fewer hands. (In the case of state capitalism it is in the hands of one, strictly speaking.) The 'Green Revolution' in wheat and rice production in recent years in certain developing countries illustrates this amply. To get the higher yield out of the new specially bred strains, the farmer requires more fertilizers, pesticides, herbicides, and more water. This requires a greater outlay of capital than growing the traditional lower-yield varieties. The richer farmer can afford this (or is in a position to get credit for the venture), while the poorer farmer cannot. The former will sooner or later drive out the latter who will then lose his means of livelihood and become unemployed, usually eventually migrating from the countryside to join the swelling ranks of the urban poor.

As is well known, possession and/or control of the means of production is power. As the means of production become concentrated in the hands of fewer people, the power of the few over the many increases. This entails a loss of freedom on the part of the latter as one important form of freedom depends on control of the means of livelihood.

To decentralize and proliferate the means of production would restore freedom to more people. This again implies the adoption of a more labour-intensive rather than a more capital-intensive type of technology. Gandhi's advocacy of the *charka* (the spinning wheel) in India is a limiting case of this argument.

The world as a whole cannot be industrialized

If industrialization is a good, and if the USA (or Japan) is taken as the model of successful industrialization, then it is a good which cannot be achieved by every economy in the world. It is an exclusive club for the affluent few. The reasons are as follows. First, the USA has 6 per cent of the world's population but she uses up nearly 40 per cent of the world's resources (see McNamara 1981: 120). Theoretically, 94 per cent of the world's population will have access to a mere 60 per cent of the world's resources. In practice, the developing world which contains 70 per cent of the world's population has access to probably only a quarter of these resources. It is just not possible for every country to achieve the level of industrialization achieved in the USA today. If the world's resources were to be equally distributed, then 1 per cent of people would have access to 1 per cent of resources, a very different type of possibility than that envisaged under industrialization (see Dasgupta 1985: 22).

If the scarcity of resources is held to be relative, then it is said the above argument does not obtain. Although it is true that most of the present resources are non-renewable, science and technology will always create new resources as substitutes, and expand the range of resources. But this is to miss the point of the argument above, which is simply that the kind of industrialization envisaged under which 6 per cent of the world's population gobbles up 40 per cent of the world's resources is just not possible for every country to pursue irrespective of the actual size of the resources.

Second, even supposing for a moment that what is impossible were to become possible and that by a touch of some magic wand every economy in the world could have access to the American level of resources, this magic wand, unless it can also overcome the absolute scarcity in the form of the limitation of the biosphere to absorb waste, would create more ecological havoc than can be dreamt of. As things stand at present, the greater amount of carbon dioxide and heat produced by the industrialized world, together with the lesser amount by the developing world, are already sufficient to give grave cause for concern about the warming of the earth's atmosphere.

Third, in any case, it is not in the nature of the game that all other countries should catch up with the American level of industrialization, for that is an ever-moving upward level. Indefinite exponential growth, ever-increasing efficiency and productivity are built into the system. It is like dangling a carrot tied to its own harness in front of a donkey; no matter how fast the donkey runs, it will never catch up with that carrot to eat it.[6]

To carry on down the road of industrialization is not compatible with promoting equity. This argument assumes that the latter goal is more worth while than the former. However, this chapter is not the place to argue for that priority.

EXPLOITATION OF NON-HUMANS AND HUMANS

The mode of mass production and the focus on manufacture

Historically, the industrial mode of production took the form of mass production and was evolved primarily in the manufacturing sector of the economy. But of late it has also been applied to agriculture so that today it is aptly called agri-business. Agriculture, horticulture and husbandry are no longer conducted in the traditional modes but have become factories producing cereals, vegetables, meat or whatever. The application of such a method is undoubtedly very successful in one sense. For instance, only a mere 4 per cent of the labour force in the USA works in the agricultural sector yet it produces so much as to make that country the bread-basket of the world.

However, on closer scrutiny this impressive performance turns out to yield, as we know, an awesome deficit which includes at least the following: it is the least efficient system of agriculture ever devised by man in energy terms as it consumes nine times as many calories as it produces (Carr 1978: 279); it is based on consuming non-renewable resources – namely, oil. In some states of the Great Plains it relies on water from the great fossil Ogallala Aquifer which is now near exhaustion (Little 1987: 43–7); it also causes extensive soil degradation and erosion, salinization and even desertification. It cannot by any stretch of the imagination be said to be ecologically sustainable.

As for animal farming, the system gives rise to grave concern about the welfare of the animals and in some cases even causes extreme cruelty to them – cows are turned into milk-producing or meat-producing machines by having drugs pumped into them, or in the case of chickens forced into spaces which leave no room for even turning round, never mind flapping their wings or flying. This kind of treatment in turn rebounds on humans when they consume such products by giving them salmonella and other poisonings, enlarged breasts (in little children) or threatening them, of late, with the possibility of contracting BSE ('mad cow' disease).

So, from the points of view of maintaining ecological integrity and animal welfare, the industrial system of food production leaves much to be desired. But it raises another issue of concern. Earlier on, I showed that it is in the nature of the industrial mode of production to generate unemployment. As the industrialized world is now rapidly reaching the stage when unemployment is not only structural but also permanent, perhaps now is the moment to enter a plea for the de-industrialization of agricultural production to return to a more ecologically sensitive as well as labour-intensive system of food production. As already mentioned, a capital-intensive technology which involves spraying pesticides and herbicides from a helicopter or from machines which cannot cope with hedgerows, can cause extensive ecological degradation even though it may be cost-effective in money terms. A more labour-intensive technology using more ecologically sensitive tools could kill not the proverbial two, but four, birds with one stone – it would reduce ecological degradation, improve the welfare of animals, and make room for a more sustainable system of food production and for more employment.

Economists compare the proportions of the manufacturing and agricultural sectors in the total labour force in order to determine whether an economy is advanced or not. An economy is then judged to be more advanced the smaller the proportion of the latter in relation to the former. An associated criterion is the proportions of the population living in cities and the countryside: the smaller the proportion of rural to urban population, the more successful the economy. That is why the USA is considered very successful on this set of criteria. In contrast, a Third World economy with 70 per cent of its labour force engaged in the rural sector and a similar proportion of its population living in the countryside is said to be retarded.

(This way of looking at the economy is geared to the ultimate aims of (a) turning the whole space into an industrial arena – hence the transformation of farming into agri-business and (b) facilitating the urbanization of all space – cities and their suburbs will grow and colonize the countryside. This is in keeping with the spirit of industrialization to turn everything, nature included, into what is sometimes called the technosphere, a totally human-controlled environment.)

To advocate a double shift in focus, first from the manufacturing to the agricultural sector and second from an increasingly intensive industrial to a less intensive industrial mode of production, is not irrational for another reason. High volume production must be backed by high universal consumption. With manufactured goods which are non-edible, such as clothes, shoes, cars, etc., high consumption can be sustained by getting people to cast off goods regularly at short intervals through devices like built-in obsolescence, the pressure of advertisement and fashions, etc. With regard to the consumption of manufactured edible goods, while still being susceptible to manipulation of the kind mentioned, it remains true that the room for manoeuvre is much less.[7] This explains why production may outpace consumption more easily than is the case with manufactured non-edibles. On the other hand, it is also true that edibles, once consumed, cannot be reused whereas a non-edible item (if constructed properly with no deliberately designed death-date) has a long usable life. Hence in a rationally organized society which respects ecological integrity, the manufacturing sector would be smaller in relation to that of the agricultural sector.

A supply-led mode of production

The motive of the producers (in a bourgeois capitalist economy) is to maximize profits. Such agents would, therefore, adopt a mode of production only if it is in keeping with that objective. The industrial mode fulfils that fundamental goal admirably. It is not designed primarily with other goals in mind, such as the meeting of demands or needs. It is, of course, an extremely powerful supplier of goods. But as it supplies these goods not with the fundamental aim of meeting demands or needs but with that of maximizing profits for the producers, the supply is first created, and if there is no obvious demand for the products, the system ordains that the demand be stimulated to meet the supply. Economists often tell us that supply exists to meet a known but as yet unrequited demand. This, however, is not always or necessarily so. Take an example. Before the technology exists to produce colour television or instant coffee, there is no demand for either product. But the search for profits via growth dictates that the industries stimulate such a demand.

The other side to the coin of this procedure is ignoring demands which are not profitable but which are known to exist. This relentlessly efficient system of production leads, as we saw, to permanent unemployment. As the unemployed have little spending power, it follows that their demands would remain unmet. The system thus caters for the rich as they are stimulated to buy what is being produced, but at the expense of nature and the poor.

IMPOVERISHMENT OF HUMAN BEINGS

De-skilling at the level of paid work

Up to now, the industrial mode of production has ensured that the majority of the gainfully employed would become increasingly de-skilled through the joint application of the division of labour leading to fragmentation and simplification of the production processes and of machines which require, as much as is feasible, uncomplicated minding. The fragmentation of the production processes is in reality a fragmentation of the person. This point is brought out admirably by Ruskin:

> We have much studied and much perfected, of late, the great civilized invention of the division of labour; only we give it a false name. It is not, truly speaking, the labour that is divided; but the men:– Divided into mere segments of men – broken into small fragments and crumbs of life; so that all the little piece of intelligence that is left in a man is not enough to make a pin, or a nail, but exhausts itself in making the point of a pin or the head of a nail. Now it is a good and desirable thing, truly, to make many pins in a day; but if we only see with what crystal sand their points were polished, – sand of human soul, much to be magnified before it can be discerned for what it is – we should think there might be some loss in it also. And the great cry that rises from all our manufacturing cities, louder than their furnace blast, is all in very deed for this, – that we manufacture everything there except men; we blanch cotton, and strengthen steel, and refine sugar, and shape pottery; but to brighten, to strengthen, to refine, or to form a single living spirit, never enters into our estimate of advantages.
>
> (Ruskin 1985: 87)

This tendency is well observed and well known in the manufacturing sector and so requires no further elaboration. However, it is not so well known that a similar process is now at work in that part of the service sector which is traditionally the domain of highly qualified experts and professionals.

The medical profession (including doctors and nurses) is an outstanding example. Up to recently, these practitioners, especially doctors, prided themselves on their expertise in the art of clinical diagnosis, an art which requires a long period of training, experience and varied skills. But today this art is being lost, for doctors are no longer required even to look at patients; they look instead at computer printouts or photographs produced by X-ray and other machines. There may be a set of skills to be acquired in interpreting printouts and photographs but the old set is lost. (New skills in this system are not added to the old but serve to displace them.) And it is arguable that the superseded set might not be a better guide to what is wrong with patients. So doctors no longer care for patients but read the data provided by machines. The next stage of development would surely be to develop even more 'user-friendly' machines which the patients can handle without the mediation of medical technocrats. The ultimate system of medicine on this view is to be machine-diagnosed, machine-prescribed and, perhaps with the help of further machines, like robots (which can perform even technically complicated operations like open-heart surgery), to be machine-cured.

Complex skills and knowledge will then concentrate in the hands of the few who design these machines. This is already happening in the latest phase of development of the industrial mode of production. But even these, in the Utopia envisaged, would be displaced by machines which design machines. The ultimate end is to render all human beings redundant in productive activities.

De-skilling at the level of basic skills of existence

What is equally worrying is also the relentless de-skilling at the level of basic, elementary tasks and activities of daily life such as cooking and eating a sensible diet. Since the coming into existence of machine-sliced pre-packed bread, many people no longer even know how to cut bread with a bread knife, never mind how to bake the bread itself. Cooking becomes increasingly a case of opening tins, or putting a container of factory-prepared oven-ready food into the microwave oven. Today, in certain countries with a rice-eating culture, many no longer know how to cook rice in an ordinary pot or pan; they are helpless minus the automatic electric or microwave rice cooker. Nor do many people seem to know how to sew a button, never mind a whole garment. Hems are no longer sewn but ironed on.

Another area of de-skilling worth mentioning is entertainment. Increasingly it is predominantly bought, pre-packed and pre-digested. The leisure so vaunted as a consequence of efficient industrialization has more or less arrived but not it seems in reality to provide the opportunity for people to exercise their skills and their capacities for creativity which gainful work has deprived them of. Instead, it has by and large simply encouraged the extension of the industrial mode of production to the leisure domain, to create the so-called leisure industries. A minority of writers had anticipated quite prophetically this gloomy outcome. To quote one of them:

> substituting machines for individual ability and uniformity for diversity . . . has brought about as great a change in man's leisure as it has in his work, and for precisely the same reasons. This is a fact which those Utopians who look forward to an age when machines, by absolving man from labour will give him increased leisure, would do well to ponder. For their theory that the spirit of man will achieve its highest expression when it has been freed from the 'slavery' of work is manifestly a fallacy since that spirit can only express itself in those creative activities which constitute that art of living of which work and leisure are not separate parts, but facets of the one whole. If that creative freedom be denied and

lost, though he work but one hour a day, man will not be freeman but slave, and just as the efficiency of his machines will determine his hours of liberty, so they will be the measure of his freedom, for boredom is the disease of minds in which the creative impulse has been atrophied, and for which sensation is the only drug.

(Holt 1947: 78)

CONCLUSIONS

This chapter has argued that it would not be irrational to de-industrialize for the following reasons:

1 To avoid ecological bankruptcy/to lessen the degradation of nature – a plea on behalf not only of humans but of all life and the biophysical foundations of all life on this planet.
2 To prevent cruelty to animals in our food-producing system.
3 To remove inequities between nations for the industrial mode of production is inherently exclusive, for the few and not for all.
4 To remove inequities within nations – between the increasingly smaller and smaller number of the privileged gainfully employed and the larger and larger number of the disadvantaged unemployed.
5 To prevent concentration in the hands of the few of the means of livelihood and hence of power.
6 To restore dignity and creativity to work which should be available not to a few but to all who are capable of it.

A society (in the developed North) which acknowledges the imperative to de-industrialize would minimally have to adopt a more ecologically sensitive technology as far as its mode of production is concerned. Simultaneously, it would have to reject a lifestyle based on consumerism and accept the need to lead a life materially more frugal but which seeks to cultivate the self by way of more creative and fulfilling activities both at work and leisure. The next more sophisticated phase of the industrial mode of production based on micro-processing, robotics, bio-engineering, etc. in the name of economic efficiency may turn out to have equally unfavourable implications for (a) the integrity of the biosphere; (b) employment; (c) the North/South divide. To avoid these, society has to become 'post-industrial' – that term has to be snatched back from those who wish to describe that technological future which is just on the horizon. But there is nothing 'post-industrial' about that eventuality. It is merely the next phase of the industrialization process.

In the developing South, the paradigm of orthodox development will have to be rejected in favour of an ecologically sensitive mode of production which at the same time aims to be more efficient than the traditional variety available. Absolute poverty has to be overcome – in this sense, there should be an increase of consumption.

However, an ecologically sustainable society must address the problems of population and generations, matters strictly beyond the remit of this chapter. While it is obvious that the population issue is more acute in the countries of the South in terms of numbers, it is not so obvious that the North ought to confront it from another perspective – namely, to recognize a limit to the prolongation of human life made possible by costly medical technology. If the average human life were extended to a hundred years, then this would pose problems for ecological sustainability at the interface of reproduction, production as well as consumption.

To sum it all up, any green model of society must minimally reflect the following theoretical considerations:

1 An ecologically sustainable society rests ultimately on respecting the integrity of the biosphere or ecosphere.
2 As such, it must also recognize that idefinite human population growth as well as indefinite prolongation of human life are not unqualified goods.
3 Similarly, while recognizing that promoting material well-being is a legitimate ideal, nevertheless, it must also admit that such a goal cannot be pursued without serious qualifications. Hence its mode of production, its technology, as well as its level of consumption, must be constrained by the requirement of respecting the integrity of the biosphere. It must, therefore, question and reject the concepts of economic efficiency and growth which underlie orthodox conceptions of the good society.
4 This then shifts the emphasis from passivity in consumption to creativity both at work and at leisure (in other words blurring the boundaries between these two domains if not totally transcending the dichotomy itself) as a source of human fulfilment.

NOTES

1 See Simon Kuznet (Todaro 1983: 56).
2 This chapter will not examine obvious ideological elements like 'the invisible hand', 'the trickle down' theory of wealth distribution, but it will be referring to others.
3 However, the author of this chapter would personally argue for the latter. In the rest of this chapter such a position is assumed.
4 Degradation of nature occurs not only in industrialized economies where capital is in private hands, but also where it is in the hands of the state. This only serves to reinforce the point that the despoliation of nature is endemic in industrialism itself regardless of the legal/political relations of production, so to speak. Degradation of nature also occurs in the developing countries, both of the Third and Fourth Worlds. But this chapter, given its brief, deals only with the despoliation that is brought about by the process of production peculiar to industrialism.
5 Of course unemployment can and does exist in so-called developing economies, aspiring to reach the level of industrialization typical of the First World today. Or to be more precise, underemployment occurs. But whether the problems of unemployment and underemployment can be successfully tackled through industrialization and urbanization is a debatable matter – on this issue, see Lee (1993).
6 I owe this to J. C. Kumarappa.
7 Ricardo, for instance, dealt with this matter as a possible limitation to the

accumulation of capital. Following Adam Smith, he said: 'Adam Smith has justly observed "that the desire of food is limited in every man by the narrow capacity of the human stomach, but the desire of the conveniences and ornaments of building, dress, equipage, and household furniture, seems to have no limit or certain boundary." Nature then has limited the amount of capital which can at any one time be profitably engaged in agriculture, but she has placed no limits to the amount of capital that may be employed in procuring "the conveniences and ornaments" of life' (Ricardo 1971: 56).

Ted Benton comments on the above as follows: 'With respect to demand, then, Ricardo explicitly makes the freedom of capital accumulation from natural limits dependent upon an assumption about human nature: limits to our appetite for food are compensated by limitless desires for "ornaments and conveniences" of life' (Benton 1989: 62).

BIBLIOGRAPHY

Benton, T. (1989) 'Marxism and natural limits: an ecological critique and reconstruction', *New Left Review*, no. 178: 51–86.

Carr, D. E. (1978) *Energy and the Earth Machine*, London: Sphere Books Ltd.

Dasgupta, S. (1985) *Towards a Post Development Era*, New Delhi: Mittal Publications.

Holt, L. T. C. (1947) *High Horse Riderless*, London: George Allen & Unwin.

Lee, K. (1993) 'Gandhi's conception of economic development', in R. P. Misra (ed.), *Rediscovering Gandhi*, Vol. IV: *Economics of Permanence*, New Delhi: Gandhi Bhavan and Gandhi School of Non-Violence, University of Delhi.

Little, C. E. (1987) 'The great American aquifer', *Wilderness* 51(178): 43–7.

McNamara, R. S. (1981) *The McNamara Years at the World Bank: Major Policy Addresses of Robert S. McNamara 1968–1981*, Baltimore and London: The Johns Hopkins University Press.

Ricardo, D. (1971) *On The Principles of Political Economy and Taxation* (ed. R. M. Hartwell), Harmondsworth: Pelican.

Ruskin, J. (1985) *Unto This Last and Other Essays* (ed. C. Wilmer), London: Penguin Books.

Todaro, M. (ed.) (1983) *The Struggle for Economic Development*, New York and London: Longman.

7

ECONOMIC THEORIES AND THE NECESSARY INTEGRATION OF ECOLOGICAL INSIGHTS

Frank J. Dietz and Jan van der Straaten

INTRODUCTION

The long-standing concern of biologists and ecologists for the environment and their warnings that it was being seriously threatened by human production and consumption, were increasingly heeded by society in the late 1960s and the early 1970s. These signs of public interest stimulated economists to pay more attention to environmental problems. They observed that what had formerly been free goods such as clean air, clean surface water, unpolluted soil, silence and natural beauty, had become scarce. This problem of 'new scarcity' (Mishan 1967; Hueting 1970, 1980) was analysed by economists.

However, in the second part of the 1970s environmental problems were pushed into the background again. Instead, economic decline, increasing unemployment rates, and the growing financial deficit of the public sector dominated social as well as scientific debates. At the end of the 1980s the ever-worsening environmental problems attracted a good deal of attention again; first in national politics and in the media, then from economists. The general impression is that this renewed interest on the part of economists could be of a more permanent nature than it was before.

This renewed attention gives rise to several questions. To us, the most crucial question is to what extent ecological issues can be adequately analysed using existing economic theories. We try to answer this question by reviewing the development of economic thought. While doing this, we come to the conclusion that mainstream economic theories can be used only to a limited extent to analyse environmental problems. This relates to the period in which these theories were developed as well as to the opinions society held at that time concerning the use of natural resources. We conclude this chapter with a sketch of a theoretical economic framework, in which ecological insights are included.

Following Opschoor (1990: 11), we define natural resources as the materials which can be taken from nature by reaping a part of the population of plants and animals, by mining for ores and fossil fuels and by draining flow resources like water and wind. Moreover, various buffers present in nature neutralize the pressure of human activities on the environment. If the pressure on the environment resulting from human activities exceeds the buffering capacity, a substantial change in the environment occurs. This means a loss of environmental quality if the change is evaluated negatively. This buffering capacity can also be defined as a stock of environmental goods, which forms part of the natural resources available.

In the past, quite different terms were used to define the potential which nature possesses for human production and consumption. Classical authors often used the term 'land' to indicate the production potential of arable land. In using this term authors were alluding specifically to the total ecological complex which makes agricultural production possible. This is currently expressed by concepts like ecocycles, ecosystems and natural resources. All these concepts can be precisely defined by reference to the existing biological and ecological literature. Although we are of the opinion that ecological concepts used in economic surveys should be carefully defined, in the following we will use them rather loosely. When using terms such as 'nature', 'the environment', 'natural resources', 'ecosystems', and 'ecocycles', we have in mind the opportunities nature offers for human production and consumption.

CLASSICAL ECONOMIC THOUGHT

Classical authors had different views in dealing with natural resources. There are authors who were of the opinion that there is no limit to the availability of natural resources. Adam Smith is the most well-known author in this group. He held an optimistic view of the possibilities for production and consumption in the future. This opinion was reinforced by social developments in the time in which he lived. The rapid advancements in science and technology, as well as the economic and military subjection of the New World, served as a confirmation of human capabilities. According to this line of reasoning, the relative scarcity of natural resources would be transformed into a relative affluence. The struggle with nature would be resolved in favour of mankind.

According to Smith, economic development, that is production growth, originates from both the increasing division of labour and the free play of markets. Division of labour increases labour productivity, subsequently increasing total production and the need for (international) trade. This process should be stimulated by breaking down the social and political barriers people have erected to stop this development (such as opposition to the concentration of production in factories and mercantilist trade policy).

Smith illustrated the huge growth potential of production with the well-known example of the manufacture of pins. At that time, however, England was much more an agrarian than an industrial country. The possibility of increasing production in the agricultural sector was considerably less than in the industrial sector. Deane and Cole estimated that the production of corn in

England and Wales increased in the first half of the nineteenth century by 11 per cent and in the second half by 28 per cent (Deane and Cole 1967: 65). In the same periods the population increased by 5 per cent and 49 per cent respectively (Deane and Cole 1967: 288). The increasing tension between the supply of and demand for corn in the second half of the eighteenth century led to continuously increasing corn prices. While the corn price decreased between 1700 and 1750 by 16 per cent, between 1751 and 1800 the price of corn rose by 133 per cent (Deane and Cole 1967: 91).[1]

The continuous tension in the corn market and the resulting upward pressure on corn prices stimulated the landed nobility to look for ways in which to increase their acreage of arable land (Turner 1984: 47–51). The English landed nobility succeeded by appropriating common land. English law gave landlords the opportunity to appropriate cultivated common land and to cultivate and to subdivide non-cultivated common land. This process is known as the Enclosure Movement (Turner 1984: 11). But in spite of the cultivation of 'waste land', which increased the acreage of arable land, the growth of agricultural production continued to lag behind the population increase.

This discrepancy strongly influenced classical economists around 1800; they therefore had a less optimistic world view than Adam Smith. The issue was raised of whether the quantity and the quality of the arable land available would be sufficient to meet food demand (Malthus 1982: 71, 75–6). Economists started looking for an explanation as to why the increase in agricultural production had fallen behind. The result was the simultaneous and coherent development of, on the one hand, the differential rent theory, to which Ricardo's name was connected in a later period, and, on the other hand, the Law of Diminishing Returns (Blaug 1978: 79–80).

The Law of Diminishing Returns states that agricultural production increases less than proportionally when additional production factors are applied. Classical economists derived this 'law' from the phenomenon that the physical yield of newly cultivated arable land was lower than that of arable land which had been cultivated for some time. The diminishing returns worried economists, as the population increased during this period at a pace never seen before. Given the poor fertility of waste land still to be cultivated, they predicted a structural shortage of food supplies in the long run.

It is remarkable that classical economists at the beginning of the nineteenth century hardly paid any attention to the possibilities of technological development for increasing agricultural production. Of course there was some technological development, but apparently this did not change the opinions of economists regarding the Law of Diminishing Returns (see, for example, Ricardo 1975: 42–5). They could not conceive of the possibility of extracting considerably more agricultural products from the ecological cycles than was already being done at this time.

We may conclude that classical economists in the first half of the nineteenth century gave the production factor 'natural resources' a central place in their theoretical reasoning. This implies that they had an integrated picture of economic and ecological processes. The limits to production and consumption were thought to be determined by the extent to which raw materials could be extracted from the land (currently we would say from ecological cycles) without adversely affecting agricultural production in the long run. In other words, both nature and economics were seen as parts of the same closed system. At first, the Industrial Revolution did not change this view of the character and quantity of the natural resources available. This changed, however, in the second half of the nineteenth century when economists focused on the market mechanism and used the utility concept as the basis for value.

THE INDUSTRIAL REVOLUTION

The start of the Industrial Revolution lent increasing importance to the quantitative aspects of the market. The production of goods took on an increasingly industrial character, whereby the necessity for trading these goods on international markets also increased. Due to this, a shift of interest occurred towards the observable economic and technical progress of that very moment, as well as the application of 'positive' science as a tool and as a measuring instrument of that progress ('science as measurement') (Goudzwaard 1978: 101).

In the same period the concept of value changed. Classical economists held the view that the labour needed for producing a particular good objectively determined the exchange value. More or less simultaneous but independent publications by Menger in 1871 (1968), Jevons in 1871 (1924), and Walras in 1874 (1954) heralded, however, a paradigm shift. The satisfaction of individual needs, provided by the goods and services available, was in their view decisive for determining the exchange value.[2]

In the Golden Age of neo-classical theory (1870–1920), refinements on marginal analysis, the elaboration of the subjectivistic concept of value and the extension of the general equilibrium analysis, vied for attention. The problem of the restricted availability of natural resources, which was an important issue for classical economists, was no longer relevant for neo-classical economists. Marshall (1925: 180), for instance, stated quite explicitly that technical development proved that Malthus was wrong. No attention has been paid, however, to the fact that this much-applauded technical development is based on the large-scale use of 'stock' natural resources such as iron ore and coal. Before the Industrial Revolution the actual use of natural resources was based almost exclusively on 'flow' resources (muscle power, wind energy, wood, wool). Since then the wealth of mankind has been based increasingly on the use of natural resources with a stock character. This has had two effects, closely connected to each other. First, ores and fossil fuels are only present in the earth's crust in limited quantities. Sooner or later these stocks will run out. Second, after being used in human production and consumption processes, these materials are discharged into the ecological cycles, as is the case with metallic compounds, fumes and synthetics. These are not naturally occurring substances in ecological cycles, or, in any case, not in such large quantities. The result is the disruption and, at worst, the destruction of ecological cycles. The Industrial Revolution thus marks the transition from a more or less closed system of production and consumption to an open economic system, characterized by an increasing use of natural resources with a stock character.

As already stated, Marshall paid little attention to natural resources. Though he analysed the price-making forces of land, ecological processes were only dealt with to the extent that they are expressed, in some way or another, in the market. For example, he mentions soil fertility while discussing agricultural production processes (Marshall 1925: 146). Moreover, Marshall makes the remarkable observation that there is 'a growing difficulty of getting fresh air and light, and in some cases fresh water, in densely populated areas'. In addition, he concluded that 'the natural beauties of a place of fashionable resort have a direct money value which cannot be overlooked' (Marshall 1925: 166). However, Marshall did not elaborate on these ideas. In the context of the price mechanism as he described it, this was hardly possible.

More as a matter of perfecting his theory than as an issue of empirical interest, Marshall introduced the concept of externality. As suggested by the name, externalities (or external economies as he called them) concern the effects of actions of individual economic agents on the production possibilities of other economic agents, occurring *beyond* the market. Marshall describes as an example the unintended influence an expanding company has on the production possibilities of other companies. These last also benefit from the presence of this expanding firm – for example, from the increased level of training and education of the labour force available in the area concerned, the growing supply of workers, or the increasing number of supply companies in the vicinity. This improvement of the investment climate occurred at no cost to the established companies (Marshall 1925: 314). It is striking that Marshall did not take external *dis*economies into account. Apparently, he had no reason to suppose that the continuing process of industrialization would also create economic disadvantages, such as depletion of natural resources and disruption of the environment.

NEO-CLASSICAL ENVIRONMENTAL ECONOMICS[3]

During the 'marginal revolution' of the last thirty years of the nineteenth century the subjectivistic concept of value won ground dramatically at the expense of the objectivistic concept of value of the classical economists. Scarcity as an individual experience was given a much more prominent place in neo-classical theory than in classical theory.[4] Economic analyses were focused on the question of how scarcity relations are expressed in terms of price relations on the market. The choices economic agents have to make under relative scarcity are portrayed as optimization problems. Economic agents in their role as consumer or producer are expected to seek maximum realization of their goals within the usual constraints, such as a limited income or limited production possibilities. This assumption is typical of rational choice theory.

These developments in economic theory have had substantial effects on the possibility of analysing the relative scarcity of natural resources. First, by putting market processes at the centre of the theoretical system, unpriced but scarce resources tended to be ignored. Many natural resources are not exchanged in a market, as a result of which they have no price and, hence, do not seem to be scarce in a world in which the market is the central institution.[5] Second, in neo-classical theories valuations made by individual economic agents form the basis for the value of the production factors available (priced and unpriced). Those early critics whom we nowadays would call ecological economists already held the opinion that considerable ecological risks were being run if the value of nature was seen as being dependent on the (short term) needs of people. As early as a hundred years ago they argued in favour of using the (objective) amount of energy needed as an indicator of the value of goods and services instead of the (subjective) wants of people (Martinez-Alier 1991). However, this ecologically based early critique of the subjectivistic concept of value passed into oblivion in this century.

Externalities

Pigou was the first neo-classical economist who paid serious attention to environmental problems based on the concept of external diseconomy or negative externality. In order to indicate the significance of this concept, Pigou distinguished the social from the private product. Between these two a divergence may occur 'out of a service or disservice rendered to persons other than the contracting parties' (Pigou 1952: 192). In other words, the actions of market parties influence the welfare of non-market parties. This influence may be positive or negative.

The examples given by Pigou of 'uncompensated services and disservices' partly concern environmental problems, which are so common nowadays. He mentions, for example, the emission of smoke by factories causing negative externalities, 'for this smoke in large towns inflicts a heavy uncharged loss on the community, in injury to buildings and vegetables, expenses for washing clothes and cleaning rooms, expenses for the provision of artificial light, and in many other ways' (Pigou 1952: 184).

In Pigou's view externalities create a difference between the social and the private cost price of goods and services. For example, in the case of a firm which discharges processing water containing heavy metals into a river, the discharging producer passes a part of his production costs onto society (in this case, the costs of restoring the quality of the river water). Due to competitive pressure, the consumer is charged too low a price – that is, the costs of the purification of the river water are not incorporated in the market price of the goods and services produced. In such a situation market prices do not reflect the actual relations of scarcity, as the increased scarcity of clean river water is not taken into consideration in consumer decisions. In other words, the factors of production are not optimally allocated.

According to Pigou (1952: 192) it is the task of government to ensure that the externalities are passed on to the buyers of products. He proposes the imposition of a levy on activities causing negative externalities (such as a levy on the discharge of polluted waste water), and the subsidizing of activities producing positive externalities. The installation of purification equipment could, for example, be subsidized. The externality will therefore acquire a shadow price, which economic agents will take into account. Negative externalities will no longer be transferred to society; the optimal allocation of production factors will have been restored.

Despite Pigou's intellectual innovation, discussions about the problem of externalities remained in the periphery of economic science, probably due to the character of the social problems in the first half of the twentieth century. Two World Wars, the stagnation of production, and large numbers of unemployed were the prevailing social concerns during this period. In the literature externalities were regarded as a theoretical refinement without any practical significance. Blaug (1978: 404) states that there was 'a common tendency in the interwar literature to regard external economies as economic curiosa'.

Apart from Pigou, King was the most important exception. He analysed the concept of 'social income', known as 'national income' since the Second World War, and concluded that there is only a partial correspondence between a high level of national income and a high level of wealth, because high income in an industrialized society is accompanied by a rising scarcity of environmental goods, which were freely available before. The examples he mentioned are game, fruit, a beautiful landscape, a decreased availability of natural resources like ores and coal, and the disappearance of complete ecological systems caused, for instance, by the cutting down of a forest (King 1919: 5–49).

After the Second World War, Fabricant (1947: 50ff) brought King's ideas up again, when a discussion started around the issue of how the concept of national income should be operationalized. In his opinion the depletion of fossil and non-fossil natural resources should be included as a cost factor, the level of national income being reduced by this amount. Denison (1947) and Kuznets (1947), by contrast, were of the opinion that such a correction was unnecessary. They saw nature as an infinite entity, the yields of which could be used without any restriction. This discussion between Denison and Kuznets on the one hand and Fabricant on the other hand ended in accordance with the dominant social opinion at that time: nature is such an infinite entity that depletion of natural resources is not an issue to worry about.

At that time social concern was focused on recovering the production capacity which had been largely destroyed during the war in Europe. Further-more, the prevention of mass unemployment, which was still fresh in every-one's memory from the economic crisis of the 1930s, was given high priority. Growth of production was thought to be the right means to achieve these goals. The emphasis on production growth also accorded very well with the atmosphere of the cold war. In both Western Europe and Eastern Europe production growth was a political and military strategy, also serving ideological ends. In this social climate there was no need to discuss environmental problems. Such a discussion could only jeopardize the social consensus of striving towards maximum production growth. As a matter of fact, environ-mental issues were consciously and unconsciously kept on the periphery of social and scientific debates.

The acceleration of industrial production which took place in the course of the 1960s combined with a rapidly changing social climate to change opinions in society fundamentally. The increasing environmental problems that accompanied continuous production growth were experienced by large sections of the population. Air pollution became more and more a 'normal' phenomenon. In industrial areas smog emerged as the unpleasant side effect of clear sunny weather. During smog episodes asthma sufferers had to be evacuated to less polluted areas. Swimming in lakes and rivers became more and more dangerous. As a consequence of pollution and intensive farming practices, certain species of flowers and animals dramatically decreased in number. In spite of the continuous construction of new motorways, roads were more and more congested with motor cars. New industrial and residential areas were developed, criss-crossing rural areas and reducing their space. The enormous growth of the petrochemical industry increased the risk of calamities. In short, a situation arose in which many people were daily experiencing the degeneration of the environment. As a consequence, scientific interest in environmental problems increased at the end of the 1960s.

Economists with a neo-classical background took their lead from Pigou. Situations of nuisance could be satisfactorily described using the concept of externalities. However, this concept is less useful for analysing problems concerning the depletion of fossil natural resources, because the nuisance is not restricted to a limited number of individuals. Depletion affects everyone and can be perceived as a 'public bad', or, when prevention of depletion is the starting point, a public good. This does not necessarily detract from the relevance of the externality concept as a tool of analysis. In fact, it reinforces Pigou's argument in favour of state intervention. But the collective nature of externalities raises additional problems regarding their valuation. These valuation problems will be dealt with in the next subsection.

The depletion of fossil natural resources is not in all cases an acute phenomenon. Especially, it is future generations who will be the victims of the present excessive use of fossil natural resources. And as we are not familiar with the preferences of future generations, the concept of externality loses its analytical strength. In fact, according to the definition of externalities, all effects of current productive and consumptive activities on future generations could and should be regarded as externalities, since future generations are not involved in any of the present market transactions, although they will enjoy or suffer the effects of these transactions on their production and consumption possibilities. For this reason, neo-classical economists were initially inclined to interpret environmental problems only as a pollution issue, excluding more wide-ranging problems like the depletion of fossil natural resources.

In the second half of the 1960s economists increasingly wrote about environmental issues. These publications were dominated by what is often called the Pigovian tradition: some sort of price manipulation is needed and sufficient to internalize (negative) externalities. In doing so, the optimal allocation of factors of production would be restored – that is, the remaining environmental degeneration is in accordance with the preferences of the economic agents.

Some authors, however, expressed serious doubts whether the 'optimum rate of pollution' can be determined. Mishan (1967: 97–8), for example, states correctly that in many cases it is not possible to quantify negative externalities – that is, to find an accurate expression of their value in money terms. Also Hueting holds the view that

> the crucial question 'What is nature worth to us?' cannot be answered by means of the instruments available to us. But in my opinion the study has shown that at the same time another question remains unanswered, namely 'What is the worth of goods that are produced and consumed at the expense of the environment?' For when the value of the environment cannot be determined in the conflict between production and environment, the market price of produced goods may no longer be accepted as an indicator of the economic value of these goods.
>
> (Hueting 1980: 185)

Here, Hueting touches upon a fundamental shortcoming of the neo-classical approach. The fixation on priced forms of scarcity, that is, scarcity manifested in the tension between supply and demand on markets, more or less excludes the unpriced forms of scarcity.

In this context Goudzwaard raised the question of whether economists should deal with unpriced scarcity. His answer is affirmative, since economic theory would lose its predictive capability if the coherence between priced and unpriced scarcity were excluded (Goudzwaard 1970: 106). He suggests considering the problem of unpriced scarcity an element of *economic policy*, where other subjective elements can already be found. Doing so, however, would exclude the production factor of natural resources from *economic theory*. In our view, this position can hardly be defended, given the long tradition among economists of distinguishing three equivalent factors of production. There are no fundamental grounds for excluding either labour, capital, or natural resources from economic theory.

126

Fundamental obstacles to the internalization of externalities

The neo-classical strategy for abating environmental problems boils down to the internalization of externalities. The idea is that after internalization the preferences for *all* goods and services, including those that cannot be supplied via the market, can be expressed. However, internalization meets with fundamental obstacles. These obstacles will be discussed in this and the next subsection with the intention of evaluating the strengths and weaknesses of neo-classical environmental economics.

The first fundamental problem concerns the *benefits* of avoided environmental damage. These benefits should be weighed against the *costs* of avoiding environmental damage. In monetary terms, estimates for the latter can be made easily and quite accurately. For example, the costs of decreasing the pollution level of a river which contains heavy metals from the effluent of a firm along that river, equals the costs of purifying the polluted river plus the costs of adapting the polluting production process. Problems arise, however, when the benefits of a clean river have to be estimated. Some benefits can be expressed in market prices, such as the lower costs of producing drinking water and the higher proceeds from fishing. Many benefits, however, cannot be expressed in market prices, simply because there are no markets for public goods such as ecosystems and landscapes. For example, what is the price of a square mile of wetlands? In conclusion, by weighing the known costs against the partly unknown benefits there is a considerable risk that the costs of environmental measures will be overestimated and not undertaken.

In the absence of markets, other evaluation methods are needed to estimate the benefits. In the last decade or so, a great deal of research has been done on alternative evaluation methods, including 'hedonic pricing' and 'contingent valuation'. Surveys of these methods can be found in Freeman (1985), Anderson and Bishop (1986) as well as in Pearce and Turner (1990: 141–58). Although some progress has been made, these methods only *indicate* individual preferences for a particular environmental quality. It is, for example, not clear whether the contingent valuation method underestimates the willingness to pay for a particular environmental quality (Hoehn and Randall 1987) or overestimates it (Crocker and Shogren 1991). Moreover, the crucial problem of how to aggregate individual preferences into a collective statement on the value of specific natural resources cannot be solved satisfactorily. Attempts at aggregation meet with problems of cardinal measuring of utility and of interpersonal comparisons of utility. Hence, unless individual preferences can be aggregated, it is impossible to weigh the value society puts on goods and services whose production and consumption pollute the environment, against the value society puts on a sound environment.

The second fundamental problem is that the preferences of future generations for natural resources are unknown. The depletion of non-renewable natural resources (such as fossil fuels and minerals), the overexploitation of renewable natural resources (such as the cutting down of tropical forests), and the irreversible pollution of ecosystems (by, for example, chemical and nuclear waste) indisputably reduce the 'stock' of natural resources available for future generations. It is not possible to deal with this problem satisfactorily using currently known evaluation methods. Consequently, the evaluation of natural resources on the basis of the preferences of individual economic agents is myopic.

Where the preferences of individual economic agents are not or only partly known, the preferences of chosen policy-makers are often used to evaluate the environment and the natural resources available.[6] Of course, this offers politicians the opportunity to tighten up or to relax environmental standards according to their own preferences. Such high-handed behaviour could cause them electoral losses at a later date if the environmental standards they choose deviate considerably from the preferences for environmental quality of the voters. Public choice literature shows, however, that there are certain circumstances (such as the short memory of voters, incomplete information, and coalition formation after elections) which would leave politicians a certain degree of latitude to act on their 'own responsibility' (Van den Doel and Van Velthoven 1990: 99–163; Mueller 1989: 277–86, 344–7).

On the basis of estimated preferences of citizens for the quality of the environment (or on the basis of their own preferences) politicians could design an environmental policy consisting of levies on polluting activities and subsidies on environmental-improving activities. Such changes in relative prices could induce economic agents to alter their behaviour and to switch to less-polluting technology. However, the desired altering of behaviour is not guaranteed, because politicians are still not familiar with the *real* preferences of the economic agents for environmental improvements as well as their *real* interests in environmental degeneration. A levy on petrol, for example, imposed with the aim of substantially decreasing car use, will hardly have the desired effect if politicians underestimate the willingness to pay for car use. The risk of incorrectly assessed preferences and, hence, of ineffective environmental policy measures, seems rather high.

Attempts have been made to resolve this problem with the help of econometric research. When the price fluctuations from preceding years are combined with the generated changes in supply and demand, the supply and demand elasticities of goods and services that cause pollution in production or consumption can be calculated. The decrease in pollution desired by politicians can then be converted into necessary changes in particular production and consumption patterns. Subsequently, the necessary price increases and price reductions can be calculated. These price alterations could be put into effect by means of levies and subsidies.

This strategy, unfortunately, is more attractive in theory than it is in reality. In a country such as The Netherlands, for instance, the emission reductions required for more or less sustainable development vary from 70 to 90 per cent (Langeweg 1988). If such large adjustments in production and consumption are to be accomplished by means of levies alone, the prices of relatively polluting goods and services will have to increase dramatically, often several times their actual prices. No doubt price fluctuations of this magnitude will change the preferences of economic agents and, hence, change the supply and demand elasticities of goods and services. If these elasticities become subject to substantial changes, politicians lack essential information concerning the behavioural adaptation that may be expected *after* the imposition of levies.

Since Pigou, several variants of economic instruments have been developed, such as deposit systems and marketable pollution rights. All these instruments are aimed at influencing individual behaviour indirectly by using financial incentives. In particular, marketable pollution rights are being increasingly advocated in economic literature. One of the advantages mentioned is that the environmental effects of marketable pollution rights are not as uncertain as those of levies (Baumol and Oates 1988: 178–80; Nentjes 1990: 159–65; Pearce and Turner 1990: 115). The maximum amount of polluting emissions which politicians consider 'permissible', are sold to the highest bidder in small, well-defined emission units. If strict enforcement is practised, total emissions in the 'bubble' will not exceed the previously specified ceiling (environmental quality goal).

At first sight the environmental effects of a system of marketable pollution rights would seem to be entirely predictable. On further consideration, however, they appear less sure. Especially, undesirable regional concentrations of emissions can hardly be prevented (Baumol and Oates 1988: 184; Pearce and Turner 1990: 116). In addition, it is difficult to see why the previously mentioned emission reductions of 70 to 90 per cent needed to establish more or less ecologically sustainable production and consumption processes should be more easily attained – that is, with less social resistance – using marketable pollution rights than by imposing regulatory levies.[7]

To summarize, the preferences of economic agents are not known (future generations) or only partly known (current generation). This knowledge is, however, indispensable for the design of an effective environmental policy based on the Pigovian internalization method.[8]

Ecological uncertainties

Internalization of externalities appears to be difficult because we lack sufficient knowledge concerning individual preferences. But even in the hypothetical case in which it is assumed that we are familiar with all individual preferences and, subsequently, are able to aggregate them into a collective decision on the environmental quality that is desired, this would still not preclude ecological disasters. This problem is linked to a fundamental limitation of rational choice theory in the context of environmental issues.

In general, the optimization strategy of rational choice theory implies that the production factors available – in most cases only labour and capital are implicitly meant – are allocated according to the preferences of the economic agents, satisfying as many needs as possible. The same strategy applies to the management of the natural resources available. The diagnosis is simple: the present allocation of natural resources is not optimal, as is demonstrated by the in most cases unwanted environmental deterioration. The neo-classical remedy is to restore optimal allocation by price manipulation. However, there is doubt as to whether this optimization philosophy is feasible for the management of the 'ecological utilization space' (Opschoor 1987). What is often lacking is essential information concerning the environmental effects of human actions.

A striking example of this is forests dying on a large scale as a result of acid rain. One of the most important causes of acid rain is the emission of large quantities of sulphur dioxide. In European industrial areas the first measures were taken to reduce the harmful effects of sulphur dioxide on public health some twenty years ago. These measures included the increased use of natural gas and nuclear energy and, especially, the construction of tall chimneys. It seemed that adequate measures had been taken, because air pollution in urban and industrial areas did decrease. However, tall chimneys have only dispersed the acidifying substances over large parts of Europe. Acid deposition beyond industrial areas increased rapidly, deteriorating forests in Central Europe and Scandinavia especially. The acidification of ecosystems was probably foreseeable. Biologists warned at an early stage that tall chimneys would at best shift the problem elsewhere. Society, however, was easily able to dismiss these warnings as exaggerations, because it was not known for certain what the effects on nature would be.

Another example is the extensive ecological damage caused by the use of DDT and other persistent agricultural pesticides. The emission of carbon dioxide may also lead to unpleasant surprises later, since the climatological effects of an increased CO_2 content in the atmosphere are not clear. The same holds for the relation between the emission of CFCs and the hole in the ozone layer. From these and many other serious and less serious examples, we see that again and again the effects of human (industrial) actions on nature are underestimated, minimized or even neglected.

If the effects of so many interventions in and influences on nature are not sufficiently known or are consistently disregarded, an optimum use of natural resources for human production and consumption, as neo-classical analyses and policy recommendations presuppose, becomes a problem. The point is that neo-classical optimization requires insight into the effects of alternative actions on nature (or into the availability of natural resources) with a probability bordering on certainty, or at least with a probability that can be calculated using the theory of probabilities. The former is the familiar assumption of the existence of fully-informed agents whereby the problem of inadequate ecological knowledge is simply neglected. The latter seems more advanced, but still needs far better ecological knowledge than we generally have for constructing a distribution of probabilities of ecological states occurring as a result of a particular human intervention (cf. Drepper and Manson 1990).

In general, processes in nature, and hence human interventions in these processes, appear to be hardly predictable for at least three reasons. First, synergetic effects increase the impact on the environment of separate emissions. For example, laboratory experiments have made clear that the combined impact of the acidifying substances SO_2, NO_x, NH_3 and O_3 on plant growth is substantially more severe than the (linear) total of the impacts of each of these substances separately would be (Tonneijk 1981). Second, thresholds are very common in ecosystems. Again acidification serves as an excellent example. The sudden acceleration of the deterioration of forests and the subsequent dying off of large parts of European forests at the beginning of the 1980s came like a bolt from the blue for most people (including a lot of scientists!). It appeared that the buffering capacity of the soil had protected trees from serious damage for decades. Once saturation point had been reached, acidifying substances could damage trees considerably and kill them within a couple of years. Third, many emissions have a delayed effect on the environment. It takes decades, for example, before the nitrogen from manure and chemical fertilizers is washed from the top soil into deeper layers, causing severe nitrate pollution of the groundwater, which serves in most countries as drinking water. Even if nitrogen leakages into the groundwater could be prevented as of today, nitrate pollution of groundwater will continue to increase considerably for decades to come.

In short, synergetic effects, thresholds, and delayed reactions cloud the issue of the relations between emissions and the deterioration of nature. As a result of human actions, ecosystems change far more capriciously than economists normally assume. The neo-classical approach to optimizing the use of the natural resources available is unsatisfactory as long as we cannot accurately assess the quantity of natural resources we have. In other words, we cannot optimize our ecological utilization space without knowing the concrete limits that must not be crossed if irreversible effects on nature are to be avoided.

MARXIST-ORIENTED APPROACHES

From the preceding section the conclusion can be drawn that for a long time neo-classical economists neglected the 'third production factor'. The question arises of whether alternative approaches in economic theory have dealt more adequately with the effects of production and consumption processes on the availability and quality of natural resources. During the last 100 years Marxist-oriented authors have been the keenest critics of neo-classical theory. Therefore we will examine this 'natural' antipode of neo-classical thought for its sensitivity to and treatment of environmental problems.[9]

Unfortunately, Marxists have hardly paid any attention to environmental problems. This is not surprising, as the work of Marx deals – first and foremost – with the exploitation of labour by capital. In handbooks accepted by Marxists hardly anything can be found that could be called a theory of the environment or natural resources. This fixation upon the exploitation of labour had the effect of making environmental problems seem irrelevant. In the 1960s and 1970s most Marxists regarded environmental problems as artificially constructed by bourgeois economists to distract attention from the class struggle. For this reason Marxists had no appreciation of, for example, the Reports for the Club of Rome.

This attitude, however, became untenable. All sections of the population suffer to some extent from increasing environmental problems. Both capitalists and workers have to deal with problems like acid rain, nuclear waste, holes in the ozone layer, the pollution of groundwater and surface water, and so forth. Ultimately, these important social problems could no longer be neglected by Marxist authors. Moreover, discontent with the deterioration of nature and the environment led to the rise of environmental interest groups, which represented a more or less autonomous resistance from all sections of the population. Marxists were hardly represented in these groups. Forced by this social development, Marxists have recently started to develop a position on environmental problems.

Initially, the orthodox approach dominated analyses of environmental problems. This approach is, in a nutshell, based on Marx's idea that the capitalist mode of production destroys the basis of life, while a socialist mode of production would not have these failings (Marx 1970: 474–5). Authors in this orthodox tradition suggest that man's alienation from nature has the same root cause as man's alienation from labour. The abolition of the alienation of human labour by transferring the control of the means of production to the working class, will, at the same time and more or less automatically, put an end to man's alienation from nature and the environment (cf. Heise and Hembold 1977: 22–38, Romören and Romören 1978: 35–47, Krusewitz 1978: 81–108, Gärtner 1979: 70).

This literature suggests that Marx had a comprehensive framework within which the analysis of environmental problems and the depletion of natural resources had been foreseen. However, this is not the case. An in-depth perception of the relation between nature and society hardly was an issue in the period in which Marx lived and worked. The rise of the Industrial Revolution and the accompanying technical development generated a widely held belief in the potential of technical progress. This idea can also be found in the work of Marx; the development of the forces of production were, in his view, a necessary condition for realizing a socialist society. Marx never developed systematic ideas regarding the relation between nature and society. Sporadic remarks on this matter are scattered throughout his work.

Marx held the opinion that nature and labour are two components of a dialectical unity and paid a great deal of attention to the value of labour (Marx 1970: 172; 1964: 112). But what value is derived from nature – the other component of the dialectical unity – remains obscure. He only stated that nature has no value in itself. Natural materials acquire value only by their mingling with human labour: 'The purely natural material in which human labour is objectified, to the extent that it is merely a material that exists of labour, has no value' (Marx 1973: 366).

Marx focused on the contradictions between labour and capital. Analysing these contradictions, he used, among other things, the labour theory of value originating from Ricardo. The use of the labour theory of value gave Marx the opportunity to demonstrate and criticize the mechanism of the creation of surplus value and the exploitation of labour. It also led, however, to a split between economy and nature in his theory. Hence, nature appears to be no longer a source of value in Marx's economic theories. This result must be attributed particularly to the assumption implicit in the labour theory of value that the resources nature offers are inexhaustible (Immler 1983a, 1983b). As an unconscious result of using the labour theory of value Marx discarded nature as a source of value, although this is contrary to his own starting-point – namely, that labour and nature are *both* sources of value. It is not clear whether Marx was aware of this inconsistency in his theories, but it is certainly connected to the almost exclusive attention he paid to the labour factor.

The division between man and nature in Marx's theories has strongly influenced the view of Marxist authors concerning environmental problems. Harmsen states that this explains why Marxists have for so long refused to recognize the social importance of environmental problems. Socialists continued to take for granted that the abolition of classes in society would automatically generate a rational management of the natural resources available (Harmsen 1974: 15).

At the end of the 1970s the first critical remarks about the orthodox approach were heard among Marxist authors. Several attempts have been made to construct alternative theories about nature and the environment using Marxist starting-points (cf. Ullrich 1979, Ernst-Pörken 1984, Govers 1988). One can conceive of concepts like exchange value and use value being used to describe the overexploitation of the environment. However, these attempts are not really convincing, and this must mainly be attributed to the fact that Marx never developed his theories for this kind of application. His theories simply lack sufficient categories for analysing current environmental problems.[10]

Summarizing, we may say that there is no Marxist-oriented theory specifically dealing with the 'ecological question'. But even if such a theory existed to more or less explain the current environmental crisis, it would not give us an answer to the crucial question as to the extent to which the pollution of the environment should be reduced. Until now, neither neo-classical nor Marxist theories have offered a satisfactory solution to this problem. This is partly due to the origin of these theories.

Both neo-classical and Marxist theories originated and were elaborated in the second half of the nineteenth century, describing and analyzing the same market processes. Neo-classical economists emphasized the issue of the efficient use of the production factors of labour and capital, while Marxist economists stressed what they considered to be an unfair distribution of power and income between labour and capital, resulting from the same market processes where, according to neo-classical economists, an optimal allocation of production factors is realized. The structure and the starting points of both theories are such that the level of socially acceptable environmental deterioration (or quality) cannot be determined. In addition, determining the borders of the ecological utilization space is hampered by a lack of knowledge about essential ecological relations, as already discussed in the previous section.

SUSTAINABLE DEVELOPMENT AS A STARTING POINT

The preceding sections demonstrate that alternative theoretical paths are needed. In neo-classical theory no special attention is paid to natural resources. Too much reliance is placed on the idea that the use of natural resources is a normal optimization problem. Internalization of externalities is the key to an optimum use of the natural resources available. In (neo)Marxist theories there is also too much dependence on ancient doctrines, in which it is assumed that the quantity and quality of natural resources are constant factors. In contrast with classical economists, obviously regarding the availability of natural resources as an explicable variable, twentieth-century economists consider the environment as a datum (neo-classicals) or as a constant factor (neo-Marxists). This change of attitude is closely connected to the already mentioned switch from the use of natural resources with a flow character to the dominating use of natural resources with a stock character since the beginning of the Industrial Revolution. This switch enabled economists, such as Marshall, to push nature as a factor of production to the periphery of economic theory and to focus attention almost exclusively on the analysis of the market mechanism. The current environmental crisis demonstrates that this attitude is untenable.

Various alternative starting points for the adaptation of economic theory are suggested in the literature. Boulding (1966) has the concept of 'spaceship earth' in mind, Goudzwaard (1974) proposes to economize within the limits set by nature, Sachs (1976, 1984) advocates an ecological development, Söderbaum (1980, 1982) suggests ecological imperatives for governmental policies, Opschoor (1987, 1990) wants to keep economic activities within the ecological utilization space available, and the WCED (1987), finally, opts for the by now famous concept of sustainable development. All that these concepts have in common is that ecologically bounded possibilities for using natural resources are taken as a starting point for the development of economic theory. In this respect we have returned to the viewpoint of the classical economists of the beginning of the nineteenth century.

Sustainable development is a normative concept. Indeed, the heart of the argument deals with a fair distribution of the natural resources available among different generations, as well as among the populations of the First, the Second and the Third World of our own generation. Though the concept is given massive support throughout the whole world, the realization of sustainable development is highly problematic (Opschoor 1990). One of the greatest problems is the operationalization of the concept. In this respect many questions arise which remain unanswered for the moment. What are, for instance, the limits nature sets to human production and consumption processes? Are these limits related to current ecological quality, which has already vastly deteriorated, or should we aim at an improved ecological quality? At what pace can we use stocks of exhaustible natural resources if we employ a maximum recycling of materials? Such questions can hardly be answered on the basis of current knowledge.

In our view, the character of the relations between the ecological system and the economic system determines to a large extent the direction in which answers to these questions are to be sought. In order to develop a framework for research, a closer look at ecological cycles (or ecocycles) is needed. For too long production and consumption processes have been portrayed as completely closed cycles, suggesting they are independent of ecological processes. If ecological insights are to be integrated into economic theory – and we think this is necessary in order to grant nature a full-fledged position in economic theory as the third production factor – the traditionally closed character of economic cycles in economic theory has to be opened up.[11]

In ecology, the notion of the 'ecocycle' describes the character of ecological processes. In general, an examination is made of the course taken by various substances in the ecological process, at what point they accumulate or decompose and how substances get blocked in the ecocycle. The description of an ecological process is complete only if the flow of information and energy in the ecosystem is also indicated. Without energy from the sun the system would not function. Furthermore, some sort of information must be present in the ecosystem on the basis of which events can take place within the system. This information causes, for example, the decomposition of organic matter or the generation of new cells. Each economic model in which an attempt is made to describe how production and consumption could be fitted into ecological processes, should take these relationships into account.

Figure 7.1 helps to distinguish between several kinds of effects of human production and consumption on the ecological system.[12] A system of human production and consumption is based, among other things, on the need to use natural resources from ecological cycles – the active part of the ecosystem. Agricultural production provides a good example of this relation. Organic matter is formed under the influence of the sun and serves as food for animals and humans. These natural resources are, in theory, inexhaustible and therefore flowing forever. Since the beginning of the nineteenth century man also started to use fossil natural resources on a large scale. However, these resources are exhaustible, as is natural oil. The hydrocarbons of which it is composed are denoted as 'stock quantities', because the stock of natural oil available in the earth's crust cannot increase within a human time horizon. The fossil part of the ecological system is hardly, if at all, affected by the flow of waste products originating from the economic system. Pollution of the environment occurs in that part of the ecological system where cycles function. These cycles can be disturbed by the discharge of waste products.

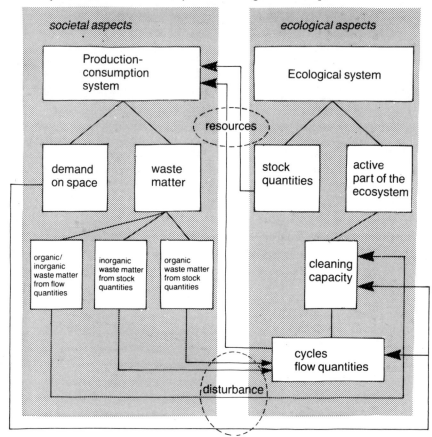

Figure 7.1 Interactions between the economic system and the ecological system

There is a great difference between the dumping of organic materials and the dumping of inorganic and synthetic materials into the ecocycles. Organic materials are normal elements of functioning ecocycles, while inorganic and synthetic substances are foreign to them. Among the latter are the waste products from fossil resources. When dumped into the ecocycles they cause disturbances, even in low concentrations, because there are no mechanisms available to process or to decompose these waste products. On the other hand, the dumping of decomposable organic matter does not necessarily disturb the ecocycles. Such matter is already part and parcel of the ecocycles and can be decomposed by bacteria in the normal way. However, if too much decomposable organic matter is dumped into, for example, surface water, the water's self-cleaning capacity can be impaired to the extent that only stinking, rotting and deoxidized expanses of water remain. Similarly, pollution from fossil matter is worse than pollution from organic, decomposable matter. Whereas the latter occurs locally and may be neutralized after a time, pollution from undecomposable stock matter is irreversible. It is almost impossible to restore the cycle in this case. Substances foreign to ecocycles accumulate, causing long-term effects on the environment and across a large area. Thus, when heavy metals are discharged into surface water, the flora and fauna in it will be seriously affected. Heavy metals do not just disappear when the organisms die, but accumulate in the ecocycles.

Attention has not yet been paid to one category of effects on nature by human actions: the use of land. Yet this very seriously violates the ecocycles. The process began as soon as people became settled in one place, took up agriculture and began to change the natural layer of vegetation. In Europe the process has reached the point where hardly anything of the original vegetation is left. Modifications in the layer of vegetation do not necessarily lead to unacceptable changes in the ecocycles, but they do interfere with the cyclical process. Further attacks on the natural vegetation by the building of houses and factories, the construction of roads and other infrastructures have seriously affected the ecosystem. Their effect is different from that of the discharge of waste products, however, in that they threaten the functioning of the ecocycles much faster and more directly, without complicated intermediary processes. For instance, ecocycles may be changed if natural woodland is turned into arable land or cut back because of road construction.

The box 'production–consumption system' in Figure 7.1 represents the human impulse to exploit natural resources. The price mechanism only partly informs individuals about the quality and availability of natural resources. The recommendation made by (neo-classical) economists to remedy this lack of information by price manipulation using levies and subsidies, appears to be hardly feasible (see pp. 127–9). This implies that the lack of information about the environmental effects of economic activities continues to exist. A (Pareto) optimum exploitation of nature seems to be hardly possible due to the unpredictable effects of human activities on nature (see pp. 129–31). Under these circumstances there is a real danger that the burden of proof for the ecological sustainability of human activities rests squarely with nature. That being so, environmental problems are likely to increase rather than decrease.[13]

In our view, existing mainstream economic theory is not the proper starting point for the development of economic theories concerning environmental problems. We would do better to take the insights of ecologists as our starting point, despite the often imperfect and contradictory nature of those insights. It is this very uncertainty concerning what and how much we can take from nature without creating irreversible effects, which should stimulate us to act carefully.

CONCLUDING REMARKS

Aiming at an ecologically sustainable society, a prerequisite is to use the ecocycles in such a way that their functioning is not damaged irreversibly. It is not easy to operationalize this starting point. In any case, the discharge of substances which are foreign to or rarely occur in the ecocycles and are mainly extracted from the stocks of fossil natural resources should be minimized or, even better, stopped. This imperative implies that the speed at which fossil natural resources are depleted needs to be considerably reduced by converting radically to the recycling of minerals and synthetics. However, it is impossible to recycle all materials completely. During production, consumption and recycling processes a part of the materials is always going to be 'lost' – that is, end up in the ecocycles. Technological development should be directed towards a continuous decrease in the percentage of 'lost' materials. Ultimately, the sustainable solution is to convert completely to renewable resources. Renewable resources can be extracted from the – on a human time-scale – ever-functioning ecocycles (provided that exploitation is careful) and subsequently, after being used in production and consumption processes, they can be disposed of without disturbing ecocycles (provided that the carrying capacity is not exceeded). The same recommendation applies to the extraction and use of energy. Fossil stocks of oil, natural gas and coal will be depleted sooner or later. This means that a complete conversion to the use of energy derived from flow quantities is inevitable in the long run.

The process of conversion to an ecologically sustainable mode of production will have considerable effects on various social relations. In any case, sustainable development will attack historically vested interests. Partly owing to the market process a situation has come about which is far removed from sustainability.

Unfortunately, one cannot expect that the reversing of the damage to the environment will be a spontaneous process. For the creation of a sustainable society there will be a strong need for collective strategies and decisions, resulting in a strict environmental policy. Policies that effectively stimulate sustainable development will not be received with great acclaim by those who privately benefit from the present degradation of the environment. Well-organized groups of polluting producers like the petrochemical industry, the transport sector and agriculture will certainly oppose strict environmental measures. In general, these interest groups do not contest the aim of sustainability, but the pace at which sustainability is to be realized.[14]

Basically, there should be no limits set on the choice of instruments in order to attain sustainable development. In our view the price mechanism can play an important role, although a different one than in neo-classical theories. The aim of sustainable development implies that limiting conditions for production and consumption processes have to be formulated. Such limiting conditions cannot be derived from the quantification and internalization of externalities as was demonstrated in previous sections. We should instead derive them from public debates and democratic collective decisions based on both ecological and ethical insights. Subsequently, both legal and economic instruments will have to be used to steer all activities in society onto a sustainable course.

Labour and capital will offer fierce resistance to the determination of ecological limiting conditions, especially when their short-term interests are unilaterally jeopardized. In fact, a social struggle concerning the distribution of the ecological space available among the various production and consumption processes will be the result. In this social struggle national and local government will play a central role, being the institution in which all decisions concerning the use of the natural resources available will have to be formalized.

The picture roughly sketched in the preceding paragraphs deviates from the ideas of economists such as Goudzwaard, reasoning back from *economic policy* towards *economic theory*. In this line of reasoning the subjective element is assigned to economic policy, in an attempt to keep economic theory objective and free from value judgements. By doing so, however, a fundamental shortcoming of neo-classical theory is ignored. The price mechanism lies at the centre of neo-classical theories, relegating environmental deterioration to the periphery of economic thought. This is demonstrated by the use of the term 'externality' for effects on production and consumption not reflected in price fluctuations. One should be aware of this one-sided orientation in neo-classical theory, as well as the consequences for environmental analyses based on this approach.

What is needed is an integration of ecological insights into economic theories. Despite the efforts of some authors to do so, adequate incorporation of natural resources in economic theories will not be an easy task. This holds particularly if mainstream economists continue to see the economy as a closed system, operating independently of nature. If an environmental problem arises, its analysis and the development of an abatement strategy is thought to be a matter for specialists in the subdiscipline of environmental economics. All critical remarks about the non-incorporation of natural resources in economic theory can be neutralized by referring to this subdiscipline. In this way an alibi is created to maintain the closed system view of society.

The consequences of an adequate incorporation of natural resources into economic theory can hardly be overestimated. For instance, the traditional system of National Accounts will be untenable in the long run, as it is based on the neo-classical approach of measuring economic variables revealed almost exclusively on the market. Such a system cannot give any insight into the unpriced scarcity of various natural resources.[15] Also, a cost–benefit analysis can only provide partial insight into environmental problems, as long as important benefits (for example, environmental quality) have no market price. As a third example, the expression of the national debt in dollars, without taking into account the national debt caused by the deterioration of natural resources, is not an adequate indicator of the solvency of a country in the long run so long as the loss of natural resources is neglected. Furthermore, accounts concerning industrial relations should no longer neglect the position of employees in industries which destroy or irreversibly affect the environment on a large scale. And finally, the concept of the optimal growth path, as defined in macroeconomics, should be regarded as a non-issue if the effects of environmental factors are not included in the concept itself.

To summarize, the developing of environmental economic theories is not enough. An adequate integration of natural resources into economic theory requires the rewriting of mainstream economic theory.

NOTES

1 The continuous rise of the corn price in the second half of the eighteenth century was constantly higher than the rise of the general price level (Deane and Cole 1967: 91). Subsequently, the Napoleonic wars pushed the corn price even higher (Deane and Cole 1967: 91, Turner 1984: 48).

2 Later, in the closing years of the nineteenth century, Marshall connected the concept of value based on the production costs principle with the concept of value based on the principle of marginal utility (see Marshall 1925). According to Marshall goods have value because, on the one hand, they satisfy human needs. On the other hand, the production of goods and services requires sacrifices in the form of the quantities of labour, capital and natural resources used.

3 In this section only a brief review of the relevant neo-classical publications on environmental issues can be provided. This implies that we cannot deal with the problem of the optimal exploitation of non-renewable resources. Most of these studies fit within the traditional neo-classical starting points, which are dealt with in this section. (For a recent neo-classical study on non-renewable natural resources see Neher 1990). We also do not deal with the discussion about the correction of GNP for environmental deterioration such as initiated by Hueting in the 1970s (Hueting 1970, 1980). After having died down at the end of the 1970s and the beginning of the 1980s, interest in this debate recently increased again considerably (see, among others, Ahmad *et al.* 1989), and has been supplied with new dimensions (see, among others, Kuik and Verbruggen 1991). Neither do we discuss the position of the New Institutionalists, who consider the absence, transfer and distribution of property rights of natural resources the ultimate cause of environmental problems. We will not discuss models which quantitatively describe the relation between the economic system and the ecological system (for a recent overview, see Hafkamp 1991). All these topics and approaches deserve extensive attention which we, however, cannot give them owing to lack of space.

4 Based on publications such as Lionel Robbins's *An Essay on the Nature and Significance of Economic Science* (1935), the concept of relative scarcity became the cornerstone of contemporary mainstream economics.

5 It must be said, however, that, in general, unpriced forms of scarcity are not excluded in mainstream economics (Robbins 1935, Hennipman 1945). Nevertheless, before the 1960s only a few economists attempted to analyse the unpriced scarcity of natural resources in a neo-classical framework.

6 In welfare economic literature this is called the Bergsonian approach. Because of the above-mentioned problems with interpersonal comparison of utility, social welfare is assumed to be dependent on the interpersonal valuations of utility by policy-makers (Boadway and Bruce 1984).

7 It is not possible to elaborate here on the pros and cons of marketable pollution rights. For economic contributions see, for example, Baumol and Oates (1988:

155: 296), Pearce and Turner (1990: 84–119), Nentjes (1990). For a legal contribution on the choice of economic instruments in environment policy see, for example, Peeters (1991).

8 Although the debate regarding the problem of which instrument is the most efficient is not unimportant and attracts much attention in economic literature, we will not discuss this issue here. In this contribution the central point is the integration of ecological insights into economic theories, so the question is how far current economic theories provide the possibility of *analysing* environmental problems.

9 We will not discuss Institutionalist analyses of environmental problems here. For such an approach see, for example, Söderbaum (1987), and Swaney (1987a, 1987b). We have made some comments on this approach elsewhere (Opschoor and Van der Straaten 1991, Dietz and Van der Straaten 1992).

10 Elsewhere (Dietz and Van der Straaten 1990) we have presented a more comprehensive review of Marxist analyses of environmental problems.

11 The following paragraphs are based on Dietz and Van der Straaten (1988), as well as on Van der Straaten (1990: 103–16).

12 Ecological systems can be described on a global level (higher air layers, including the ozone layer in the stratosphere) where processes regulating radiation and temperature are located; on a continental level (continents and oceans) where processes take place such as air and ocean currents; on a fluvial level (large river-basins and coastal seas) comprising various processes related to the water ecology; on a regional level (landscapes) involving various processes within the soil; and on a local level (work and living environment) dealing with the environment made by man.

13 This is one of the explanations for the lack of linkages between mainstream environmental economic theory and current environmental policy (see Dietz and Van der Straaten 1992).

14 Recent debates, political decisions and the influences of interest groups concerning the reduction of acidifying emissions in specific sectors are described and analysed in Van der Straaten (1990, 1991) (especially oil refineries and electric power plants); Dietz et al.(1991) (traffic); Dietz and Hoogervorst (1991), as well as Dietz and Termeer (1991) (agriculture).

15 Here we encounter the debate concerning the possibility of a green GNP; see for a recent state-of-the-art overview Ahmad et al. (1989). However, attempts to calculate a green GNP meet with the fundamental obstacles discussed in the section on neo-classical environmental economics. In our view a much more promising initiative in this context is the attempt to develop indicators of sustainable development, by which the 'extent of sustainability' of a whole nation, economic policy or specific sectors could be determined (cf. Kuik and Verbruggen 1991, for potentials and pitfalls).

BIBLIOGRAPHY

Ahmad, Y. J., Serafy, S. E. and Lutz, E. (1989) *Environmental Accounting for Sustainable Development*, Washington: The World Bank.

Anderson, G. D. and Bishop, R. C. (1986) 'The valuation problem', in D. W. Bromley (ed.), *Natural Resource Economics; Policy Problems and Contemporary Analysis*, Boston and Dordrecht: Kluwer Academic Publishers.

Baumol, W. J. and Oates, W. E. (1988) *The Theory of Environmental Policy* (2nd ed), Cambridge: Cambridge University Press.

Blaug, M. (1978) *Economic Theory in Retrospect*, Cambridge: Cambridge University Press.

Boadway, R. and Bruce, N. (1984) *Welfare Economics*, Oxford: Basil Blackwell.

Boulding, K. (1966) 'The economics of the coming Spaceship Earth', in H. Jarret (ed.), *Environmental Quality in a Growing Economy*, Baltimore: Johns Hopkins.

Crocker, T. D. and Shogren, J. F. (1991) 'Preference learning and contingent valuation methods', in F. J. Dietz, F. van der Ploeg and J. van der Straaten (eds), *Environmental Policy and the Economy*, Amsterdam: North-Holland.

Deane, P. and Cole, W. A. (1967) *British Economic Growth 1688–1959; Trends and Structure* (2nd ed), Cambridge: Cambridge University Press.

Denison, E. F. (1947) in *Studies in Income and Wealth*, vol. 10, New York: Conference on Research in Income and Wealth.

Dietz, F. J. and Hoogervorst, N. J. P. (1991) 'Towards a sustainable and efficient use of manure in agriculture: the Dutch case', *Environmental and Resource Economics* 1(3): 313–32.

—— and van der Straaten, J. (1988) 'The problem of optimal exploitation of natural resources: the need for ecological limiting conditions', *International Journal of Social Economics* 15(3–4): 71–9.

—— —— (1990) 'Economic analyses of environmental problems: a critique of Marxist approaches', in S. Brander and O. Roloff (eds), *Politische Oekenomie des Umweltschutzes*, Regensburg: Transfer-Verlag.

—— —— (1992) 'Rethinking environmental economics: the missing links between economic theory and environmental policy', *Journal of Economic Issues* 26(1): 27–51.

—— —— and Van der Velde, M. (1991) 'The European Common Market and the environment: the case of the emission of NO_x by motorcars', *Review of Political Economy* 3(1): 62–78.

—— and Termeer, K. J. A. M. (1991) 'Dutch manure policy: the lack of economic instruments', in D. J. Kraan and R. J. In't Veld (eds), *Environmental Protection: Public or Private Choice*, Dordrecht: Kluwer Academic Publishers.

Doel, J. van den and Van Velthoven, B. C. J. (1990) *Democratie en welvaartstheorie* (3rd edn), Alphen aan de Rijn: Samsom Tjeenk Willink.

Drepper, F. R. and Manson, B. A. (1990) 'On the role of unpredictability in environmental economics', Paper presented at the conference 'Economics and the Environment', 17–19 September, Tilburg University.

Ernst-Pörken, M. (ed.) (1984) *Alternativen der Oekonomie – Oekonomie der Alternativen*, Argument Sonderband AS 104, Berlin: Argument-Verlag.

Fabricant, S. (1947) in *Studies in Income and Wealth*, vol. 10, New York: Conference on Research in Income and Wealth.

Freeman, A. M. (1985) 'Methods for assessing the benefits of environmental programs', in A. V. Kneese and F. L. Sweeney (eds), *Handbook of Natural Resource and Energy Economics*, vol. 1, Amsterdam: North-Holland.

Gärtner, E. (1979) *Arbeiterklasse und Oekologie*, Frankfurt am Main: Verlag Marxistische Blätter.

Goudzwaard, B. (1970) *Ongeprijsde Schaarste*, Den Haag: W. P. van Stokkum en Zn.

—— (1974) *Schaduwen van het groeigeloof*, Kampen: Kok.

—— (1978) *Kapitalisme en Vooruitgang*, Assen: Van Gorcum.

Govers, H. (1988) *Natuur, techniek en milieupolitiek*, Utrecht: Jan van Arkel.

Hafkamp, W. A. (1991) 'Three decades of environmental-economic modelling: economic models of pollutant emissions', in F. J. Dietz, F. van der Ploeg and J. van der Straaten (eds), *Environmental Policy and the Economy*, Amsterdam: North-Holland.

Harmsen, G. (1974) *Natuur, Geschiedenis, Filosofie*, Nijmegen: SUN.

Heise, K.-H. and Hembold, M. (1977) 'Umweltgefährdung und Kapitalverwertung', *Marximus Digest* 2: 22–38.

Hennipman, P. (1945) *Economisch motief en economisch principe*, Amsterdam: Noord-Hollandsche Uitgeversmaatschappij.

Hoehn, J. P. and Randall, A. (1987) 'A satisfactory benefit cost indicator for contingent valuation', *Journal of Environmental Economics and Management* 14(3): 226–47.

Hueting, R. (1970) *Wat is de Natuur ons waard?*, Baarn: Wereldvenster.

—— (1980) *New Scarcity and Economic Growth* (2nd edn), Amsterdam: North-Holland.

Immler, H. (1983a) 'Ist nur die Arbeit wertbildend?', *Sozialismus*, no. 5: 53–8.

—— (1983b) 'Natur ist wertbildend', *Sozialismus*, no. 10: 27–30.

Jevons, W. S. (1924) *The Theory of Political Economy*, London: Macmillan.

King, W. J. (1919) *The Wealth and Income of the People of the United States*, New York and London.

Krusewitz, K. (1978) 'Opmerkingen over de oorzaken van de milieukrisis in historisch-maatschappelijke samenhang', in H. Verhagen (ed.), *Inleiding tot de politieke economie van het milieu*, Amsterdam: Ekologische Uitgeverij.

Kuik, O. and Verbruggen, H. (1991) *In Search of Indicators of Sustainable Development*, Boston and Dordrecht: Kluwer Academic Publishers.

Kuznets, S. (1947) 'National income and industrial structure', in The Econometric Society Meeting, 6–18 September, Washington, DC, *Proceedings of the International Statistical Conference*, vol. 5: 218–19.

Langeweg, F. (ed.) (1988) *Zorgen voor Morgen*, Alphen aan de Rijn: Samsom Tjeenk Willink.

Malthus, T. R. (1982) *An Essay on the Principle of Population*, Harmondsworth: Penguin.

Marshall, A. (1925) *Principles of Economics*, London: Macmillan.

Martinez-Alier, J. (1991) 'Ecological perception and distributional effects: a historical view', in F. J. Dietz, F. van der Ploeg and J. van der Straaten (eds), *Environmental Policy and the Economy*, Amsterdam: North-Holland.

Marx, K. (1964) *The Economic and Philosophical Manuscripts of 1844*, New York: Martin Milligan International Publishers.

—— (1970) *Capital*, Vol. 1, London: Lawrence & Wishart.

—— (1973) *Grundrisse, Foundations of the Critique of Political Economy (Rough draft)*, translated by M. Nicolaus, Harmondsworth: Pelican.

Menger, C. (1968) *Grundsätze der Volkswirtschaftslehre*, Vienna: Braumeller.

Mishan, E. J. (1967) *The Costs of Economic Growth*, London: Staples Press.

Mueller, D. C. (1989) *Public Choice II*, Cambridge: Cambridge University Press.

Neher, P. A. (1990) *Natural Resource Economics, Conservation and Exploitation*, Cambridge: Cambridge University Press.

Nentjes, A. (1990) 'Economische instrumenten in het milieubeleid: financierings- of sturingsmiddel?', in P. Nijkamp and H. Verbruggen (eds), *Het Nederlandse milieu in de Europese ruimte*, Preadviezen van de Koninklijke Vereniging voor de Staathuishoudkunde, Leiden: Stenfert Kroese.

Opschoor, J. B. (1987) *Duurzaamheid en Verandering: over ecologisch inpasbare economische Ontwikkeling*, Oratie, Amsterdam: Vrije Universiteit.

—— (1990) 'Ecologisch duurzame ontwikkeling: een theoretisch idee en een weerbarstige praktijk', in P. Nijkamp and H. Verbruggen (eds), *Het Nederlandse milieu in de Europese ruimte*, Preadviezen van de Koninklijke Vereniging voor de Staathuishoudkunde, Leiden: Stenfert Kroese.

—— and van der Straaten, J. (1991) 'Sustainable Development: An Institutional Approach', Paper presented at Annual Conference of the European Association of Environmental and Resource Economists, 11–14 June, Stockholm.

Pearce, D. W. and Turner, R. K. (1990) *Economics of Natural Resources and the Environment*, London: Harvester Wheatsheaf.

Peeters, M. (1991) 'Legal aspects of marketable pollution rights', in F. J. Dietz, F. van der Ploeg and J. van der Straaten (eds), *Environmental Policy and the Economy*, Amsterdam: North-Holland.

Pigou, A. C. (1952) *The Economics of Welfare*, London: Macmillan.

Ricardo, D. (1975) *The Principles of Political Economy and Taxation*, London: Everyman.

Robbins, L. (1935) *An Essay on the Nature and Significance of Economic Science* (2nd edn), London: Macmillan.

Romören, E. and Römoren, T. I. (1978) 'Marx en de ekologie', in H. Verhagen (ed.), *Inleiding tot de politieke economie van het milieu*, Amsterdam: Ekologische Uitgeverij.

Sachs, I. (1976) 'Environment and styles of development', in W. Matthews (ed.), *Outer Limits and Human Needs*, Uppsala: Dag Hammarskjöld Foundation.

—— (1984) 'The strategies of ecodevelopment', *Ceres; FAO Review on Agriculture and Development* 17: 17–21.

Söderbaum, P. (1980) 'Towards a reconciliation of economics and ecology', *European Review of Agricultural Economics* 7: 55–77.

—— (1982) 'Ecological imperatives for public policy', *Ceres; FAO Review on Agriculture and Development* 15: 28–32.

—— (1987) 'Environmental management: a non-traditional approach', *Journal of Economic Issues* 21(1): 139–65.

Swaney, J. A. (1987a) 'Building instrumental environmental control institutions', *Journal of Economic Issues* 21(1): 295–308.

—— (1987b) 'Elements of a neoinstitutional environmental economics', *Journal of Economic Issues* 21(4): 1793–79.

Straaten, J. van der (1990) *Zure regen, economische theorie en het Nederlandse Beleid*, Utrecht: Jan van Arkel.

—— (1991) 'Acid rain and the single internal market: policies from the Netherlands', *European Environment* 1(1): 20–4.

Tonneijk, A. E. G. (1981) *Research on the Influence of Different Air Pollutants Separately and in Combination in Agriculture, Horticulture and Forestry Crops*, Wageningen: IPO Report R 262.

Turner, M. (1984) *Enclosures in Britian 1750–1830*, London: Macmillan.

Ullrich, O. (1979) *Weltniveau*, Berlin: Rotbuch Verlag.

Walras, L. (1954) *Elements of Pure Economics or the Theory of Social Wealth*, Homewood, Ill.: Allen & Unwin.

World Commission on Environment and Development (WCED) (1987) *Our Common Future* (Brundtland Report), Oxford: Oxford University Press.

8

ECOLOGICAL VERSUS SOCIAL RATIONALITY

Can there be green social policies?

John Ferris

INTRODUCTION

If it is accepted that green politics should be clearly distinguished from environmentalism then it follows that green politics should aspire to be more than a form of single issue politics. This is the position adopted by Andrew Dobson who argues that ecologism is indeed an ideology in the conventional sense in that it seeks to offer an account of the social and political world, prescribes action, and at the same time motivates appropriate activity (Dobson 1990). If ecologism is indeed such an ideology it should be able to inform social choice across a range of policy areas. Social Democrats tend to favour forms of state intervention and regulation and justify this by reference to the value of equality. Liberals believe that free markets are the most effective way to provide necessary and desired goods and services, and appeal to the value of freedom to legitimate this belief. These divergent legitimating principles have given rise to quite distinctive models of social welfare (George and Wilding 1985). This chapter is addressed to the question of whether green political theory does yield such a model of welfare, or at least implies a distinctive approach to social policy.

ECOLOGICAL VERSUS SOCIAL RATIONALITY

Sara Parkin can be taken as representative of those who subscribe to 'ecologism' and moreover adhere to an essentially biocentric view of green politics: 'Greens are suggesting that we should abandon our obsession with ourselves and put the Earth into the centre of all the models and plans we make for our personal and collective activities' (Parkin 1989: 18). She argues that instead of back-pedalling on the environment the Greens should be putting down roots on the political high ground and from that position develop multiple examples of how the environment touches every aspect of the lives of ordinary people. Parkin thinks that the Greens should not seek to be the complete political party in the conventional sense:

145

For example, if conservation and protection of the Earth were made the motor of our economic and social regime rather than its fuel, it would effect the health and well being of the people too. Social justice would be possible through conservation as it never was through consumption – our success – with real life indicators such as health, cultural variety, clean air, safe water, unpoisoned food, secure and convivial neighbourhoods.

(Parkin 1989: 23)

Clearly Parkin believes that a model of welfare can be derived from 'nature' in some sense. This earth-first argument certainly points towards a model of ecological rationality and Parkin accepts such a model at least implicitly. Drysek has made a useful contribution to thinking about this issue by putting forward an explicit model of ecological rationality:

Ecological rationality as a principle and as a form of functional rationality is concerned with low entropy, or order in human systems as they combine with natural systems. . . . There is a sense in which this 'nature knows best' contention just has to be correct. Recall that in the absence of human interests ecological rationality may be recognized in terms of an ecosystem's provision of life support to itself.

(Drysek 1987: 43–5)

Drysek presents his argument for the moral priority of ecological rationality in the following terms:

The preservation and enhancement of the material and ecological basis of society is necessary not only for the functioning of societal forms such as economically, socially, legally and politically rational structures but also action in pursuit of all such values is predicated upon the avoidance of ecological catastrophe.

(Drysek 1987: 58)

This position would be accepted by most Greens and justifies the formulation 'the needs of the planet are the needs of the person' (Roszack 1979: 23). Fundamentalist biocentric Greens prioritize ecological rationality but go further than Drysek and implicitly or explicitly 'read off' social policies from their model of ecological rationality without reference to other forms of reason and rationality. They are not usually willing to consider that it might be necessary to trade off ecological rationality with competing rationalities in order to advance the claims of eco-rationality. Two examples can be offered to illustrate the potential dilemmas. The Brundtland Commission in its report *Our Common Future*, attempts to reconcile ecological rationality and competing forms of rationality with the overriding aim of promoting intragenerational and intergenerational justice (WCED 1987: 43). Garrett Hardin (and other neo-Malthusians) gave absolute priority to ecological rationality and explicitly reject welfare state policies.

146

If each human family were dependent only on its own resources; if the children of improvident parents starved to death, if this overbreeding brought its own 'punishment' to the germ line – then there would be no public interest in controlling the breeding of families. But our society is deeply committed to the welfare state. . . . If we love the truth we must openly deny the validity of the Universal Declaration of Human Rights, even though it is promoted by the United Nations.

(Hardin 1968: 1247)

Even if we concede with Drysek that ecological rationality has moral superiority there are nevertheless competing values and forms of rationality (Drysek identifies legal, social, economic, political) and it becomes far from evident that human welfare can simply be 'read off' from an 'earth first' position. Drysek acknowledges this:

Social rationality is a form of reason less controversial in the ecological realm than economic rationality, but also less obviously applicable. Under social rationality the prime value is social harmony and integration, generally achieved through processes of interpersonal adjustment and which are not mediated by price or numerical calculation . . . this form of reason has no obvious application to ecology. A society might be socially rational, yet still be in a state of disequilibrium with its natural environment.

(Drysek 1987: 56)

We would add that an ecologically rational society might still neglect social rationality.

It will be generally acknowledged that concerns with 'social harmony and integration' have indeed played a major, if far from exclusive role, in the development of social policy and welfare states. Inequality and distributional problems have been softened if not eliminated by state welfare. From a purely functional standpoint there is no doubt that capitalist accumulation has been legitimated by social policies (Gough 1981, Habermas 1976, Frankel 1987). Social policy has also been used to promote economic growth (George and Wilding 1984) and to exercise control and surveillance over minorities of all kinds (Frankel 1987). The potential conflict between social and ecological rationality was widely acknowledged in the zero-growth debates following the publication of 'Limits to Growth' (Stretton 1976).

Drysek's arguments for the moral precedence of ecological rationality are logically persuasive but less than politically convincing. It is the case that ecological rationality is a newcomer to the family of rationalities that seek to govern human affairs on this planet and is far from establishing moral superiority to date. It is virtually a sociological truism to say that in conditions of modern society there is no 'centre' or 'apex' that could confer moral priority to any particular forms of rationality or values. Non-competitive positions are no longer available. If we, by way of illustration, use the

147

language and categories of systems theory we might say that every subsystem will seek to maximize its own priorities and the values embodied within it. Even relative success in this competitive struggle to maximize rationality for a particular form of reason can lead to a loss of overall rationality and system failure (Luhmann 1989: 135). Soviet Communism, in seeking to maximize social and economic justice, sacrificed efficiency and, paradoxically, justice itself. Similarly it can be plausibly argued that the neo-liberals in Britain and the USA, while prioritizing a particular interpretation of economic reason, have sacrificed social rationality. In so doing they have polarized society and created additional social problems. The structural complexity and normative fragmentation of modern society leads to the reflection that some authoritarian imposition of ecological rationality (and every fundamentalist position has authoritarianism embedded in it) would impose similarly unwelcome costs and have paradoxical side effects.

Modern social and political theory based on structuralist perspectives, whether radical or conservative in intent, stresses powerful constraints on change. Such theorizing is not kind to Utopian thought, green or otherwise. In order to provide a basis for action a more robust political theory is required. With the decline of the socialist left it is still nevertheless important to many radicals in the Green movement that the normative claims of the historic left are not forgotten. Murray Bookchin has forcefully argued that there is a danger that uncritical 'earth-firstism' abandons the emancipatory critique of domination that has motivated left politics since the eighteenth century (Bookchin 1990). Leftist versions of social harmony have always been premised on the normative claims of equality and mutuality. While there may indeed be no obvious or necessary links between social and ecological rationality it would be a grossly distorted and misanthropic green politics that sought to end the domination of nature without explicitly addressing the many forms of social domination that still exist. Even within the constraints of capitalist industrialization social policies have been directed towards providing alternatives to those offered by market rationality. Because socialism has been deficient in ecological rationality is insufficient reason to reject what it might have to offer in terms of social rationality.

Conversely, socialists can learn from Greens not just about the requirements of ecological rationality but also in respect of developing less statist policies to develop more self-reliant individuals – and communities – able to engage in the social experiments that will be necessary to achieve ecological security for this and future generations. Despite many changes over the past decade the welfare state forms that emerged post-1945 still exist in rich industrial nations and continue to provide basic security for these populations. For this reason they cannot be ignored or arbitrarily abandoned as some 'new paradigm' critics seem to propose (Robertson 1984). Nevertheless, it is important to recognize that the 'centre-less society' does generate social problems that are not effectively resolved by welfare state strategies. A plausible characterization of the present era might be to call it a conjuncture of transition. On the one side we have welfare state institutions and processes that are dependent upon ecologically (and socially) destructive economic growth policies; on the other there is a variety of social movements with 'alternative values' and radical demands but few institutional resources available to secure the kinds of transformation they call for.

Green politics have been shaped by (but are not synonymous with) three distinct social movements: those of feminism, ecology and peace. The demands that now press upon public policy, and which it can only accommodate by incorporation and dilution of motivating values, originated in social movements as moral crusades, consciousness raising and calling for changes in lifestyle, communal action, etc. Whether all this amounts to a unified ideology that might lead to a distinctive social policy is doubtful. Helmut Weisenthal has used the comparison of drug dependency to liken our situation in capitalist economies to the condition of a drug addict who would suffer fatally, both from sudden withdrawal of the drug as well as from its continual use (Weisenthal 1988). Instead of the grandiose ideological constructs of 'old' liberal and socialist politics there are a scattered set of issues and demands that do not add up to a unified vision or coherent ideology. The major unambiguous demand of the green movement is for ecological rationality. The problem is how to relate this to social, legal, economic, political and other forms of reason. The absence of a totally compelling global vision that is persuasive cannot be blamed on ecological movements. It is a result of substantive difficulties inherent in the view that we are indeed living through a conjuncture of transition. The links between ecological and other forms of rationality are necessarily eclectic and pragmatic, rather than given by care for the planet, if this interpretation is persuasive. For these reasons, then, it is not necessary that there should be a universal class with a comprehensive ideology striving for 'green' power. Pragmatic experiments in the field of social policy might offer a more promising way of reconciling social and ecological rationality. The future we now face, informed hopefully by ecological reason, is one where there will be a need for social experiments of many kinds and correspondingly for a willingness to minimize ideological dogma.

The demands for ecological reason that have emerged from civil society as responses to ecological threats pose new challenges for institutional learning. The means adopted by 'old' politics have proved incapable of realizing the values proclaimed. They promised more than could be delivered. This is the Achilles heel of modernism which green politics now seeks to remedy with more modest aspirations and less grandiose methods. This surely has implications for social policy.

The flawed construction of green politics

The West German Greens have been singled out by many observers as an example that other national Green parties should be careful not to emulate. The virulent intra-party conflicts and debates have been the despair of many who had previously been inspired from a distance (Spretnak and Capra 1985, Porritt 1984, Parkin 1989). The lesson that appears to have been drawn is that the unique West German Constitution, plus the influx of left secretarians into Die Grünen when it was formed, makes Germany a special case. A survey of this literature reveals a 'peculiarity of the Germans' kind of argument. Against this position it can be argued that what has distinguished the German Greens from other nationalities is that green ideology in Germany has been subjected to the realities of participation in power at both national and local level. In no other country have Greens seriously participated in power. The splits in Die Grünen, especially those between the 'fundis' and 'realos', have revealed flaws in green ideology that are blandly smoothed over elsewhere – although it must be said that Murray Bookchin has been busy attempting to penetrate the mystical fog in the USA in his polemics against deep ecology (Bookchin 1990). When we examine the intellectual and social foundations of green politics in Britain, we find that the potential for fragmentation – ideological and social – is just as sharp as that experienced by Die Grünen, US Greens, and would be revealed just as painfully were significant electoral success to come the way of the Green Party in the UK. The dilemmas of movement protest and institutional power have been usefully explored by Claus Offe, even though he has also been influenced by German 'exceptionalism' arguments (Offe 1990).

The oft quoted green slogan 'neither right nor left but forward' is superficially attractive but ignores the importance of history and especially the fact that green politics have been constructed from elements of both leftist and rightist ideology. While a more careful investigation into the history of recent political ecology is certainly needed, even a superficial review of the literature reveals this eclectic formation of green ideology and lumping together of contradictory ideas. The theoretical foundation of green politics must therefore be regarded as less than rigorous. A quick sketch of this will have to suffice to support the argument developed here.

Between 1970 and 1980 the dominant tendency in ecological argument was distinctly Malthusian. The public debates, certainly in Britain and the USA, had been shaped by the 'foundation' reports (Meadows *et al.* 1972, Goldsmith *et al.* 1972). This was the period of debate about the feasibility of zero-growth policies. The main informing science was biology – a point sharply made by Enzenberger (1988) in his critique of political ecology. There were, of course, counter tendencies that were not Malthusian such as those represented in the popular writings of Illich and Schumacher, as well as the more orthodox political economy of Barbara Ward and her colleagues who adopted world-order perspectives. The tension between these contrasting views is reflected in O'Riordan's well-known typology of political ecology (O'Riordan 1981). It was possible in 1979 to sharply contrast ecocentric and environmental standpoints and this reveals very clearly that the main thrust of political ecology prior to 1979 was Malthusian, albeit overlaid with 'decentralist' anarchism.

What changed political ecology after 1980, was the coming together of the peace movement and feminism with green concerns. This injected into ecological thought the historic concerns of the left, especially the critique of social domination and concern with equality and justice. These concerns had been signally absent in the contributions of the biologists like Hardin and the Ehrlichs as well as in the limits to growth debates. Again it must be emphasized that there were forerunners – notably, Bookchin and Gorz – who approached ecological problems with different leftist orientations (Gorz 1981). Offe and other political scientists who have paid attention to the phenomenon of the 'new' social movements have emphasized the non-reactionary universalist critique of modernity that did not fit easily with socialist or conservative politics (Offe 1990: 233).

Obviously a more careful documentation of these conflicting currents in green ideology is required, but the point to be made here is that the spectacular synthesis claimed by populist 'earth firstism' and transmitted by writers like Parkin and Porritt is far from having been achieved either intellectually or politically and that this has consequences for what greens do with political power should they gain it. This has particular salience for social policy because the Utopian anti-statism and Malthusian prescriptions that are embedded in green ideology fail to seriously address the very real problems we face in an increasingly impoverished and urbanized world. It leaves sceptics who are disposed to take ecological rationality seriously, little scope for adopting anything other than instrumental environmental positions. Green fundamentalism and the failure to learn from experience is not necessarily an irrational response to the manifest inadequacies of public policy as currently pursued, but the alternatives that have been proposed are not politically persuasive either.

CAN THERE BE DISTINCTIVELY GREEN SOCIAL POLICIES?

A review of some recently published green manifestos indicates that where social policy is specifically mentioned it is generally informed by two strands of 'ecologism' (Kemp and Wall 1990, Irvine and Ponton 1988). First, eco-rationality and the need to conserve energy. Second, by a belief in the need to establish more 'convivial' (human scale) communities. These two stands are interwoven and informed by the principle of 'voluntary simplicity'. Two particular authors have been influential in shaping these perspectives. Critiques of social policy are made by Illich in books on education, health, transport, the service professions, and gender. Schumacher, in his writings, emphasized qualitative approaches to work and the use of appropriate technology. It is fair to say that while both writers were certainly concerned with the possibility of ecological disaster, they paid more attention to rescuing the idea of community and resisting the dehumanizing effects of corporate/ bureaucratic modes of service delivery characteristic of industrial societies. Both authors implicitly assumed that 'convivial' human-scale alternatives would only emerge from grassroots initiatives and would not be led by professional or state elites who were dependent upon the prevailing institutions. Neither it seems, was optimistic about the possibilities of institutional learning. The main thrust of their work was to promote the idea of self-reliance because the corporate and professional elites themselves either would not or could not indicate necessary changes.

There can be no doubt that the influence of both Schumacher and Illich on the formation of green political ideology during the 1980s has been considerable. Paradoxically, it has been even more influential practically in the sphere of corporate organization and among the service professionals who were the subjects of Illich's critique. Illich, and to a lesser extent Schumacher, was primarily concerned with disadvantaged and marginalized groups in the Third World. Support for the new social movements in Europe and the USA, which became important carriers of these ideas, is derived mainly from groups who themselves play an active role in the steering and managing of what many writers call the 'post-industrial society'. These core groups are relatively well off and include people from the new middle classes and professional service sectors who have high levels of education and skills (Offe 1990). New forms of decentralized service delivery in the Welfare State are innovations that have often been informed, at least in part, by the same sources as those which informed green ideology (see, for example, Ashworth and Seymour 1989, Power 1989, Hadley and Hatch 1981, Wates and Knevitt 1987). Local economic development initiatives which are often consistent in their aims with many of Schumacher's ideas have arguably been one of the few positive achievements in this field over the past decade, at least in Britain, and can be seen in a similar way (Ekins 1986, Davidson 1988, Inglis and Kramer 1985). While these projects are frequently aimed at disadvantaged and marginalized social groups they have usually been initiated by service professionals and been underpinned by government grants and incentive schemes – for example, enterprise and employment programmes. The rhetoric and reality of 'self-reliance' is certainly part of the story but so are the cash-flows from the state to initiate such experiments. Should this be regarded as institutional incorporation of local initiative or institutional learning? Is it some kind of Foucaultian power net that entraps everyone, or authentic innovation? This is a matter of meta-interpretation and it is difficult to see how it could be resolved in any conclusive way other than by empirical research. Only one-dimensional positivism could make the contradictions disappear from view.

What does seem evident is that while such innovations in service delivery might be considered consistent with green ideology, those who initiate and finance such programmes as well as those who benefit do not necessarily share such ideological motivations. A fundamentalist standpoint and the literalist orientation that goes with it would presumably require consciousness and activity to be linked in some form of green praxis (see Devall 1990: ch. 2, on the 'ecological self'). A realist position is premised on the assumption that such ideological unity is neither possible nor necessary; plurality of values and motivations is a given that has to be accommodated. Service delivery initiatives and innovations are part of a wider process of institutional learning and transformation that changes both those who provide and those who receive services. As Weisenthal has most forcefully argued from a rational choice position, this is not a conflict over political ends but strategy: 'as a combination of means and ends, ends and the means to realise them' (Weisenthal 1989: 143).

Both green fundamentalists and realists will agree on the need for ecological rationality and human scale (conviviality). Where they differ most profoundly is in their view of the gains that can be won from institutional participation. (This is a separate issue from the reactionary neo-Malthusianism that still pervades much green ideology.) A willingness to participate in institutional processes, even where it is acknowledged that both the values and practices of dominant institutions are inadequate, is not necessarily a capitulation to instrumental environmentalism as is often argued by the left and by anarchist fundamentalists (Bookchin 1982).

The 'people' who earn their living in the state apparatus are also 'neighbours'. Populist appeals to 'people power' mystify the mundane realities of community and corporate power. In so far as social democracy has always been concerned with equality and redistribution the foregoing discussion points to a potentially fruitful synthesis of green and social democratic ideas. (It could of course be argued that European Christian Democrats and Liberals have also supported redistributive social policies and could just as well take on board green ideas. We would nevertheless assert that equality and redistribution are central to democratic socialism in a way they are not to rightist parties.) Such a position best reflects the insight that social rationality cannot simply be read off from a biocentric position in green politics because the social policy measures that would follow from this kind of analysis would probably be very controversial – for example, very strong immigration controls and stringent population control policies (we are assuming that biocentric politics would include neo-Malthusian influences, which also tend to find a sympathetic response in conservative political parties).

Another reason to suppose that socialist parties might be more likely to find common ground with radical Greens is that it is not plausible, or in our view ethically acceptable, to expect poor communities to succeed in becoming more self-reliant without redistributive grants and subsidies from the state. The same argument applies to lesser-developed nations as the Brundtland report demonstrated.

It is now widely conceded by social democrats that the Welfare State has been overly statist. Green anarchists like Bookchin adopt a maximalist position that the state always reflects the interests of the ruling groups and therefore perpetuates the long history of hierarchy and domination. While there is no doubt some truth in this view it is too simplistic, as debates within Marxism have shown. We would argue that from such a position it is very difficult to develop transformational strategies beyond consciousness raising, sectarian politics, or alternative but ultimately dependent lifestyles. The statism which green anarchists rightly oppose has to be resisted by structural reforms, participatory politics and a broader view of citizenship. It is no doubt true that social democratic welfare has often been paternalistic and rhetorically rather than substantively committed to welfare rights. Citizenship implies obligations as well as rights. At its core is an ethic of responsibility, and this should include social and ecological concerns. Some examples taken from British social policy innovations can be given here as illustrations of the ways in which citizen and institutional learning might be encouraged. Similar examples can certainly be found elsewhere in the European Community and in the USA as well as in lesser-developed nations.

These decentralist innovations might perhaps provide a new direction for social policy that can reconcile social and ecological rationality. They would not necessarily require individuals to espouse deep ecology, or any other ideology for that matter.

Housing and urban policy

During the 1980s housing co-operatives have grown quite rapidly in Britain and elsewhere in Europe. It seems to be an expanding form of housing tenure in countries with widely varying political, cultural and economic conditions. There are now over 10 million people in eighteen nations living in housing co-operatives (Wates and Knevitt 1987). Such housing can be more easily linked with shared community facilities than private and state-run housing. Not-for-profit development schemes are emerging in Britain as a type of organization for involving local communities in development at town or neighbourhood level. Such activity may be initiated by professionals in local government but they are directed by local citizens. Another idea discussed by Wates and Knevitt is that of environmental and technical aid centres where individuals and community groups can find appropriate advice and assistance. Community architecture and planning will need state support because the communities that need them most do not have the resources to pay for such services. Municipalities clearly have a role to play in promoting and supporting such participatory initiatives. While there have been experiments of this kind in Britain there are even more examples in other European nations and the USA (Middleton 1987). In a wide-ranging international comparative study Harloe and Martens (1990) have explored a wide range of alternatives to state housing and concluded that with appropriate financial aid and subsidies they do have potential.

Work and welfare

Although no nation has yet adopted a guaranteed basic income scheme in any of the forms proposed by Greens it is surely an idea that seriously addresses one of the major problems of advanced industrial societies: structural unemployment that has arisen with new labour market practices and new technology. Central to green thought is the idea that we do need to transcend the protestant work ethic. A variety of schemes have been advanced with this object in mind. Common to all is the idea that taxes and benefits could be integrated and that every citizen would have a basic right to an income that would meet subsistence needs. Above an agreed level additional earnings would be taxed to pay for the scheme. Advocates of basic income systems argue that it would transform attitudes to work and labour markets by making labour more competitive with capital. They also argue that it would allow people to engage in necessary work that is not presently 'economic' – for example, ecological reclamation, child care, etc. While it is evident that such proposals are not a panacea to remove poverty, and would have to be complemented by a range of other social policies, they do indicate a means by which poor people might gain increasing self-reliance and autonomy (Walter 1990, Jordan 1987). It is difficult to imagine a basic income scheme working in an anarchist society where there is no state to collect taxes, although some green anarchists can advocate such measures without blushing! (Another reason for links between red and green perhaps.)

Community care

This is a complex area of social policy embracing a wide range of needs categories and different patterns of service delivery. What is very clear, however, is that growing numbers of elderly people in the industrialized nations will generate new demands on the care services and institutions. It is generally agreed that it is desirable that elderly people, the mentally ill, children in need, and other needs categories should as far as possible be cared for in the community.

Currently, in Britain and other European nations, the main arguments focus on the appropriate balance between the different sectors of welfare, public, private, voluntary and informal care. What is at stake is not whether care should be community-based but how to finance such care. Over-reliance on private and informal care would impose heavy costs on women and the poor. Green Utopians envision small-scale rural settlements and communes where such care is assumed to be automatically available. This ignores the difficulties faced by poor communities in assuming such burdens and, of course, the all-too-human propensity to stigmatize the infirm and deviant members of society.

There is now a mixed economy of welfare in all industrialized nations that is to a considerable extent decentralized. The role of government in such a situation is to act as provider of resources where markets will not work and to regulate the decentralized system of care. Romantic green visions which simply invoke the extended family and local community as carers ignore the fact that we now live in an urbanized world where we have to find ways of caring for 'strangers'. Green Utopias are worlds without strangers. Nevertheless it is the case that the decentralized structures now emerging could be positively welcomed if they were supported adequately by government in terms of finance and regulation. This would not be inconsistent with the ideas of human scale and 'conviviality' that are valued by Greens. The main problems in this area in Britain have been market dogma and shortage of resources for innovative forms of care. User power could be increased by making money available. Community care and personal social services are not areas that offer much scope for Utopian or fundamentalist thinking, but a green society that was unable to institutionalize compassion and offer care to strangers could hardly be described as socially rational. This area is one where there is need for diversity and experiments to alleviate the stresses of urban-industrial society. Many of these observations could also be applied to rapidly urbanizing cities in the lesser-developed nations.

Health policy

Of all the major areas of social policy there can be no doubt that mainstream green thought has had the greatest impact in relation to health policies. While 'new age' ideas have influenced green thinking and publicized alternative medicine, much of which has been faddish and irrelevant, it has also served to make people aware of what they can do to take responsibility for their own health and cope with it when curative medicine fails. Initiatives like the WHO 'healthy cities' programme are changing professional and official attitudes to preventative health care. The social and economic causes of illness, including diet and stress related illness, now receive much more attention than they did a decade ago (Ashton and Seymour 1988). Green concerns with the purity of water supplies and food, as well as atmospheric pollution, are all near the top of the political agenda nationally and internationally. The slogan 'quality of life' has been given real meaning by green campaigns addressed to these health issues. We are still a long way from creating low stress living and working environments and this might become a major agenda item in an approach to green social policy. On the other hand the negative stance adopted towards medical science and curative medicine by some green writers will hardly find support with public opinion (Porritt 1984: 82–4).

CONCLUSIONS

The examples of social policies given above address major green concerns and/or the demand for human scale. Variants are often advocated in green manifestos. These and similar initiatives are now emerging in many different nations and are supported by citizens who are not necessarily 'green'. While green ideology has influenced some of the experiments, as often as not the stimulus has been economic recession, privatization by neo-liberal govern-ments, and above all the need to find ways of delivering services to those in need. While Greens have certainly been important in identifying major social problems in industrial society the resolution of these problems requires much

156

wider involvement and an extended societal learning process. In our view, this will come to involve a reconciliation of conflicting rationalities, to use Drysek's language.

Typologies of shades of green no doubt have pedagogic uses, but 'real world' politics requires tolerance of differing views, trade-offs, as well as coherent values. Normative green theories are part of the process of learning and help to shape new social actors. The argument presented here comes from a realist perspective but it has to be acknowledged that every political movement has its realists and fundamentalists, with tensions and conflict therefore being inevitable; and there is no reason to suppose that green politics will be different.

The social and political world we live in is plural. This leads to the answer posed by the question at the beginning of this chapter – there is as yet no consensually agreed green social policy although it is necessary to reconcile ecological and social concerns. It also seems important to say that we should not be seeking a single green political theory if this means trying to construct some kind of all-embracing ideology comparable to liberalism and Marxism. If this view is accepted then Greens can experiment with ideas and practical experiments aimed at improving living conditions without destroying the natural world. Realistic green politics is premised on the belief that we do not have to sacrifice normative perspectives or basic ethical principles in order to explore possibilities of effective action in a threatened world. Greens need to think about means and ends and how they can be combined. The problem that arises with fundamentalism, biocentric or otherwise, is the exclusive pre-occupation with ends. This is also true of social policy where socialist and liberal dogmatism has led to ecological blindness in the pursuit of economic growth to pay for welfare.

BIBLIOGRAPHY

Ashton, J. and Seymour, H. (1988) *The New Public Heath*, Milton Keynes: Open University.

Bookchin, M. (1982) *The Ecology of Freedom*, Palo Alto: Cheshire Books.

—— (1990) *Social Ecology*, Montreal: Black Rose Books.

Davidson, J. (1988) *How Green is Your City?*, London: Bedford Square Press.

Devall, B. (1990) *Simple in Means, Rich in Ends – Practising Deep Ecology*, London: Green Print.

Dobson, A. (1990) *Green Political Thought*, London: Unwin Hyman.

Drysek, J. (1987) *Rational Ecology*, Oxford: Blackwell.

Ehrlich, P. R. and Ehrlich, A. M. (1972) *Populations, Resources, Environment, Issues in Human Ecology*, San Francisco: Freeman.

Ekins, P. (ed.) (1986) *The Living Economy*, London: Routledge.

Enzensberger, H. (1988) 'A critique of political ecology [1984]', in H. Enzensberger, *Dreamers of the Absolute – Essays on Politics, Crime and Culture*, London: Radius.

Frankel, B. (1987) *The Post Industrial Utopians*, Cambridge: Polity.

George, V. and Wilding, P. (1984) *Impact of Social Policy*, London: Routledge.

—— —— (1985) *Ideology and Social Welfare* (2nd edn), London: Routledge.

Goldsmith, E., Allen, R., Allaby, M., Davoce, J. and Lawrence, S. (1972) 'Blueprint

157

for survival', *The Ecologist* 2 (also published by Penguin Books, Harmondsworth, 1972).

Gorz, A. (1981) *Ecology as Politics*, Boston: South End Press

Gough, A. (1981) *The Political Economy of Welfare*, London: Macmillan.

Habermas, J. (1976) *Legitimation Crisis*, London: Heinemann.

Hadley, R. and Hatch, S. (1981) *Social Welfare and the Failure of the State*, London: Allen & Unwin.

Hardin, G. (1968) 'The tragedy of the commons', *Science*, no. 162: 1243–8.

Harloe, M. and Martens, M. (1990) *New Ideas for Housing*, London: Shelter.

Illich, I. (1977) *Limits to Medicine*, London: Penguin.

Inglis, M. and Kramer, S. (1985) *The New Economic Agenda*, Forres: Findhorn Press.

Irvine, S. and Ponton, A. (1988) *A Green Manifesto*, London: Optima Books.

Jonas, H. (1982) *The Imperative of Responsibility*, Chicago: Chicago University Press.

Jordan, B. (1987) *Redefining Welfare*, London: Routledge.

Kemp, P. and Wall, D. (1990) *A Green Manifesto for the 1990s*, London: Penguin Books.

Luhmann, N. (1989) *Ecological Communication*, Cambridge: Polity.

Meadows, D. H., Meadows, D. L., Randers, J. and Behrens, W. W. (1972) *The Limits to Growth*, London: Pan Books.

Middleton, M. (1987) *Man Made the Town*, New York: St Martins Press.

Offe, C. (1990) 'Reflections on the institutional self transformation of movement politics: a tentative stage model', in R. Dalton and M. Kuchler, *Challenging the Political Order*, Cambridge: Polity.

O'Riordan, T. (1981) *Environmentalism* (2nd edn), London: Pion.

Parkin, S. (1989) *Green Political Parties*, London: Heretic Books.

Power, A. (1989) *Property before People*, London: Unwin Hyman.

Porritt, J. (1984) *Seeing Green*, Oxford: Blackwell.

Robertson, J. (1984) *Future Work*, London: Temple-Smith.

Roszack, T. (1979) *Person/Planet*, Granada Books.

Schumacher, E. F. (1972) *Small is Beautiful*, London: Abacus Books.

Spretnak, C. and Capra, F. (1985) *Green Politics*, London: Paladin.

Stretton, H. (1976) *Capitalism, Socialism, and Environment*, Cambridge: Cambridge University Press.

Walter, T. (1990) *Basic Income*, London: Marion Boyars.

Wates, N. and Knevitt, C. (1987) *Community Architecture*, London: Penguin Books.

Weisenthal, H. (1988) 'Deer at the World Market', in J. Ferris (ed.) (1992), *Realism in Green Politics*, Manchester: Manchester University Press.

—— (1989) 'Interview with Helmut Weisenthal', J. Ely and V. Heins, in *Capitalism, Nature, Socialism – A Journal of Socialist Ecology*, no. 3, November.

World Commission on Environment and Development (WCED) (1987) *Our Common Future*, Oxford: Oxford University Press.

Part IV

GREEN POLITICAL THEORY: THE BOUNDARIES

9

ANIMAL RIGHTS AND SOCIAL RELATIONS

Ted Benton

INTRODUCTION

Alongside, and to some extent intertwined with, the rise of environmental politics has emerged a new and increasingly politicized concern about human mistreatment of other animals. In both cases there is an evident concern to extend – or, properly, restore – the scope of moral responsibility to include the non-human world. However, there are also interesting points of tension between the moral discourses of environmental concern and the most influential voices in the debate about the moral status of (non-human) animals. For example, radical environmentalism ('deep ecology') claims to reject anthropocentric approaches to morality, whilst the advocates of animal rights argue for an extension of moral concepts to non-human animals only on the basis, and to the extent that, the latter share certain favoured psychological abilities with humans. Also, the discourse of animal rights preserves the abstract individualism of liberal moral thinking, in sharp contrast to the 'holistic' thinking of deep ecology. In general, radical environmentalists have seen a need for profound changes in human ways of social living and have tended therefore to be sceptical about the prevailing (liberalist-individualist) moral vocabulary. By contrast, the most influential advocates of an improved moral status for animals have taken their stand *with* the prevailing moral discourses, and attempted to show that they cannot consistently be confined within the species boundary.

This strategy has been relatively effective in getting the moral status of animals onto the agenda of 'established' moral philosophy, but it has had the consequence of detaching animal rights advocacy from potential allies among the radical critics of the established moral discourses and practices. This chapter is a small part of the wide-ranging investigation of the issue of the moral status of animals from just such a radical, or oppositional moral standpoint (Benton 1993). Where the leading champions of the moral status of animals have tried to show that we should consider them as holders of rights, they seek to confer on animals the benefits already accruing to humans from the current popularity of the idea of '*human* rights'. But there are, of course, several long traditions of radical scepticism about the epistemological basis, political desirability and practical effectiveness of the discourse of rights even in its paradigm application to the human case. If rights advocacy is 'nonsense upon stilts' when applied to humans, why should we suppose it makes any better sense when applied to animals? And, if some other moral discourse – for example, a socialist, needs-based morality – might be held to offer better prospects for humans, how does *it* fare across the species boundary?

ANIMAL RIGHTS: THE OBJECTIONS

The standard objections to animal rights do not call into question the status of *human* rights. They are aimed either at exhibiting morally significant differences between humans, and all non-human animals, or at demonstrating the paradoxical or counter-intuitive consequences of extending rights beyond the species boundary. First, animals may be held to lack the crucial psychological powers to be bona fide rights-holders. Can they be said to have intentions, beliefs, desires, autonomous will, a sense of past and future, and of their own identity? It is easier, of course, to get consensus around the claim that animals can experience pleasure and pain. A utilitarian defence of the moral status of animals, whatever its disadvantages in other aspects, faces less resistance from those who hold a dim view of the mental life of animals. However, animal rights advocates are able to call in animal ethologists and psychologists, proud pet owners, and the principles of evolutionary biology as witnesses in support of their claim that *at least some* non-human animals have the necessary psychological complexity to count as what Tom Regan calls 'subjects-of-a-life' (Regan 1988: 243).

But is subject-of-a-life status sufficient to qualify as a bearer of rights? Some opponents of animal rights argue that only beings who can comprehend the force of moral requirements, and choose to act in conformity to or deviance of them – 'moral agents' – can so qualify. No (non-human) animal is a moral agent in the appropriate sense. Against this, animal rights advocates argue that some groups of humans (young infants and the severely mentally handicapped are standard examples which, of course, raise rather different issues) are not moral agents either. Yet, it is precisely such vulnerable individuals who are most in need of the protections afforded by rights. If one accepts that such *human* 'moral patients' have rights, then it is inconsistent to deny rights to non-human animals which, whilst lacking moral *agency*, are certainly vulnerable to suffering harms in broadly comparable ways to human moral patients. Here, the dispute opens out into a more detailed discussion of how and in what respects the various categories of 'moral patient' differ from one another, and what moral significance should attach to such differences as there are.

Yet another common line of attack on the idea of animal rights is closely linked to the point about moral agency. Lacking full linguistic capacity and, connectedly, lacking moral agency, animals are intrinsically incapable of claiming rights on their own behalf. There is an inescapably paternalistic or vicarious element in the ascription of rights to animals. This is a powerful argument against those advocates of animal rights who argue from parallels between the demands for women's liberation, black people's rights and so on, and their moral claims on behalf of animals. Acquiring the power to make and enforce rights claims on one's own behalf is a crucial part of the content of such human emancipatory movements, yet it can be given no sense at all in the case of non-human animals. More generally, the argument is effective against the animal rights case because of the clear affinities between that discourse and liberal-individualist moral perspectives in which personal autonomy and self-avowal have a canonical status.

There are, further, two difficulties having to do with the scope of the rights discourse if we seek to extend it beyond the boundaries of the human species. Both of these difficulties are especially pressing when viewed from the standpoint of a broader environmental concern. The first of these difficulties derives, again, from the individualism of the rights-perspective. Though, on the rights view, it is prima facie wrong to harm any individual subject of life, it would also be wrong to discriminate between such individuals on the basis of their belonging to rare or endangered species. No moral significance attaches to the extinction of species over and above that of the deaths of the individuals concerned. The denial of this is even denounced as environmental Fascism! (Regan 1988: 361–2). The second difficulty has to do with the moral status of those animals which fail to satisfy the subject-of-a-life criterion. For Tom Regan satisfaction of this criterion is a sufficient, not a necessary, condition for having 'inherent value' and therefore rights, but it is hard to see what kind of case could be made out for attributing rights to beings which failed his criterion. Unless this were done, the rights view gives, or purports to give, the full protection of rights to subjects of a life (mammalian individuals, and, possibly, some birds), whilst apparently withholding any direct moral status at all from the immense majority of animals (amphibians, reptiles, fish, insects, crustaceans, and so on) which unambiguously fail the subject-of-a-life test.

The difficulty of squaring this last consequence with any moderately environmentalist 'reflective intuition' is intensified by the resolute cross-species egalitarianism (*within* the class of subjects of a life) which goes along with animal rights advocacy. Rats must be accorded rights on equal terms with humans, whilst frogs, bees and butterflies are a moral free-fire zone in which 'anything goes'. It is, indeed, cross-species egalitarianism which draws most resistance to the animal rights cause. Most opponents of animal rights take it to be absurd to require that the same consideration should be given to the interests of a human being, and, say, a dog, or a rat. One strategy for softening this line of resistance is to point out that 'equality of consideration' does not imply 'sameness of treatment'. Where beings differ, then equality of consideration will positively require appropriate differences of treatment. This defence of egalitarianism, is, indeed, quite adequate when it is applied to individuals which differ only in a small number of respects (for example, across human differences of gender, race, or ability/disability). However, where beings differ so radically in their nature and modes of life as, say, mice, seals, orang-utans and humans, the question must arise as to whether any determinate sense can be given to the requirement to treat them with equal consideration.

Short of a solution to that problem, we are returned to the favoured ground of animal-rights opponents – stark choices between saving a child or a dog from drowning, and the like, where few have any doubts which way their 'choice' would go. A common stand taken by many opponents of animal rights at this point is to abandon the appeal to abstract and formal moral reasoning of the kind favoured by animal rights advocacy, and to acknowledge, instead, the powerful sentiments that lead us to favour our own kind in such situations: 'species loyalty' as one such opponent of animal rights calls them (Rose 1991: 21). But there is a ready response to this from the side of animal rights. Such spontaneous sentiments in favour of one's own kind can be, and often are, used to justify, or otherwise give legitimacy to racist and patriarchal practices, *within* the human species. How can we accept the one, but reject the others?

HUMANS, ANIMALS AND SOCIAL RELATIONS

An ambitious response to this question was attempted by Leslie Pickering Francis and Richard Norman (1978). Ultimately, their response was not, I think, successful, but it did take the argument about animal rights onto a new terrain, and I propose to follow them. Their main argument is that humans may justifiably give more weight to the interests of other humans than they give to those of other animals, not because of characteristics possessed uniquely by humans, but because of the relations in which humans stand to one another. Though human social relations are by no means *always* characterized by reciprocity, mutual understanding, and self-conscious intentionality, our capacity for such relationships in activities such as communication, economic life, the family and politics, enable and dispose us to identify more strongly with other humans than with non-human animals with which, in general, we do not have such relationships.

Francis and Norman (1978) do, indeed, offer a plausible account of how it comes about that humans generally are disposed to give greater weight to the interests of other humans, but they do not show why this is morally justifiable. A closely similar argument could be advanced to show how it comes about that people give greater weight to the interests of members of their own gender, racial or ethnic group. It would not show that such preferential treatment is just. However, though it does not succeed in its own terms, Francis and Norman's argument has the merit of bringing into the debate about the moral status of animals the key feature which is excluded by the rights view: namely, social relationships. By this means, a long tradition of politically radical (mainly socialist, but also feminist) criticism of the discourse and practice of rights in the human case can be brought into dialogue with advocacy of a new moral status for animals.

164

However, a further step beyond Francis and Norman's position has to be taken. For them, moral commitments and responsibilities arise in the contexts of human relatedness in social life. A moral view (such as the rights view) which abstracts from social belonging as a dimension of well-being, and considers the moral standing of individuals independently of their positioning in social practices and structures will have little or no purchase on the actual conditions of life in which morally significant decisions have to be taken. So far, so good. Where I part company with Francis and Norman is in their exclusion of animals from the domain of human social life. They achieve this exclusion by assigning a distinctive (exclusive?) moral significance to certain kinds of social relation as against others. Special moral value attaches to autonomous, self-conscious, reciprocal recognition-according relationships, and so special moral condemnation is reserved for those human social relations in which these aspects are withheld or suppressed.

Since these are precisely the kinds of social relations we cannot have with individuals of other species, it is left unclear in Francis and Norman's account what positive moral value can be given to those social relations we *are* capable of having with other animals, and, indeed, what moral grounds there would be for objecting to the various ways in which those relations might go wrong. We cannot be criticized for deceiving, cheating, or even exploiting an animal, since fair trading and honest discourse do not carry across the species divide. But surely both humans and animals can be tortured, treated cruelly, deprived of their freedom, neglected and abused in a whole panoply of ways which *do* depend on social relations and which also may span the species-boundary. From the practice of maintaining nature reserves, through zoos and circuses, to pet keeping, animal experimentation and intensive stock-rearing, humans are bound to non-human animals by a great diversity of patterns of social relationships. Just as the basic interests of individual humans may be affected in morally significant ways by the place they occupy in society, so may the basic interests of animals be affected by their mode of inclusion in such human social practices. A moral view which seeks to offer effective protection from harm would need to be conceptually sensitive to such social-relational conditions of harm and well-being, and context-specific enough to provide moral regulation across a wide range of very diverse social situations. Prima facie the liberal-individualist discourse of universal rights is not well suited to this task in the human case. What I have just suggested about the social placing of non-human animals indicates some cause for scepticism about the likely effectiveness of the extension of that same discourse to protect them.

ANIMALS IN SOCIETY: AGAINST RIGHTS?

In what follows I'll explore some of the further implications of this thought, whilst holding in mind one 'core' argument in the radical case against (human) rights: in societies governed by deep inequalities of political power, economic wealth, social standing and cultural accomplishment the promise of *equal* rights is delusory, with the consequence that for the majority, rights are merely abstract, formal entitlements with little or no *de facto* purchase on the realities of social life. In so far as social life is regulated by these abstract principles, and in so far as the promise is mistaken for its fulfilment, then the discourse of rights and justice is an ideology, a form of mystification which plays a real causal role in binding individuals to the very conditions of dependence and impoverishment from which it purports to offer emancipation.

How much of this line of criticism of the discourse of rights applies to the liberal-individualist argument for the recognition of rights in the case of (non-human) animals? First, we can dispense rather quickly with the contention attributed to the early Marx that all (bourgeois) rights amount, in effect, to property rights. Except in rather special legal contexts (which do not, anyway, affect my argument) non-human animals cannot be property owners. This is not a merely contingent, historical-cultural fact, but is rooted in a recognition of real differences of psychological constitution and moral attributes as between (most) humans and individuals of all currently known non-human animal species. The capacities to exercise ownership rights are, if not identical with, then closely allied with those that constitute moral agency.

If the claim that animals have rights amounts to the claim that they have a right to acquire property, then it directly falls. But, clearly, the *interests* of animals which advocates of animal rights seek to protect remain unaffected by this argument. Whatever force the argument for animal rights has, it cannot derive from any claim that animals have a basic interest in the protection of their property! If there is moral force in that argument, it must derive from an acknowledgement that non-human animals have basic interests, other than property ownership, which ought to be protected. If this is so in the case of animals, then it is reasonable to consider whether humans, too, may have such right-grounding basic interests, irreducible to property. This consideration tells against any Marxian temptation to reduce liberal-individualist rights to property rights. However, the serious point of Marx's association of rights with property is still sustainable. For some categories of property – most obviously property in means of production – ownership rights are simultaneously powers to affect the basic interests of non-owners: to give or withhold the means of livelihood, health, safety, and personal liberty.

Just as economically dependent, or relatively powerless humans are at risk of harms from the exercise of property rights by other humans, so, too, may be non-human animals which are caught up within human social relations and practices which involve the exercise of property rights – intensive livestock farming, for example. Here, an analysis could be given of the distortion and fragmentation of the mode of life of animals in such regimes which parallels that given by the young Marx of the consequences for wage labourers of capitalist private property (Benton 1988). Also, however, animals may suffer harm as a result of the exercise of property rights in land, as when land-use changes result in habitat destruction. Again, there are parallels with the effects on human rural society wrought by the extension of commercial agriculture, enclosure of common land, and the destruction of natural and semi-natural biotopes used as traditional sources of food and fuel resources. In each of these cases, animals suffer harms as a result of the exercise by humans of property rights in ways which parallel (and, indeed, are often intertwined with) the effects on relatively powerless humans; but, of course, animals are significantly less well-placed than even the most disadvantaged humans.

ANIMALS IN SOCIETY: FOR RIGHTS?

However, there are also situations in which the discourse of rights appears, at first sight, to offer a good chance of substantive protection to animals. One implication of the radical criticism of rights is that we should expect the liberal discourse of rights to work best in protecting individuals from basic harms in real circumstances which approximate to what we might call the presumed social ontology of the rights discourse: that of autonomous individuals, contingently related, each resisting encroachment/interference on the part of the other, and seeking authoritative arbitration. For reasons which I cannot explore here, these conditions are never satisfied in the case of competing rights claims across the species divide. However, some moral controversies affecting animals are analogous in certain respects. In the case of blood sports, for example, where the quarry is a wild animal, there is a (highly qualified) sense in which the hunters and the hunted are autonomous, contingently related beings: they are not bound together, as in the case of farmers and stock animals, for example, in socio-economic relations of power and dependency. Moreover, the right of the quarry animal (asserted on its behalf by human allies) is a claim not to be interfered with in its own, non-right-infringing activity. This is a right closely assimilable to the liberal paradigm of negative liberty, and the situation is, *ex hypothesi*, one in which it does make sense to think of the wild animal's enjoyment of its freedom as something which can be taken for granted, so long as restraint is imposed upon the hunters.

Of course, the situation is not an exact parallel. Most obviously, the rights attributed to quarry animals conflict with those claimed by hunters to enjoy traditional rural sports which do not infringe the rights of other humans. These rights are aggressively asserted when they are threatened, either by the direct action of 'hunt saboteurs' or by attempts at legislation. The disanalogy with the human case is, of course, that the countervailing rights of animals not to be hunted cannot be claimed by the animals themselves. The outcome then depends on the retrospective powers of advocacy and access to political and legal institutions of rival human social groups. Notwithstanding this disanalogy, however, this is one type of situation in which an extension of the liberal-individualist notion of rights to non-human animals could have some hope not only of carrying rational conviction, but also of being practically efficacious in protecting some categories of animals from substantive harms to which they would otherwise be vulnerable.

Another sort of case in which practical efficacy on the part of the liberal-rights discourse might be hoped for is that of acts of cruelty committed by human individuals against animals kept in confinement. The deliberate infliction of unnecessary pain on domestic pets will serve as an example here. Although differentials of power and dependency are intrinsic to the relation between a pet owner and pet, this situation is unlike the employer/employee one with respect to, for example, freedom of speech in that the right to inflict unnecessary pain cannot reasonably be claimed as a part of what it is to be a pet owner. Cruel practices are a contingent, and not an essential feature of the relationship. On the contrary, the widely shared cultural norms which prescribe and regulate pet-keeping include a strong presumption *against* cruelty. In such a case, where a powerful consensus favours a presumption against causing unnecessary pain, where causal and moral responsibility for causing pain can be readily placed at the door of an identifiable (human) moral agent, and where there are no powerful countervailing socio-economic interests, the prospects for an effective defence of the rights of the animals concerned against the rival claims of pet-owners to privacy and rights of property in their pets are relatively good.

But even in these two kinds of case, there is a point to the radical critique. First, in the case of blood sports, the sense in which the quarry are 'wild' animals will generally need to be highly qualified. Commonly, game animals are deliberately hand reared, or, in some cases, allowed to breed under highly protected 'semi-wild' conditions for sporting purposes. Even where this is not done, links between landowners and blood-sports interests are generally crucial in sustaining conditions for the practice. Only if sufficient areas of suitable habitat are left free of incompatible commercial management or development will enough game animals survive to make the sport worth while. The relation between hunters and quarry, in this perspective, looks less like a 'contingent' relation between autonomous beings, and more like a systemically structured relation of differential socio-economic power and dependency, albeit an ecologically mediated one. To the extent that this is true, the practical effectiveness of the rights strategy in getting the sport abolished could well have the self-defeating effect of undermining the conditions under which it was reasonable to take as 'given' the ability of the animals concerned to enjoy their freedom once protected from the depredations of the hunters. These conditions are, precisely, the preservation of the general ecological conditions for the living of the life appropriate to that species over a sufficiently large geographical extent to sustain its population. The often quite cynical use of this argument to give a 'conservationist' cover to blood-sports interests does not affect its validity, so far as it goes![1]

Application of the radical critique to this kind of case, at first sight one very amenable to the 'rights' approach, suggests that *under prevailing patterns of social and economic relationship* the objectives of protecting the basic interests of the animals concerned are more likely to be achieved by complementing – or even replacing – a rights-based strategy with a broader strategy for large-scale shifts in patterns of land ownership, and redistributed powers and altered criteria for regulating land use and land management. This strategy would, in turn, presuppose integrated socio-economic and ecological analysis, and involve animal rights and welfare campaigners entering into coalitions with other social groups which might favour such changes on other grounds: amenity access, nature conservation, aesthetics, social justice, and so on. More specifically, the strategy would be one of integrating concern for the well-being of animals into a broader political programme.

The second kind of case – that of cruelty to animals kept in confinement by humans – is also to a degree vulnerable to considerations of a socialist or radical kind. For one thing, notwithstanding the power of the cultural consensus against cruelty, it would be a mistake to underestimate the rival cultural power of the appeal to privacy and property rights. The privacy of the pet owner is not only the ground for powerful 'non-interference' rights but is also a major barrier against both detection of abuses and collection of reliable evidence. In this respect there are strong parallels between the situation of 'privately' abused non-human animals, and humans – usually children and women – abused in domestic contexts. To the extent that property rights may be adduced to defend cruelty to animals, the advocates of the ascription of rights to animals have two options. One would be to argue for a limitation of property rights in this case on grounds of the nature of the property: as the subject of a life the pet animal has a right to respectful treatment. But it is difficult to see how this line of argument could stop short of (the second option) calling into question the institution of private property itself in relation to this class of being. From a 'fully fledged' animal-rights perspective the keeping of pets – even at its most benign – would be seen as a form of slavery.

Again, however, we might reasonably ask whether the rights perspective, if it has these implications, offers the best strategy for achieving its own objectives: protecting the individual animals concerned from harms to their basic interests. In this case, as often elsewhere, the rhetoric of rights (of the pet owner) is implicated as both a substantive condition (privacy) of abuse and its legitimation (private property). The extension of rights to those vulnerable to abuse, though prima facie an attractive option, is liable to be limited in its practical effectiveness. What the radical line of argument suggests in this kind of case, too, is that a transformation of the social relations of power and dependency which characterize the private, domestic sphere would be likely both to be effective on its own account, and also to provide conditions under which the extension of moral concern could begin to offer effective rather than merely formal 'protections'.

ANIMAL RIGHTS AND HUMAN INTERESTS: IN THE LAB AND ON THE FARM

Other cases which give rise to moral concern over the treatment of animals in captivity include the use of captive animals in medical experimentation or in safety testing of new commodities, and also modern regimes of intensive rearing of livestock in meat production. Here, the liberal-individualist moral framework of rights and justice can be shown to be still more directly vulnerable to criticisms which foreground the social relational and economic conditions under which such rights are conceptualized and are to be recognized.

Animal experimentation

The use of animals as experimental subjects is in some respects analogous to the case of cruelty to pet animals. In both cases the animal is kept in confinement, and in both cases the concept of ownership may play a part in the moral justification of the disposal over the conditions of life of the animal by some individual or group of humans. However, there are also significant disanalogies. The keeping of animals as pets has as its central point the intrinsic value of the relationship itself. The relation is asymmetrical in terms of the social powers and communicative competences of the human individuals and animals involved, but it is, nonetheless, a 'quasi-personal' relationship in which each takes pleasure in the company of the other and has regard to the other's desires as well as needs. If these features are not present, the relation is not one of pet owner to pet, but, perhaps, more closely assimilable to a utilitarian one, in which the animal is kept as an extra protection for the household from burglary, to keep vermin at bay, or for some other purpose *extrinsic* to the social relation involved. By contrast, keeping animals for use as experimental subjects involves humans and animals in just such external, utilitarian social relations with one another, and this is, moreover, the point of keeping the animals in confinement.

This is not, of course, to overlook the fact that moral and/or legal regulation is typically present in these situations. For one thing, many experiments on animals make sense only if there are believed to be good reasons for thinking that human/animal comparisons are valid with respect to the characteristics or responses under test. Depending on what those are, some degree or other of practical recognition of their conditions of well-being will have to be accorded in the way the test-animals are kept and treated. Also, there is often a tendency for those human individuals whose work tasks include caring for the animals to spontaneously develop affective ties and a sense of moral responsibility for the well-being of the animals for which they are responsible. Finally, the whole situation will be bounded by broader cultural predispositions against maltreatment of captive animals, and a juridical framework which, to varying degrees, sets conditions and limits on the range of legally tolerable treatments and interventions.

However, these limitations are themselves an implicit acknowledgement that the point of the practice of animal experimentation is that human experimenters intervene in the lives of the animals under their control in ways which are liable to cause them harm. This is a morally significant difference between the practice of animal experimentation and the keeping of pets. Standards of care which would be acknowledged and routinely maintained in the one sphere, are deliberately, but conditionally and within limits, suspended in the other. So, for example, the deliberate causing of unnecessary pain, from which animal rights advocates would seek to protect the pet animal, becomes a problematic concept in the case of animal experimentation. Difficulty focuses on both the terms 'deliberate' and 'unnecessary'. Let us suppose that a specific intervention be deemed necessary to achieve the purpose of an experiment, but that it is incidental to the experiment whether the intervention causes suffering to the animal. We could say in this sort of case that the *intervention* is deliberate, but not under the description 'causing suffering'. Here it would be morally relevant to ask whether the experiment would retain its epistemic value if some available anaesthetic were used to spare the animal's suffering, and, if so, whether care had been taken to administer it. Where suffering really is, and is known by the experimenters to be, an unavoidable concomitant of the experiment they wish to carry out, then the moral focus is on the term 'unnecessary': if the suffering is necessary to the experiment, is the experiment itself necessary?

In the terms available to the liberal-individualist rights discourse, it is of course possible to hold that individuals, including individual (non-human) animals have absolute rights. This position does, however, have implications which are difficult to square with the reflective moral intuitions of most supporters of the idea of individual rights, who tend to regard rights rather as prima facie morally valid claims. From this standpoint, an experiment which caused suffering to an animal (or person) might in some circumstances be justified, despite involving an infringement of its (prima facie) rights. If the moral grounds (for example, competing rights of other individuals) are strong enough, then rights *may* be overridden. On the rights perspective, a utilitarian calculation of possible benefits to humans (or, indeed, other animals) in the form of cures to major diseases or the like cannot justify an infringement of basic rights. However, competing rights *could* do so.

Steven Rose, for example, advocates a high priority for research to replace animals in safety testing, and in medical research. But, he argues, there will always be some areas where the use of animals is unavoidable:

> There is no way, for instance, that the biochemical causes of the lethal disease diabetes, or its treatment with insulin, could have been discovered, without experiments on mammals. And we can't use tissue-cultures, or bacteria, or plants, to develop and test the treatments needed to alleviate epilepsy, Parkinsonism or manic depression.
>
> (Rose 1991: 21)

This sort of argument, on the face of it, is flatly opposed to the rights perspective in its preparedness to license basic harms to members of other species for the benefit of members of our own.

However, it is quite possible to cast such arguments in the language of countervailing rights – those of human sufferers from terminal or chronically disabling diseases to some hope of alleviation, or of research scientists to intellectual liberty. For example, a recent newspaper article on the case for animal research combined both. Focusing on a sufferer from an inherited disabling disease called Friedreich's ataxia, the article went on:

> In the years that he has left, he hopes to further the chances of a cure for his and other disabling conditions by campaigning for the right of doctors and scientists to use animals in scientific research. . . . He has founded Seriously Ill for Medical Research, an organisation which places the human right to health above any claim animals may have on our consciences.

(Stepney 1991: 34)

Animal experimentation is a kind of case, then, where the rights perspective is limited in its power to protect animals at risk by several prevailing features of the social–relational conditions under which such experimentation is conducted. First, the rights of the experimental subjects have to be balanced against countervailing 'basic' rights of experimenters *and* against powerful popular moral sentiments which differentiate in ways not available to the rights perspective between a range of different benefits which may or may not result from experimentation (between, say, attempts to find a cure for cancer, and testing of novelty cosmetics). Both these countervailing social forces have access to political representation and therefore to legislative influence.

Second, the character of the practice is one within which such rights as are ascribed to experimental subjects are liable to be overridden or abused in pursuit of the intrinsic purposes of the practice. This contrasts with pet keeping, in which the power and opportunity to abuse are structurally present, but in which the practice of abuse runs counter to the intrinsic normative order and 'spirit' of the practice. Third, the institutional framework – whether public institution research science, or private corporation research and development – within which animal experimentation takes place, is one which resembles the domestic sphere in its relative imperviousness to external monitoring and, in the event of suspicion of abuse, to the gathering of reliable evidence leading to successful prosecution. Though the rights perspective is not consensual among animal welfare pressure groups, it is none the less true that widespread popular opposition to animal abuse in experimental laboratories has not yet been effective in preventing extreme suffering, often with quite trivial justification (Ryder 1985; Sperlinger 1981; Rollin 1989; Fox 1986). The socialist argument's emphasis on the social relational conditions and contexts under which formal rights may or may not be substantively enjoyed is, I claim, a persuasive diagnosis of this state of affairs.

But, more than this, it places on the agenda alternative strategies for, first, changing the social and economic relations which enable and favour abuse, and, second, developing moral perspectives on the status of animals which may have more purchase on the complex social realities of animal research than does the rights view on its own. Recent feminist work points in a promising direction here, linking laboratory abuse of animals with a broader critique of the culture and institutions of contemporary science. Lynda Birke, for example, is both critical of the abuse of animals in the name of science *and* sceptical of the value of the attribution of rights. Desensitization to animal suffering, she points out, is an established part of science education, a condition of the appropriate attitude of dispassionate 'objectivity' required to become a 'real' scientist. She continues:

> In our critiques, we have stressed the social context of contemporary science. Within that context of capitalism and patriarchy, specific forms of science have developed and with them, specific ways of conceptualizing animals and using them in science. But those forms are not inevitable. At present, our biological knowledge is grounded in a material base that includes the bodies of experimental animals. A science that did not see animals as expendable (if sometimes expensive) bits of apparatus might, then, have a somewhat different understanding of the material world.
>
> (Birke 1991: 456–7)

A more humane and egalitarian society would be one in which many current laboratory uses of animals would no longer have any point, but 'even if that more humane society still sanctioned the use of some animals in research in specified conditions, it would see the ethical issues as centrally important' (Birke 1991: 457).

The costs of food

In many cases of animal abuse in experimental situations, many of the above social-relational obstacles to the substantive enjoyment of formal rights (even where they are juridically acknowledged) are complemented by yet another obstacle: an economic or commercial dynamic and its effects on the priorities and intentional attitudes of the human agents bound up in it.

This applies even more forcefully to yet another class of case – modern intensive stock-rearing, or 'factory farming'. The development of commercial, and then fully capitalist agriculture exerts contradictory pressures with respect to the treatment of stock animals. For any specific technical organization of agricultural labour processes there are pressures towards an instrumental treatment of animals as mere 'things' whose output is to be maximized by whatever technical means are available; but there are also countervailing obstacles and restraints on the full realization of these pressures, which derive from the organic, psychological and social requirements of the stock animals themselves. These restraints are not, or are not necessarily, of a normative kind, but are ontological. If the social needs of captive animals are not met, they cease to breed, they show developmental anomalies, become ill, behave aggressively or self-destructively, and so on. In his description of the early stages of intensive rearing in the poultry industry, for example, Jim Mason notes:

> Large-scale indoor production caught on fast around the urban market
> centres, but the new methods created a host of problems. Nightmarish
> scenes began to occur in the crowded sheds. Birds pecked others to death
> and ate their remains. In the poorly ventilated poultry sheds contagious
> diseases were rampant and losses multiplied . . .
>
> (Mason 1985: 90)

Of course, as Mason also points out, research science was able to come up with
technical responses to many of these problems – for example, automatic
'debeaking' machines for reducing the damage birds could do to one another,
antibiotics and other drugs to reduce disease losses. However, none of these
responses was free either of costs, or of undesirable unintended consequences.
Obstacles and constraints deriving from the biological nature and psychological and social requirements of confined animals remain as limits to
'reifying' commercial pressures whatever technical reorganization of animal
'husbandry' is adopted.

However, there are clear qualitative differences both in the extent to which
needs are acknowledged and the ways in which they are met as between
different production regimes. Traditional, non-commercial pastoralism
requires human/animal communicative interaction, extensive sharing by
humans of the conditions of life of herd animals, and human adaptation to
those conditions. There are generally deeply held affective dispositions and
culturally authoritative moral regulations at work in these practices, notwithstanding the fact that animals are commonly being reared to be killed as
food. Commercial agriculture, with the 'formal' subsumption of ecological
conditions, animals and human labour, retains many of these features, though
the element of a requirement for humans to adapt to the conditions of life of
stock animals is reduced or eliminated with physical confinement and eco-
regulation.

A sharp differentiation in the affective and normative content of human/
animal relations comes with intensive rearing. The fragmentation, distortion
and partial suppression of the mode of life of the stock animal is paralleled by
an elimination of 'quasi-personal' elements in the relation between humans
and animals in the labour process. The human-social division of labour and
specialization of tasks imposed by the overriding intentionality of value-
maximization, de-skills, fragments, and 'operationalizes' necessary human/
animal contacts in ways which give them the character of episodic interventions and routines as distinct from long-run relationships, as in other
husbandry modes.

CONCLUSION

The paradox for the 'rights' perspective is that it is just this animal 'husbandry' regime whose predominance in modern agriculture has led to the
most intense moral outrage. Yet, at the same time, the forms of human/animal

interaction at the core of these practices are precisely the ones which are least likely to be responsive to moral appeals. There are several reasons why this is likely to be so. First, the appeal to the rights of the animals involved can be effective only if the moral agents to whom it is addressed are already able to recognize or acknowledge these animals as subjects of a life, or as bearers of inherent value. The mode of involvement of human agents in these labour processes is one which, as we have seen, obstructs the formation of long-run, 'quasi-personal', communicative relations between humans and animals. In this respect, intensive rearing of livestock is quite unlike traditional animal husbandry, pet-keeping and other such social practices which combine humans and animals. To the extent that intensive stock-rearing regimes do 'acknowledge' or 'recognize' the subject-of-a-life status of the animals involved (and I have suggested that they necessarily do so to some extent) they do so in a sense not reducible to the forms of calculation employed by individual human actors in the process. Such 'recognitions' are, rather, built into the design of the overall structure of the labour process, for which no single individual is likely to be wholly responsible:

'I am just a small cog in a big industry', Mr Turton said. 'Today poultry management is dictated by the company accountant rather than the stockman, but the big companies are not so much villains, as victims of a system that dictates that only the economically ruthless shall survive.'

(Erlichman 1991: 4)

A second reason why the appeal to rights in the case of intensive stock-rearing regimes is unlikely to be effective is closely related to the first. Even if an argument in favour of the rights of animals subjected to these regimes could be made rationally convincing to the human moral agents involved, the *affective* conditions under which such a conviction might issue in relevantly altered conduct are liable to be missing. In the absence of long-run, quasi-personal, communicative relations between humans and animals, the affective ties of trust, loyalty, compassion and responsibility cannot develop either. This is still more significant if we take into account the powerful socio-economic interests of the workers in these regimes which run strongly counter to their giving subjective recognition to any feelings of repugnance or moral disquiet they may have about the nature of their work.

Finally, the human-social structure of these regimes is one in which a division of labour and hierarchy of authority diffuses both the causal and moral responsibility of the individual human agents involved. Electrical maintenance workers at intensive plants may well strongly disapprove of the regime, but quite sensibly take the view that there is very little they can do to alter it. They have no access to top management, withdrawal of their labour would make the situation of the animals even worse, whilst giving up the job would deprive them of income without helping the animals at all: other electricians with less of a conscience will be employed to replace them. I am not, of course, here arguing that where individual causal responsibility is diffused by

175

the structure of an oppressive practice there is no moral responsibility on individuals. The point is, rather, that in such a case, the bare moral appeal is liable to be ineffective. It needs to be complemented by a critique of the social-relational structure of the practice and a strategy for transforming it. This is precisely what is obstructed by the abstract-individualist social ontology which underpins the most influential animal rights arguments.

NOTE

1 In a recent Leicestershire County Council debate on fox-hunting a Labour motion was opposed by a Liberal Democrat, Mr David Bill, on the grounds that 'The Hunts had planted much of the wild animal habitat left in the county. Abolishing hunting would be a move towards a prairie landscape' (*Horse and Hound*, 6 February 1992, p. 28). Predictably enough, the argument failed to call into question the economic system which restricts our options in the countryside to a choice between fox-hunting and a 'prairie landscape'!

BIBLIOGRAPHY

Benton, T. (1988) 'Humanism = speciesism? Marx on humans and animals', *Radical Philosophy*, no. 50: 4–18.
——— (1993) *Natural Relations: Ecology, Animal Rights and Social Justice*, London: Verso.
Birke, L. (1991) 'Science, feminism and animal natures II', *Women's Studies International Forum* 14(5): 456–7.
Erlichman, J. (1991) 'The meat factory', *The Guardian*, 5 October.
Fox, M. A. (1986) *The Case for Animal Experimentation*, Berkeley: University of California Press.
Francis, L. P. and Norman, R. (1978) 'Some animals are more equal than others', *Philosophy* 53: 507–27.
Mason, J. (1985) 'Brave new farm?' in P. Singer (ed.), *In Defence of Animals*, Oxford: Blackwell.
Regan, T. (1988) *The Case for Animal Rights*, London: Routledge.
Rollin, B. (1989) *The Unheeded Cry: Animal Consciousness, Animal Pain and Science*, Oxford: Oxford University Press.
Rose, S. (1991) 'Proud to be speciesist', *New Statesman and Society*, 26 April.
Ryder, R. D. (1985) 'Speciesism in the laboratory', in P. Singer (ed.), *In Defence of Animals*, Oxford: Blackwell.
Sperlinger, D. (1981) *Animals in Research*, Chichester: John Wiley.
Stepney, R. (1991) 'Body before conscience', *The Guardian*, 11 October, p. 34.

10

ECOFEMINISM AND THE POLITICS OF THE GENDERED SELF

Judy Evans

INTRODUCTION

Second-wave feminism has in large part moved from a belief in the existence or potential of androgyny and an aim of equality with men, to a politics of difference. And for much of the journey difference has meant, above all, differences between women and men.

A certain emphasis on differences so construed, as something to be celebrated, and on the importance of female values, probably is – at least among those who explicitly theorize – now the dominant stance. Ecofeminism, however, is a minority tendency which stems from a school that holds this view at its most extreme. Ecofeminists, that is, are linked to cultural feminism, which celebrates womanhood and believes in a unique female closeness to, and alliance with, nature and the earth. Here I have chosen Mary Daly as an exemplar of cultural feminism, and Andrée Collard as an ecofeminist inspired by her, to illustrate such views. (As Daly is well-known and her ideas are often discussed, I have given the merest indication of them here.)

There are ecofeminists unhappy with both this view of woman and androgyny (whether it is suggested that androgyny exists now, or as an aim), and who search for another view of the self. The two most prominent such writers are Valerie Plumwood and Ynestra King. I have outlined their arguments in detail in this chapter.

Feminism has produced massive and wide-ranging debates on gender and epistemology. The dualisms such as culture/nature, mind/body, and reason/emotion that preoccupy green theory, and are addressed by Collard, Plumwood and King, lie at their heart. Ecofeminism has, however, tended to be peripheral to the debates, and is remarkably undertheorized compared with the major schools. I have therefore employed material from other feminist discussions – for example, on psychology and moral philosophy, methodology, and the philosophy of science[1] – to interrogate ecofeminism's ideas, and to take further the discussion of the politics of a gendered self.

The first section of this chapter briefly portrays early second-wave feminism's quest for androgyny: for equality via, and in part as, the abolition of the stereotypes of 'man' and 'woman' that we know now. It argues that large

177

parts of the movement, and in particular of its ecofeminist wing, have renounced this stance to so great an extent that the movement has turned full circle and embraced the stereotype earlier feminists had tried to combat. This development, it is said, is inimical to female advance. The second section expands on these points via a more detailed discussion and critique of this, the cultural feminist part of the ecofeminist school, while the third assesses the attempts of other ecofeminists to steer between the mystique and an androgyny they cannot accept. In the fourth section I turn to mainstream feminist thought and current models of the female self, to assess their viability and the political consequences they hold. Though the point is not explicitly theorized, part of my aim here is to address the implications of the model(s) for political alliances of the kind in which feminism has engaged, of which ecofeminism is presumably the newest form. My conclusion, which derives from my beliefs as an equality and androgyny feminist, summarizes my views on this point. It relates, therefore, not to the ecofeminist project alone.

A FEMINIST JOURNEY: ANDROGYNY AND BEYOND

The feminist mystique says that the highest value and the only commitment for women is the fulfilment of their own feminity. It says that the great mistake of Western culture, throughout most of its history, has been the *undervaluation of this femininity*. It says that this femininity is *so mysterious and intuitive and close to the creation and origin of life that man-made science may never be able to understand it*. But however special and different, it is in no way inferior to the nature of man; *it may even in certain respects be superior*. The mistake, says the mystique, the root of women's troubles in the past is that women envied men, women tried to be like men, instead of accepting their own nature, which can find fulfilment only in sexual passivity, male domination, and nurturing maternal love.[2]

(Friedan 1982: 38)

Early liberal second-wave feminists such as Betty Friedan demanded that women be treated as persons – that is, as men. 'Early radicals' such as Marge Piercy and Shulamith Firestone demanded that all systems of domination be overthrown and women treated as persons – that is, as persons could become. And both in effect sought androgyny.

The liberal claims would seem to be flawed by assumptions that men were treated like persons, or rather as persons should be, and that men were the persons women wanted to become. And indeed Friedan's somewhat unreflective text tends to that view. Radicals, however, with sadder and more jaundiced eyes, saw men 'warped and programmed' (Piercy 1970: 438). They sought the abolition of extant gendered selves; they did not want to be as males were, then (Firestone 1971: 133 and *passim*). Undertheorized as it was, early radicalism possessed a systemic analysis of oppression that saw how men had been maimed.

We see a clear expression of this in Firestone; in for example her description as 'tragic' of 'The division of the psyche into male and female . . . the hypertrophy in men of rationalism, aggressive drive. . . . The emotionalism and passivity of women' (Firestone 1971: 133), and her aim to abolish 'The double curse . . . that man would till the soil by the sweat of his brow in order to live, and that woman should bear in pain and travail' (ibid. 1971: 274) which humankind had known hitherto.

Feminist theory has changed greatly in the ensuing years, and one school of thought in particular has moved so far from these aims and beliefs as to invert them, and readopt the feminine mystique. Certain cultural radical or 'woman-centred' feminists such as Mary Daly[3] have sought to claim that women, by virtue of their closeness to the body, to nurture, and to nature itself, possess qualities superior to men's. Further they reject rationality, reason, and humanism as 'male'. And of all feminists these are the most closely associated with ecofeminism, particularly in its mystic, spiritual feminist mode.

These writers are essentialist. They propose, that is, a static female character comprising or displaying itself in qualities such as nurture, kindness and care; a character that does not vary historically, or across culture, race, and class. As Elizabeth Grosz, one of the few writers to define the concept of essentialism adequately, says, this character is normally biologically derived, though on occasion a God-given nature or an 'as it were ontological' existentialist or psychoanalytic view is held (Grosz 1990: 334).

Many feminists might sympathize with the wish of these authors to revalue, say, motherhood, undervalued by society and denigrated by certain early second-wave writers, too. And many, also, would understand Daly's attack on androgyny as 'something like John Travolta and Farrah Fawcett Majors scotch-taped together' (Daly 1979: xi). But they will dislike essentialism because of its conservative implications, its potential and actual use against women, the fact that it echoes 'woman' as described by patriarchy, and the belief that if we assume it we walk into a trap. For as Jean Elshtain has pointed out, proclamations of female virtue by suffragists contended with arguments from female virtue that women should be denied the vote (Elshtain 1974: 462–3).

Further, this line of thought resembles Marxist/socialist Standpoint theory in its initial and best-known form. This postulates a female viewpoint more accurate than that of men, derived from women's experience(s) in their subordinate status of 'slave'.[4] As Mary Hawkesworth says, this type of thinking '[raises] the specter of an authoritarian trump', ruling out reasoned debate. However it can be relativist at the same time, when it appeals to intuition and experience as the only guides (Hawkesworth 1989: 239, 331). Alternatively, as I have suggested elsewhere, it possesses a pre-emptive view of what bona fide female experience is (Evans *et al.* 1986: n. 15). Thus it tends to elitism *vis-à-vis* other women.

But were these last charges untrue, an essentialist feminist thought would none the less hamper women, given its tendency to ally us with the characteristics society has allotted us, and cited in evidence against our advance. It is an essentialist feminism – what will be called 'classic' ecofeminism – to which I turn.

CLASSIC ECOFEMINISM:
ARE WOMEN 'MADE OF THIS EARTH'?

Daly has inspired ecofeminism and as will be seen, has endorsed, in part at least, its work. Her project is to reclaim via language woman as devalued by man. She proclaims herself an ecofeminist: '*Women and our kind* – the earth, the sea, the sky – are the real but unacknowledged objects of attack, victimized as The Enemy of patriarchy – of all its wars, of all its professions' (Daly 1987: 28). Her views cannot however lend comfort to the ecological cause, for she says:

> I am not suggesting that women have a 'mission' to save the world from ecological disaster. I am certainly not calling for female Self-sacrifice in the male-led cause of 'ecology'. I am affirming that those women who have the courage to break the silence within our Selves are finding/ creating/spiraling a new Spring.
>
> (Daly 1987: 21)

Daly introduces Andrée Collard's *Rape of the Wild* (Collard with Contrucci 1988) as 'a major work of ecofeminism, demonstrating and explaining the unity of women and nature and the oneness of women's struggle to save our Selves and to save the planet' (Daly 1988: ix–x). Is Collard an essentialist?[5]

Collard recounts the overthrow of 'Earth/Goddess' worshipping, non-hierarchical matriarchies and their replacement by the individualist, hierarchical and power-based gods and societies of men. A knowledge and memory of this is vital to women who will otherwise adopt male values and seek 'equality' rather than the 'kinship, egalitarianism and nurturance-based values' of those times (Collard 1988: 8). In the centuries since then women have been subjugated as and with nature: 'processed in the same way as foods: breaking down, removal of essential parts, replacement with man-made additives, reconstruction into artificial aggregates. . . . Properly reared pets have a great deal in common with the well-adjusted women and people of colour whom the white man has conquered/colonised/enslaved . . .' (Collard 1988: 83, 87). Thus women are maltreated; our true views devalued; our interests and those of the 'natural' world denied or ignored. But women's prior non-devalued link to nature and the good qualities we possess have not been banished by patriarchy. For women share the existence of childbearing and rearing with 'the rest of the living world', whether we are or have been mothers or not (Collard 1988: 106).

I infer from this last, most controversial claim, that Collard is an essentialist, whose analysis raises all the problems that stance entails.

Women further partake of epistemic privilege, of superior ecological insight and awareness, not only via this link but 'also and primarily because we recognise the many faces of oppression'[6] (Collard 1988: 97). This form of reasoning resembles, as I have noted, Standpoint theory, which also posits women's privileged access to knowledge from the perspective of the 'slave'. Women (and others oppressed) are able, it is said, to possess a greater knowledge than their oppressors, as we can and must learn their ways as well as our own (Harding 1986: 141ff).

Uri Narayan, taking issue with such views, points out that Third World women like her[7] inhabit a culture that assigns a high value to traditional female tasks, and suggests that it will be comparatively easy for traditionalists there to co-opt a revaluation of femininity to their own use, though that could happen in industrial society, too. And 'dual-context epistemic advantage', she says, may lead not to a critical stance, but to segmentation, or adoption of dominant values, or an assertion of the virtues of womanhood at the risk of exclusion from power (Narayan 1989). Further and more damningly she argues that certain types of oppression may be so great as to rule out critique, and if not that, contrary acts. Finally and powerfully she proclaims:

> the alternative to 'buying' into an oppressive social system need not be a celebration of exclusion and the mechanisms of marginalization. The thesis that oppression may bestow an epistemic advantage should not tempt us in the direction of idealizing or romanticizing oppression and blind us to its real material and psychic deprivations.
>
> (Narayan 1989: 259, 266–8)

Gayatri Spivak's views are also relevant here, for she attacks both imperialism and 'nativism or reverse ethnocentrism' as responses to the female condition, and she believes that 'all . . . clear-cut nostalgias for lost origins are suspect, especially as grounds for counter-hegemonic ideological production' (Spivak 1988: 307). This could clearly be applied to various of the arguments Collard makes. And Jane Flax comments on Standpoint failure to see the depths of oppression, and their consequences, and on the assumption that 'women, unlike men, can be free of determination from their own participation in relations of domination such as those rooted in the social relations of race, class, or homophobia' (Flax 1990: 56), thus providing a critique which can be applied to essentialism, too.

ANOTHER WAY OF BEING?

Ynestra King seeks to solve the type of problem mentioned above. In *Healing the Wounds* (King 1989a) she summarizes ecofeminist tendencies as I have described them, and argues for another way of conceptualizing the self.[8]

King sees three options for feminists aware of the woman–nature link. The first, said by her to be characteristic of socialist and rationalist radical feminists, is to break the tie. The second, chosen by ecofeminists, is to opt for nature,

181

again not questioning dualism itself and failing to see that 'women's ecological sensitivity and life orientation is a socialized perspective that could be socialized right out of us depending on our day-to-day lives' (King 1989a).[9] Her preferred path is to choose to maintain the link with nature (via an avoidance of male culture) '[to create] a different kind of culture and politics that would integrate intuitive, spiritual, and rational forms of knowledge, embracing both science and magic insofar as they enable us to transform the nature/culture distinction and to envision and create a free, ecological society' (King 1989a: 23).

King here faces, and indeed articulates, the problem that if female values are innate and take the form ecofeminism suggests, they may be unable to overcome male power, but that if they are socialized then as she says, they can be changed. It is difficult to see how this powerful objection to the postulation and acceptance of a gendered self can be overcome.

For King the specific importance of ecofeminism is that it can combat and overcome the male ecological flaw of misogyny which is hatred of nature too; it can, given its dual concerns, help develop an appropriate set of ethics; and it can explain to men that there is no natural hierarchy at all, but only that which they have produced, beginning with the domination of women from which all other forms of subjugation flow (King 1989a: 24).

Finally King supports 'harmonious, diverse, decentralized communities, using only those technologies based on ecological principles'; albeit, she views these as a Utopia (King 1989a: 25). Against this I note Iris Young's opposition to feminist ideals of community and face-to-face relations, not in themselves but as 'the organizing principle of a whole society' and her pointing to cities, with all their problems, as supporting the politics of difference and providing benefits for 'deviants' including independent women (Young 1990: 302–3, 316–17).

King ends 'Healing the wounds' by saying: 'there is no point in liberating people if the planet cannot sustain their liberated lives or in saving the planet by disregarding the preciousness of human existence' (King 1989b: 134). This is of course true. But here King opens the door to the belief that reason, human interest, and human rights offer grounds for serving (or not) the ecological cause, and that while (or perhaps) humans are indeed tied – and some, inextricably bound – to their environment, human self-interest may dictate ecological concern.

Why can King not accept any extant model of the self? Unlike some feminist thinkers, she accepts that liberalism possesses liberatory potential for women and other oppressed groups. However, she regards it as being the stance most inimical to ecology because of its 'rationalist, utilitarian bias and underlying assumption that "male is better" '. These characteristics entail that liberal feminists will be environmentalists, viewing non-human nature as a resource to be managed better, but for human goals (King 1982b: 119–20).

Socialist feminism, as King says, is a synthesis of other views, though most would see it as having allied aspects of radical feminism – and in particular, the notion of patriarchy – with Marxist method and aims. Its origins entail, in her view, that it support the subjugation of the natural world (King 1989b: 127).

Can ecofeminism overcome the problems illustrated here? Valerie Plumwood (1990) rejects essentialism but argues that we cannot simply ignore the woman/nature link and/or opt for culture given *inter alia* that we deal not only with a devalued womanhood but a 'de-natured male'.[10] By choosing culture, we do not, then, opt for a neutral position *vis-à-vis* the natural world but for dominance over it, and that position is intolerable now. Further and for the same reason, we cannot justify our rise via the continued subordination of the group whose status we shared and from among whom we have come (Plumwood 1990: 214–15).

We must, she says, consider the converging critiques of masculinity, rationality, and subordination of nature: converging because of the links between the masculine and the human, and the major role played by rationality in both. As Plumwood notes, it is not only ecofeminists who have produced these critiques.

Possible ecofeminist views of female character are threefold.[11] It could be complementary to the male; as Plumwood says, this is a conservative notion. Indeed, it is conservative both because it is static and because it accepts, prima facie, the view of women patriarchy gives. Or a rival idea of the human can be produced, entailing the desirability of certain female characteristics for, and their attainability by, men. Finally, ecofeminists could adopt the stance which seeks the celebration of difference via a 'feminine' as yet unvoiced (Plumwood 1990: 223–4).[12]

For Plumwood, the second and third possibilities are no solution to the various problems she seeks to address. To adopt a rival model of the self is to assume that we know which traits to choose and, furthermore, which, if any, are authentic and therefore will endure. And in the case of difference theory are we not left either with traits as yet to be discovered, but now totally unknown, or a retreat to essentialism and a reverse of the dualism already condemned – that is, an exaltation of body over mind (Plumwood 1990: 224–6)?

Her suggested escape is a concept of the human which embraces neither gendered model we now know, which would also, she believes, abolish dualism. But she cannot accept an androgynous self for a reason many have given: that it leads to an amalgam and uniformity (Plumwood 1990: 229–30) – a point put more picturesquely by Daly in the passage quoted above. Rather, she would affirm transcendence (synthesis?), or a maintenance of difference without dualism and essentialism and the notion of a uniquely human; which would allow the revaluing of certain 'female' traits (Plumwood 1990: 231–3).

Women's link to nature must, she believes, be conceptualized in a way that avoids the trap that would confine women to childbearing and exclusion from culture and the qualities valued therein. There would need to be a change in conceptualizing the masculine, and an attack on dualism, too (Plumwood

1990: 232). Then, 'We would be able to see value not only in the natural world but in the characteristics which we as humans share with it, which have been allocated to the feminine and treated as culturally problematic' (Plumwood 1990: 233).

Plumwood does not tell us how we do this. It is hard to see how the link between women (rather than persons) and nature could be made without invoking biological reproduction as key. Further and more generally it is unclear how her project can escape the problems she has already singled out. For we still do not know which traits to choose, and cannot be sure they will remain. And there is also the problem that we take a risk in linking persons to nature while nature remains devalued, the more so as we have reason to believe we know which persons would be linked.

Further, however, Plumwood has not sought to prove, or even to argue, rather than assert, either that what we in fact have in common with nature is what has been viewed as feminine, or that what we have in common with nature is good. Though of course this flaw is not unique to her.

A THINLY OR TACTICALLY GENDERED SELF?

While feminists are increasingly wary of the essentialism displayed by most ecofeminists, many believe that there are womanly virtues and a woman's voice. There is, for example, much sympathy for the psychologist Carol Gilligan's view that opposed to a male ethic of justice stands a female ethic of care (Gilligan 1982).

Gilligan's argument differs crucially from those of cultural feminism in that she would not forsake justice but rather introduce a complementary view where appropriate. However, she has been assailed for universalism (as opposed to essentialism), and it has been pointed out that such a value might disappear under different circumstances (Segal 1987: 14–147ff). Further, Joan Tronto has, in a thorough and nuanced analysis, pointed *inter alia* to the difference between a feminine and feminist analysis of caring and, at the extreme, at the way in which care can be seen as the ethic of those who, indeed, serve (Tronto 1989: esp. 184).

Lynne Segal, who shares my antipathy to womanliness and produces various counter-examples, none the less states:

> The popular faith in women persists . . . because it is also true that women's values and maternal thinking can serve . . . to inspire women to resist destructive and oppressive forces, especially on behalf of others. Nearly all feminists today are more likely to stress the importance of 'women-centred' values . . . by whatever complex route and at whatever cost women may have acquired . . . the virtues that accompany such values. Some of us would more readily admit, however, the possible contradictions within those values . . .[13]

(Segal 1987: 199)

This might be called a tactical (and partial) acceptance of a gendered self and voice. Others have postulated a tactical acceptance, though in a different cause. While Segal is concerned with the relevance of female character to socialist ends, Grosz points to the problem that if 'woman' is but a social construct there is no constituency and indeed no grounding to which feminism can appeal. Rather, there will be but local and specific groups of women. Here, seeking an escape from the essentialism/deconstruction impasse, she cites Spivak on the feminist impure versus the patriarchal impure and on a necessary impurity within feminism itself. For feminism is implicated within patriarchy. It could not criticize patriarchy if it were not. But its criticism is limited thereby. Given that we are bounded by patriarchy's power any choice is complicit and corrupt, and tactical utility therefore guides our choice (Grosz 1990: 341–3, Spivak 1984: 184). Susan Bordo (1990) argues more explicitly for the retention of 'gender' as a political need against the forces that would dissolve feminism's case. These forces are, I take it, twofold: a universalist humanism wherein human means man, and a deconstruction into categories and subcategories of woman: both tending to our being unable to say, 'women are oppressed'. Thus the concern is that expressed by Grosz. This tactical self is, I assume, gendered to the extent that it is not man; what else it may be remains unresolved.

Kate Soper (who is not addressing these specific texts) is wary of both the essentialism of the post-structuralist logic of difference and the ultimate deconstruction of gender that logic can dictate (the latter is, of course, Bordo's concern too) (Soper 1990: 240). Her solution is a dual and contrary future for a feminism that pursues both the humanism that post-structuralism, at its extreme, paradoxically becomes, and *feminism* – that is, a clinging to the notion of gender as a construct, a lived reality, and a motive force (Soper 1990: 243).

While I too believe that the logics of post-structuralism and post-modernism tend to a liberal individualist stance, I here note Hawkesworth's indictment of post-modernism's other and perhaps more characteristic face:[14]

At a moment when the preponderance of rational and moral argument sustains prescriptions for women's equality, it is a bit too cruel a conclusion and too reactionary a political agenda to accept that reason is impotent, that equality is impossible. Should post-modernism's seductive text gain ascendancy, it will not be an accident that power remains in the hands of the white males who currently possess it. In a world of radical inequality, relativist resignation supports the status quo.

(Hawkesworth 1989: 351)

Soper would tend to tactical dualism because of a tension in her thought. If we are to aim for equality we must be able to abstract 'from some differences between people'; and if we jettison impartiality then we cannot, for example, say of the application of the law that it is unjust (Soper 1990: 207–9). However, society requires 'feminine values', somewhat at variance to beliefs and

185

values such as this, which would currently seem to reside more with women than elsewhere (Soper 1990). Further, she wants to retain the concept of women to redress those aspects of women's situation second-wave feminism has not managed to change (Soper 1990: 241–3). Thus it is, I believe, the category of gender she would retain and not a gendered self.

If female values alone were the issue then we would ask: Why is this side of the dual project feminist and not, say, a bonus for the cause of peace? But if changing women's situation is primary, while we need to be able to say 'women', yet, why not make the humanist cause foremost? For as Hester Eisenstein says:

> the impact of feminism is connected to the insistence upon agency, sub-jectivity, self-determination and self-transformation, all old universalising non-trendy humanist . . . concepts, I know, but none of them yet really tested and tried out with their full implications for the women of the world.
>
> (Eisenstein 1991: 112)

To the essentialism of Daly and others are counterposed, we have seen, a socialized gendered self whose values are to be cherished, a tactically gendered self or an adoption thereof, and, a tactical retention of the concept of gender.

The weakness in all these positions has already been shown. Essentialism is conservative and plays into patriarchy's hands; socialized attributes can dissolve; the concept of gender must be based on something. Is that something essential or not? If it is not, why not be humanist?

Because '*claims* to universality and objectivity' are 'the alibis of a largely masculinist, heterosexist and white Western subject' (Mani 1990: 25–6)[15] we give those values up. Because rationality is hegemonic male rationality, we renounce that too. Because 'truth' is a masquerade, we embrace a permanent partiality of our own (Haraway 1990: 215). As both Hawkesworth and Soper have said – though Hawkesworth the more strongly – this leads to political paralysis, if not worse. Certainly it deprives feminists of a chance to say, you are wrong.

CONCLUSIONS

I began this chapter by outlining second-wave feminism's early, androgynous aims, contained in a liberal humanist quest for equality and a Marxist-inspired 'early radical' search for the overthrow of subordination of all kinds, though premised on the liberation of women.

I then outlined various views of gender that have since come to the fore. What might be called 'classic ecofeminism',[16] I have said, falls foul of the arguments against essentialism: its conservatism, its ability to be used against women, and its epistemological pre-emptive strike. Others, however, fall prey to the hazard of wagering all on a socialized self, which can again be used against women but can also disappear. (That is, I assume, also true of the tactical acceptance and use of such a self.) And the 'transcenders' not only face the problems of the second group but like all these writers rest their case on assumptions about men, women and nature that await their proof.

I then discussed a line of thought that is basically socialist in orientation and, while sympathetic to Soper's project *in toto*, tended to endorse her humanist face. And here I would invoke aspects of the early writings and suggest that the best if not the easiest[17] transitional path for feminists is to revert to calling liberalism's bluff. For I have come, like Barrett (1988: xxiii), to believe not only that there can be no equating of feminism and Marxism but that the feminist enterprise is indeed a liberal humanist one. Although such a viewpoint may be regarded as a philosophical distinction between types of emancipation[18] I regard it, as Eisenstein clearly does,[19] as having obvious political implications too.

These implications, I will add, are not, for example, that feminists are liberals and nothing more than that. Rather, while there are many causes for which women may, and some of us will think, should, work, by only one – a demand for equal treatment – is our cause *as women* advanced.[20] And thus it makes sense, I suggest, to speak, for example, not of liberal feminists, but of feminist liberals; not of ecofeminists, but of ecologists who are feminists too.

It follows from my arguments above that women have no especial, innate tendency towards, or interest in, ecological concerns; and that while ecology will be one of the causes for which we may work, if we do so *as feminists* it must be on a basis of equality with men, or rather, while striving for that. An engagement with ecology will, however, have to bear in mind the dangers of celebrating the natural. For that could entrench more or less every aspect of the female condition many of us have sought to renounce. Having fought to emerge from 'nature', we must not go back.

NOTES

1 These discussions are, of course, on occasion interlinked.
2 Emphases mine.
3 We can regard these writers as a school, but must accept that there are important differences between them. While Daly merits a more nuanced reading than can be given here, Rich conforms to almost none of the stereotypes normally presented and attacked.
4 See the discussion on pp. 180–1.
5 Contrucci prepared *Rape of the Wild* for publication after Collard's death. I have assumed that this made no difference to the analysis.
6 This is a common statement for which evidence is never adduced.
7 Narayan speaks as a Third World feminist, but does not want to be seen as speaking *for* the Third World.
8 I have here adhered closely to King's discussion.
9 A belief in socialization is normally regarded as the province of liberal feminists and as shallow compared to Marxist/socialist views of the historically constituted self.
10 My discussion here closely follows that of Plumwood.
11 It should be noted that Plumwood herself is an ecofeminist.
12 The reference is to contemporary French feminism.
13 A contemporary counterpart to Segal's evidence is the finding that women were

significantly more likely than men to oppose the Gulf War and significantly more likely to agree that it would be best ended quickly by killing Hussein.

14 Liberalism can be said to be Janus-faced, too. But I shall not pursue that inquiry here.

15 Emphasis mine.

16 I refer to King's 'ecofeminism' category. See pp. 181–2.

17 Though Chris Weedon has principled objections to liberal feminism, she also believes its project infeasible given the scope and amount of male power (Weedon 1989: 131–2).

18 I am grateful to Ted Benton for pointing this out.

19 See pp. 185–6.

20 I am aware that this comment is somewhat redolent of the 'all women are white, all blacks are men' syndrome that has marred feminism's first and second waves.

BIBLIOGRAPHY

Barrett, M. (1988) *Women's Oppression Today: The Marxist/Feminist Encounter*, London: Verso.

Bordo, S. (1990) 'Feminism, postmodernism and gender skepticism', in L. Nicholson (ed.), *Feminism/Postmodernism*, London: Routledge.

Collard, A. (with J. Contrucci) (1988) *Rape of the Wild*, London: The Women's Press.

Daly, M. (1987) *Gyn/Ecology*, London: The Women's Press.

—— (1988) 'Foreword' to A. Collard (with J. Contrucci) *Rape of the Wild*, London: The Women's Press.

Eisenstein, H. (1991) *Gender Shock: Practicing Feminism on Two Continents*, North Sydney: Allen & Unwin.

Elshtain, J. B. (1974) 'Moral woman and immoral man: a consideration of the public–private split and its political ramifications', *Politics and Society* 4(4): 452–73.

Evans, J. *et al.* (1986) *Feminism and Political Theory*, London: Sage.

Firestone, S. (1971) *The Dialectic of Sex*, London: Jonathan Cape.

Flax, J. (1990) 'Postmodernism and gender relations in feminist theory', in L. Nicholson (ed.), *Feminism/Postmodernism*, London: Routledge.

Friedan, B. (1982) *The Feminine Mystique*, Harmondsworth: Penguin.

—— (1983) *The Second Stage*, London: Sphere Books.

Gilligan, C. (1982) *In A Different Voice*, London: Harvard University Press.

Grosz, E. (1990) 'Conclusion: a note on essentialism and difference', in S. Gunew (ed.), *Feminist Knowledge: Critique and Construct*, London: Routledge.

Harding, S. (1986) *The Science Question in Feminism*, Milton Keynes: Open University Press.

—— (1989) 'Feminist justificatory strategies', in A. Garry and M. Pearsall (eds), *Women, Knowledge and Reality: Explorations in Feminist Philosophy*, London: Unwin Hyman.

Hawkesworth, M. (1989) 'Knowers, knowing, known: feminist theory and the claims of truth', in M. Malson *et al.* (eds), *Feminist Theory in Practice and Process*, London: University of Chicago Press.

Jaggar, A. (1983) *Feminist Politics and Human Nature*, Brighton: Harvester.

—— and Bordo, S. (eds) (1989) *Gender/Body/Knowledge: Feminist Reconstructions of Being and Knowing*, London: Rutgers University Press.

King, Y. (1989a) 'The ecology of feminism and the feminism of ecology', in J. Plant (ed.), *Healing the Wounds*, London: Green Print.

—— (1989b) 'Healing the wounds', in A. Jaggar and S. Bordo (eds), *Gender/Body/*

Knowledge: Feminist Reconstructions of Being and Knowing, London: Rutgers University Press.

Mason, M. *et al.* (eds) (1989) *Feminist Theory in Practice and Process*, London: University of Chicago Press.

Mani, L. (1990) 'Multiple mediations: feminist scholarship in the age of multinational reception', *Feminist Review*.

Narayan, U. (1989) 'The project of feminist epistemology: perspectives from a non-western feminist', in A. Jaggar and S. Bordo (eds), *Gender/Body/Knowledge: Feminist Reconstructions of Being and Knowing*, London: Rutgers University Press.

Nicholson, L. J. (ed.) (1990) *Feminism/Postmodernism*, London: Routledge.

Piercy, M. (1970) 'The Grand Coolie damn', in R. Morgan (ed.), *Sisterhood is Powerful*, New York: Vintage Books.

Plant, J. (ed.) (1989) *Healing the Wounds*, London: Green Print.

Plumwood, V. (1990) 'Women, humanity and nature', in S. Sayers and P. Osborne (eds), *Socialism, Feminism and Philosophy: A Radical Philosophy Reader*, London: Routledge.

Segal, L. (1987) *Is the Future Female?: Troubled Thoughts on Contemporary Feminism*, London: Virago.

Soper, K. (1990) *Troubled Pleasures. Writings on Politics, Gender and Hedonism*, London: Verso.

Spivak, G. (1984) 'Criticism, feminism and the institution', *Thesis Eleven*.

—— (1988) 'Can the subaltern speak?', in C. Nelson and L. Grossberg (eds), *Marxism and the Interpretation of Culture*, London: Macmillan.

Tronto, J. (1989) 'Women and caring: what can feminists learn about morality from caring?', in A. Jaggar and S. Bordo (eds), *Gender/Body/Knowledge: Feminist Reconstructions of Being and Knowing*, London: Rutgers University Press.

Weedon, C. (1989) *Feminist Practice and Poststructuralist Theory*, Oxford: Blackwell.

Young, I. (1990) 'The ideal of community and the politics of difference', in L. Nicholson (ed.), *Feminism/Postmodernism*, London: Routledge.

11

CRITICAL THEORY AND GREEN POLITICS

Andrew Dobson

INTRODUCTION

Comparisons between early critical theory and green politics can be drawn because both of them, in different ways, amount to a critique of various Enlightenment themes. They both bemoan the dark side of scientism, industrialism and modernity, and citical theorists, like ecocentrics, seek the emancipation not just of human beings but of nature as a whole. The stress here is on early critical theory, and a fuller picture of the relationship between critical theory and green politics would involve a detailed examination of the work of Jurgen Habermas. I only touch briefly on Habermas in this chapter, and these present considerations are excellently complemented by Robyn Eckersley's (1990) paper on Habermas and green theory.

Cursory understandings of green politics might lead us to question this assessment of it as in at least partial opposition to Enlightenment themes. On such a cursory understanding, green politics is precisely about mobilizing the resources of the Enlightenment – particularly technological ones – to ameliorate the ugly side of industrialist progress: acid rain, global warming, and holes in the ozone layer. Technology is mobilized to ameliorate the damage that technology has brought about.

Less cursory understandings of green politics, though, call these strategies into question. The 'technological fix' – as dark-greens call it – amounts to an evasion of political responsibility, in the sense that most of the environmental problems we confront are not technological but political. Greens agree with critical theorists that the nature of the political-cultural arena is such that the 'right' kinds of political decisions are hard to make. This is because the political-cultural arena is so saturated with a particular 'way of thinking' that it is difficult even to ask the right questions, let alone put into effect the policies that might follow from answering them correctly.

Fundamental to a change of direction in dark-green terms is a profound shift in the strategies and assumptions of our lives, founded on a changed relationship with the natural world – and in this respect the critical theory of the Frankfurt School mirrors many standard green sentiments. In the burgeoning literature in the field of environmental ethics one theme stands out big and bold: that our instrumental relationship with the natural world needs to change to one that recognizes its intrinsic value – either through standard rights-talk strategies, or through encouraging us to a metaphysical sense of closeness to nature so that we would see harm to nature as self-harm.

The word 'instrumental', mentioned a moment or two ago in respect of a description of our relationship with the natural world is, of course, a word closely associated with the work of critical theorists, and it also accurately describes the manipulative, means-oriented relationship with the natural world that Greens are keen to criticize.

Similarly, in terms of an analysis of the history of such instrumentality, the word Enlightenment bulks large in both green and critical theoretical descriptions. More specifically, the British scientist Francis Bacon plays a leading role in the tale of terror. He is pilloried in Fritjof Capra's *The Turning Point* (widely read in the green movement) as one who argued that the goal of scientific knowledge is to 'control and dominate nature', and who made his point in terms that were

> not only passionate but often outright vicious. Nature, in his view, had to be 'hounded in her wanderings', 'bound into service', and made a 'slave'. She was to be 'put in constraint', and the aim of the scientists was to 'torture nature's secrets from her'
>
> (Capra 1985: 40–1)[1]

Bacon also occupies the first two-and-a-half pages of Adorno and Horkheimer's *Dialectic of Enlightenment* as Voltaire's 'father of experimental philosophy' who put into effect the 'program of the Enlightenment', which involved the 'disenchantment of the world' (Adorno and Horkheimer 1973: 3) and whose ultimate aim was to enable 'man' (for it was he) 'to hold sway over a disenchanted nature' (ibid.: 4). The instrumentality is clear, too, in Bacon's own quoted belief that

> the true end, scope, or office of knowledge . . . [does not] . . . consist in any plausible, delectable, revered or admired discourse, or any satisfactory arguments, but in *effecting and working*, and in the discovery of particulars not revealed before, for the better endowment and help of man's life.
>
> (Adorno and Horkheimer 1973: 5, my emphasis)

As well as a clear expression of instrumentality, Bacon emphasizes the anthropocentric nature of this project in the last few words, and this, too, is a principal green theme in their assessment of the roots of our environmental predicament.

The superficial similarities of concern between critical theory and green politics, then, are clear. But I was drawn to this comparison as much by what I expected to be difference as by similarity. More particularly I have become increasingly aware of, and disturbed by, the *undertheorized* nature of green politics. By this I do not mean that no thinking is going on, or that theoretical aspects of the relationship between human beings and their environment are not sophisticatedly dealt with – I have already indicated that the literature in environmental ethics is already vast and still growing. What is lacking, though, is a material and historical analysis of the relationship between human beings and the non-human natural world – and a corollary of this is that the issue of social change is undertheorized in green politics.

Green tracts are conspicuously written in the conditional tense: 'If there were a green government, it would phase out nuclear power in the lifetime of a parliament'; or 'a green society would be more conserving and less wasteful'. Only very rarely do we get any hint as to how the conditional is to be redeemed, and when we do it is invariably couched in rather feeble terms. Thus, for example, 'education' is seen as the panacea for a whole range of desirable projects ranging from birth control to a pacified relationship with the natural world. Of course education has a role to play, but the shunting into service of this strategy without theorizing its drawbacks and limitations is tantamount to naïvety. I think it is essential, for example, that Greens take seriously the material and ideological circumstances within which the 'call to education' is made, and which are surely in danger of appropriating and dis-figuring the project before it has even got off the ground. This embeddedness or contextualizing of strategy (and of the green programme in general) is what I believe to be undertheorized in green literature.

Now, one of the aspects of Karl Marx's thought that is presently the butt of a great deal of smug irony is his anti-Utopianism. Marx's work is conspicuous for the absence of sentences constructed in the conditional tense. It is very hard for students to write essays on topics like 'what would a communist society look like?' because Marx never tells us. We have to make do with aphorisms, such as that the principle of distributive justice in a communist society would be 'from each according to his ability to each according to his needs'. This is instructive, but it hardly amounts to a full-blown description of communist society, and it certainly pales into insignificance alongside the lengthy descriptions of green society which constitute the major genre in green literature – in Britain at least (see, for example, Porritt 1984, Irvine and Ponton 1988, Icke 1990, Kemp and Wall 1990). Marx refused to entertain such descriptions, and his most frequent reply to those who asked him to describe what communist society would look like was that he wasn't in the business of 'writing recipes for the cookshops of the future'.

Of course, Marx had a good reason for this position. He believed that material practices and the value systems that they produce and help reproduce are first and foremost *historical* practices and value systems. To the extent that the future is an unknown land which is itself forged by practice, its precise contours are unknowable. More importantly in the present context, programmes for social change can only be innocent of embeddedness and of context at the price of being Utopian in Marx's specialized sense of the word. So contemplative solutions to social problems (in the guise of the positing of an invented 'Utopia') may contribute to the culture of oppositional movements, but they can never constitute practical solutions to the problems which gave rise to those movements. In his Eighth Thesis on Feuerbach, Marx wrote that, 'Social life is essentially *practical*. All mysteries which mislead theory to mysticism find their rational solution in human practice and in the comprehension of this practice' (Feuer 1976: 285). On some readings, the green position of 'deep ecology' is precisely an example of a mystical answer to a problem whose rational solution needs to be found in material human practice rather than in contemplation.

This chapter, then, is intended to test two hypotheses. First, that critical theory's critique of Enlightenment will lead to fruitful comparisons with the green political critique of the same phenomenon. Second, that critical theory's grounding in Marxist theory might provide the material and historical analysis of the relationship between human beings and the natural world which green politics so conspicuously lacks. If it does, then it might also provide the ground for a non-Utopian (in Marx's sense) resolution of the counter-productive aspects of that relationship.

In what follows I refer mostly to those texts in the early to middle periods of critical theory which most obviously deal with the relationship between human beings and the natural world. They are: Theodor Adorno and Max Horkheimer's *Dialectic of Enlightenment*, Horkheimer's *Eclipse of Reason* (particularly ch. 3), and Herbert Marcuse's *One-Dimensional Man* and *Counterrevolution and Revolt* (particularly ch. 2).

INSTRUMENTAL REASON

The central theme to emerge is critical theory's observation that it is the spread of a certain form of Enlightenment rationality to all areas and most corners of conscious existence that underpins our exploitative relationship with the natural world. This rationality has different names at different points of critical theory, and is variously called subjective rationality, instrumental rationality, formalized rationality, and technological rationality.

The themes of this rationality are manipulation and domination, so that on the Baconian view, and in the context of the natural world, 'What men want to learn from nature is how to use it in order to dominate it and other men' (Adorno and Horkheimer 1973: 4), and, 'Enlightenment behaves towards things as a dictator toward men. He knows them in so far as he can manipulate them' (ibid.: 9). The desire (or on some critical theoretical readings, the need) to dominate nature leads to the development of instrumental reason which, as it extends its territory of application, leads to the ever more exclusive apprehension of the social and natural worlds in an instrumental fashion. From an instrumentalist point of view, nature has no meaning in itself; rather its meaning comes from our instrumental apprehension of it. Thus the 'disenchantment of the world is the extirpation of animism' (Adorno and Horkheimer 1973: 5, 13). The implication is that at the end of this process everything would be apprehended instrumentally and 'independent thought', as Horkheimer calls it (Horkheimer 1946: 127) would become impossible.

Horkheimer formulates this as what he calls a paradox, but which reads more to me like a consequence: 'On the one hand', he writes, 'the destructive antagonism of self and nature, an antagonism epitomizing the history of our civilization, reaches its peak in this era', and on the other, 'philosophical thinking, whose task it is to essay a reconciliation, has come to deny or to forget the very existence of this antagonism' (Horkheimer 1946: 162). Once again, the more our apprehension of the world becomes saturated with instrumental reason, the more difficult it is to mobilize any opposition to it. This is obviously a central issue in respect of any attempt to heal our wounded relationship with the natural world and I shall have more to say on it later.

As far as a comparison between green politics and critical theory is concerned, Greens will often say that our relationship with the natural world is troubled because we treat it as a means, and to this extent they will agree with critical theorists. The difference lies in the level of sophisication. In distinguishing between instrumental and other forms of reason critical theorists help to make clearer the nature of the enemy, because by naming it we understand better both what it is and what the alternatives might be.

HISTORY

Greens recognize the historical nature of the environmental malaise which has given rise to their movement in that they focus on Enlightenment scientific method as the source of our exploitative relationship with the natural world. Given this starting point, there is a distinct tendency in green literature (and particularly in ecofeminist literature) to view the pre-Enlightenment human relationship with the natural world as more desirable than the one we presently have. This leads to the elevation to vanguard status of contemporary peoples who practise such a 'pre-Enlightenment' relationship (for example, North American Indians and rain-forest tribes), and to the exhortation that we should learn from these peoples and somehow copy their benign practices in the context of our own societies. We read, for example, that 'Deep ecology . . . requires openness to the black bear, becoming truly intimate with the black bear, so that honey dribbles down your fur coat as you catch the bus to work' (Robert Aitken, in Fox 1986: 59).

The difficulty with this green position is that it is Utopian in the sense outlined earlier, and critical theory is at odds with most green thinking in this respect. There is little indication in green theory that specific historical and material circumstances might have 'produced' our contemporary relationship with the natural world, nor – more importantly – that we carry that inheritance with us as an inherent and irreversible part of our present practices. Our troubled relationship with the natural world cannot simply be wished away.

Critical theory is clear (with Horkheimer as a partial exception; see p. 207) that the terroristic sway of instrumental reason is a historically specific experience. But critical theory's view differs from the green one in that no critical theorist believes that pre-Enlightenment attitudes towards the natural world can be uncomplicatedly massaged back to life in the contemporary context. Horkheimer asks: 'Is it possible to void the conflict [between human beings and nature] by a "return to nature", by a revival of old doctrines?' (Horkheimer 1946: 109), and the answer he gives is no, because, 'The complete transformation of the world into a world of means rather than of ends is itself the consequence of the historical development of the methods of production' (Horkheimer 1946: 102). This development is irreversible and we carry around its mental and material consequences as pieces of baggage that we cannot simply throw overboard. They constitute what we are as practical creatures.

Again, Horkheimer writes that, 'we are the heirs, for better or worse, of the Enlightenment and technological progress. To oppose these by regressing to more primitive stages does not alleviate the permanent crisis they have brought about' (Horkheimer 1946: 127). Marcuse confirms that because of the historical nature of our relationship with the natural world, the ' "liberation of nature" cannot mean returning to a pre-technological stage, but advancing to the use of the achievements of technological civilization for freeing man and nature from the destructive abuse of science and technology in the service of exploitation' (Marcuse 1972: 60).

There is support here for those who would want to persuade Greens away from flirtation with pre-industrial forms of society. Greens have found it hard to shake off accusations that they are anti-progressive, and in this respect they could help their cause by wholeheartedly embracing the critical theoretical observation that not only is history a one-way street, but also that we are irremediably, presently and wholly constituted by that history. Put simply, there is no going back, and going forward entails going forward as we are, and not as we would like to be.

HUMAN BEINGS AND THE NATURAL WORLD

This refusal to contemplate a revival of the past, and the insistence, rather, on the present as containing the seeds of an improved future, is crucial in at least one respect in the context of comparing green theory with critical theory. In trying to edge us towards a more harmonious relationship with the non-human natural world, some Greens blur the distinction between that world and human beings almost to the point of erasure. Arne Naess, the Norwegian philosopher and 'founder' of deep ecology, for example, grounds his environmental ethic in the notion of a 'Self' (capital 'S') which encompasses both my embodied 'self' (small 's') and the environment within which I live – an environment which begins with my immediate surroundings but which, given the implications of ecological interdependence, extends in principle to the entire universe (Naess 1989). Once this metaphysics is in place, irresponsible activity in the environment amounts, literally, to Self-mutilation (see also Mathews 1991).

Greens who subscribe to this sort of view (and even those who subscribe to less extreme versions of it) often point to pre-Enlightenment times as a period when such a view was so commonplace that it was acted upon without a second thought. They then urge us to recover this sensibility, arguing that if we did, our relationships with the natural world would immediately become less exploitative and more sustainable. Critical theory's point, however, would be that even if this were an accurate description of the pre-Enlightenment period, its recovery in the modern world is out of the question. If critical theory is right in this regard, then deep ecological exhortations in the context of modern industrial society to develop an ecological sense of 'Self' are, strictly, Utopian.

Not all Greens, though, subscribe to the dissolution of the human and non-human natural worlds in a holistic 'oneness'. Many are prepared to accept some sort of separation and to argue for pacts of reduced interference in the non-human natural environment. Roughly speaking, the justifications for such pacts split into two. First, there are those who argue that we should be more benign because it is in our own best interests as human beings to be so; while others suggest that the natural world (or at least parts of it) has intrinsic value from which a generalized 'right to exist' is derived.

Many Greens will reject the first position as being too instrumental, in the sense of viewing nature principally as a vehicle for human satisfaction. The second position is probably the more common in green literature, although the problems involved in establishing intrinsic value for the natural world, working out which of its categories should be awarded intrinsic value status (individuals?, species?, ecosystems?), and in deciding whether this applies equally to California Redwoods and to the AIDS virus have proved enormous.

Interestingly, critical theory comes up with a view about the relationship between human beings and the non-human natural world similar to this second green position. The fact is, say the critical theorists, that instrumental reason has so come to dominate our apprehension of the natural world that the only value we can conceive it having is use-value. Horkheimer remarks that,

> The story of the boy who looked up at the sky and asked, 'Daddy, what is the moon supposed to advertise?' is an allegory of what has happened to the relation between man and nature in the era of formalized reason. On the one hand, nature has been stripped of all intrinsic value or meaning. On the other, man has been stripped of all aims except self-preservation.
> (Horkheimer 1946: 101)

The implications are twofold: that nature can have intrinsic value, and that 'man' needs aims beyond self-preservation so that such value can emerge.

But critical theorists, and particularly Marcuse, are adamant that the cause of nature is not advanced by positing a spurious 'closeness' of human beings to nature, nor do they believe that nature will ever exist other than 'for' human beings. 'There is', writes Marcuse, 'a definite internal limit to the idea of the liberation of nature through "human appropriation" ' because ' "Appropriation", no matter how human, remains appropriation of a (living) object by a subject' (Marcuse 1972: 68, 69). He asks:

> Can the human appropriation of nature ever achieve the elimination of violence, cruelty, and brutality in the daily sacrifice of animal life for the physical reproduction of the human race? To treat nature 'for its own sake' sounds good, but it is certainly not for the sake of the animal to be eaten, nor probably for the sake of the plant.
>
> (Marcuse 1972: 68)

He concludes that, 'The end of this war, the perfect peace in the animal world – this idea belongs to the Orphic myth, not to any conceivable historical reality', but that, 'no free society is imaginable which does not, under its "regulative idea of reason" make a concerted effort to reduce consistently the suffering which man imposes on the natural world' (Marcuse 1972: 68).

So Marcuse's ideal is what he calls a 'pacified world', but this will be a world in which human beings and nature are still in opposition. He writes that he is proposing no ideal reconciliation between human beings and nature because, 'Pacification presupposes mastery of Nature, which is and remains the object opposed to the developing subject. But there are two kinds of mastery: a repressive and a liberating one' (Marcuse 1964: 236), and he argues that nature will always exist for human beings, but that the question is whether this will be 'for its own sake' or as 'brute raw material' (Marcuse 1972: 62). To a large extent the answer to this question, for Marcuse, depends on the development of a 'new science', one that will not only make more use of existing alternative technologies but develop new ones unimaginable within capitalist horizons (see Alford 1985: 49–68).

Jurgen Habermas has written relatively little on either the environmental crisis in general or on the relationship between human beings and the natural world in particular. However, in view of his interest in knowledge and human interests he has been obliged to say something about the 'proper' relationship between human beings and the natural world in the context of 'knowledge accumulation'. What he says places him firmly in the critical-theoretical tradition as outlined above. From the point of view of a theory of knowledge, he writes, 'there is for *this* domain of reality only one *theoretically fruitful* attitude, namely the objectivating attitude of the natural-scientific, experimenting observer' (Habermas 1982: 243–4). Habermas recognizes the existence of an 'ecological problematic' but is convinced (despite the well-known objections of some sections of the green movement; see, for example, Eckersley 1990) that 'this problematic can be dealt with satisfactorily within the anthropocentric framework of a discourse ethic' (Habermas 1982: 247). In sum, he agrees with Joel Whitebook that 'the proper norms for regulating the relation between society and nature would *somehow* follow from the communicatively conceived idea of the human good life without reference to nature as an end-in-itself' (Habermas 1982: 247, my emphasis).

In other words, healing the rift between human beings and the natural world, for Habermas, is not a matter of joining what was once put asunder, but of getting the relations between human beings right first. Indeed, in this respect Habermas goes further than his critical-theoretical predecessors. Horkheimer, Adorno and Marcuse all admit of the possibility – even the necessity – of a 'nature-in-itself', while Habermas is so concerned with the theoretical difficulties of gaining either moral or epistemological access to 'nature-in-itself' that he prefers to stay on this side of it and to generate solutions to the environmental crisis from within a principled anthropocentrism. The worst thing about this from a green point of view is that the crisis seems to be of secondary importance. Even once the public sphere has been invigorated in the way that Habermas demands, there is no guarantee that the free and equal conversations that ensue will grant a more valued status to the non-human natural world than it has at present. In other words, the liberation of nature is only a possibility for Habermas (and is not necessarily entailed by human emancipation), and Greens will want stronger guarantees than this.

To sum up so far, critical theorists believe instrumental reason to be at the root of our exploitative relationship with the natural world. They do not suggest, though, that this can be righted by an appeal to pre-Enlightenment sensibilities – such sensibilities are irrecoverable. At the same time, we must live with our separation from the natural world rather than try to dissolve it away. Indeed, as we shall see, this very separation is the condition for a new and pacified relationship between human beings and the natural world.

REASON

Critical theorists in general, and Horkheimer in particular in this context, are clear that while instrumental reason is an obstacle to such a pacified relationship, this must not be taken to mean that reason as such should be abandoned, or that nature should be exalted above reason, or that reason should be dissolved in nature. There is a tendency in green literature to follow any one of these routes under the general guise of encouraging us to recognize the wisdom of nature and to allow it to speak to us, as if such spontaneous and pre-reflective attunement were the way forward to renewal.

Horkheimer sees this as positively dangerous. He argues that dissolving reason in a 'fight for survival' 'entails the rejection of any elements of the mind that transcend the function of adaptation and consequently are not instruments of self-preservation' (Horkheimer 1946: 126). This is dangerous because it is precisely instrumental reason that causes all the problems, and so any strategy which reinforces the instrumentality of reason is counter-productive. This, according to Horkheimer, is exactly what happens when reason abdicates in favour of nature. What is required is more of a different sort of reason, rather than the dissolution of reason itself. Thus:

198

The equating of reason and nature, by which reason is debased and raw nature exalted, is a typical fallacy of the era of rationalization. Instrumentalized subjective reason either eulogizes nature as pure vitality or disparages it as brute force, instead of treating it like a text to be interpreted by philosophy that, if rightly read, will unfold a tale of infinite suffering. Without committing the fallacy of equating nature and reason, mankind must try to reconcile the two.'

(Horkheimer 1946: 125)

The point is that such reconciliation will be impossible so long as the tool of reconciliation – reason – is only ever comprehended and used in its instrumentalist guise. Instrumental reason can never effect a reconciliation because it operates with a set of assumptions and intentions precisely opposed to reconciliation. Moreover, if reason needs to be rescued from instrumentality, then the very worst we can do is to try to effect an equation of reason and nature because this obscures the very non-instrumental features of reason which we need to preserve.

Solution 1: The material conditions for new thinking

By now it will have become clear that a central feature of critical theory's programme for a reconciliation between human beings and the natural world is the domestication of instrumental reason and its supplementation with non-instrumental forms of reason – variously called objective, substantive, or post-technological reason. What is needed is a reason that is not blind to values and that is capable of being used to decide on the desirability of ends. Horkheimer describes this as 'independent thought', and he appears to tie it into a historical moment when we shall be free to think beyond mere self-preservation. Indeed he suggests that there have been moments like this: 'During his long history, man has at times acquired such freedom from the immediate pressure of nature that he could think about nature and reality without directly or indirectly thereby planning for his self-preservation' (Horkheimer 1946: 102).

To this extent the second hypothesis about critical theory that I outlined at the beginning of this chapter seems partly borne out. I suggested that critical theory might provide us with a material and historical account of our relationship with the natural world which would improve on green theory's somewhat idealistic and Utopian version. Horkheimer here points to the material conditions required for healing the rift between human beings and the natural world: a productive capacity so fantastic that the realm of necessity is transformed into the realm of freedom, thereby freeing everyone to think beyond self-preservation.

This certainly provides the material basis for an account of improved relations between human beings and nature. But, interestingly, it emerges at the price of making precisely the cornucopian assumptions that Greens say we are not entitled to make in the context of a finite earth. In other words, if freedom from scarcity is the condition for a pacified relationship between human beings and nature, then Greens will argue that such a relationship can never come about because the condition is unfulfillable.

Put differently, green politics is founded precisely on a critique of the possibility of the very condition which Horkheimer appears to posit as necessary for improved relations between human beings and the natural world: high levels of production and consumption. Of course these hypotheses raise the question as to just what kind of level of production Horkheimer had in mind. Us comfortable members of the Western European middle-class, for example, hardly feel ourselves under 'the immediate pressure of nature' (as Horkheimer puts it), and in this respect we've already entered Horkheimer's realm of freedom. To the extent that the majority of green support is derived precisely from post-materialist groups drawn from that relatively wealthy class, Horkheimer's thesis would seem to be borne out. Is this the level of production and consumption he had in mind? But then what of green warnings that these levels are only generalizable across the planet at the cost of devastating environmental destruction?

Then there is still the problem of all those many members of modern industrial societies, freed from the immediate pressures of nature, who have no interest in green politics at all. At best Horkheimer's formulation would seem to be a necessary but not a sufficient condition for better relations between human beings and the natural world. And at worst, we might point out that the people with the healthiest relationship with the natural world are not those freed from the pressure of nature but those most consistently and crudely confronted with it at every turn. This most obviously applies to peoples such as rain-forest tribes and North American Indians, but it might also apply to the modern organic vegetable grower trying to raise decent carrots and potatoes.

Interestingly, Marcuse reaches precisely the opposite conclusion to Horkheimer in respect of the material conditions necessary for a pacified relationship with the natural world. He bemoans contemporary society's 'containment' of liberation and argues that,

> To a great extent, it is the sheer *quantity* of goods, services, work, and recreation in the overdeveloped countries which effectuates this containment. Consequently, qualitative change seems to presuppose a *quantitative* change in the advanced standard of living, namely reduction of *overdevelopment*.
>
> (Marcuse 1964: 242)

This is a clear echo of green demands for de-industrialization, or what Ted Trainer has called 'de-development' (Trainer 1985: 176–8; see also Keekok Lee, Ch. 6 this volume).

The difference, though, is that the Greens' demand for reduced production and consumption is based on their assessment of the necessary limits to growth in the context of a finite planet. It is simply impossible, they say, to sustain economic growth at present levels for much longer than the next few decades. Marcuse's recommendation for a reduction in overdevelopment, on the other hand, stems from his concern about the tightening of the screw of instrumental reason which development presupposes. Put differently, present fantastic production rates have been made possible (at least partly) by the application of instrumental reason to various fields of human enquiry and practice. The implication is that increased production (of the sort advocated by Horkheimer in order to boost us from the realm of necessity to the realm of freedom) will involve increased application of instrumental reason. Given that it is precisely the domination of instrumental reason which critical theory identifies as the basis of the conflictful relationship between human beings and the natural world, the last thing we should want to do, argues Marcuse, is to follow an upward spiral of production which would tighten instrumental reason's stranglehold. He concludes that, 'The standard of living attained in the most advanced industrial areas is not a suitable model of development if the aim is pacification', because of, 'what this standard has made of Man and Nature' (Marcuse 1964: 242).

In respect of the desirability of reduced production and consumption, then, Marcuse and green theorists are in agreement – but for different reasons. In the context of our search for a materialist account in critical theory this is ironic, because in this case it seems to be green theory which makes the hard-headed assessment of the material impossibility of ever-expanding growth in a finite system (that is, the planet), and Marcuse who bases his critique on the counter-productive aspects of a particular mode of thought.

Solution 2: The role of philosophy

Indeed, despite these gestures in the direction of the material preconditions for a pacified relationship between human beings and the natural world, it is of course true that in general critical theory is more interested in a new type of reason and the role it might play than in its material base. Philosophy, particularly in Horkheimer, has a crucial role to play. In the *Eclipse of Reason* he writes that, 'An underlying assumption of the present discussion has been that philosophical awareness of these processes may help to reverse them' (Horkheimer 1946: 162). And by 'philosophical', Horkheimer means something quite specific because, for him, good philosophy aims at an understanding of the natural world in and for itself. Thus there have been times when 'philosophy aimed at an insight that was not to serve useful calculations but was intended to further understanding of nature in and for itself' (Horkheimer 1946: 102).

But philosophy is not simply confined to the passive role of understanding the natural world, for Horkheimer it is also the voice of the natural world. He bemoans the passing of an era when,

Once it was the endeavor of art, literature and philosophy to express the meaning of things and of life, to be the voice of all that is dumb, to endow nature with an organ for making known her sufferings, or, we might say, to call reality by its rightful name. Today nature's tongue is taken away. Once it was thought that each utterance, word, cry or gesture had an intrinsic meaning; today it is merely an occurrence.

(Horkheimer 1946: 101)

Horkheimer is not suggesting that philosophy can tell nature's story in any narrative sense. He means, rather, that philosophy speaks nature's language, which is a language of ends and not of means. For instance, in a resounding cry of support for the ideals of the Enlightenment, he writes that, 'Distorted though the great ideals of civilization – justice, equality, freedom – may be, they are nature's protestations against her plight, the only formulated testimonies we possess' (Horkheimer 1946: 182). Horkheimer cannot mean that nature desires – in any self-conscious sense – justice, equality and freedom. But these ideals are conspicuous by their location in a discourse of ends and not of means, and in this respect they are part of a discourse which, if it could be widened, so repelling the onslaught of means-oriented instrumental reason, would provide the foundation for improved relations between human beings and the natural world. Under these new circumstances there would be room for talk of nature as an end in itself and as having intrinsic value, rather than as a means to the reproduction of production. All this underscores the importance, noted earlier in the context of Horkheimer, of keeping reason and nature separate. If reason abdicates in favour of nature then nature loses its champion and forfeits any chance of having limits placed upon the activities of human beings in respect of it: 'nature is today more than ever conceived as a mere tool of man. It is the object of total exploitation that has no aim set by reason, and therefore no limit' (Horkheimer 1946: 108). Bounds can only be set by 'objective reason' (Horkheimer 1946: 180), and so attempts either to dissolve reason in nature, or to widen still further the scope of instrumental reason, must be firmly resisted.

Solution 3: The aesthetic

Romantic defences of the natural world have often been couched in aesthetic terms, but beauty is a notoriously flimsy basis on which to build a sound and lasting redoubt. Greens have come to use the appeal to aesthetic sensibility as one among a number of forms of defence, operating on the assumption (for instance) that while it might work for whole ecosystems (for example, a rain forest), it might not work for particular bits of it (for example, snakes). Basing arguments for intrinsic value on the beauty of the object, then, while it might work for some objects, will clearly not do for enough of them to satisfy green demands for a generalized environmental ethic.

Critical theory's recourse to the aesthetic in the context of our relationship with the natural world is notable for its concentration not on particular objects of aesthetic sensibility, but on the realm of the aesthetic in general. Critical theorists are pushed to consider this realm by the implications of their own enquiry. I have already noted critical theory's suggestion that our social context might become so wholly saturated with instrumental reason that apprehending the world from any point of view other than the instrumental would become impossible.

The very possibility of critical theory, then, presupposes a space from which to make the critique – a space which must, by implication, be relatively free of instrumental reason. For critical theorists this space can be defined as one which constitutes a realm of ends and not of means. We have already seen Horkheimer referring to 'art, literature and philosophy' as the 'voice of all that is dumb' (see p. 201), and I suggested that we should understand this voice as a voice of ends and not of means.

Marcuse, too, points towards a sort of aesthetic rationality when he writes that,

> Civilization produces the means for freeing Nature from its own brutality, its own insufficiency, its own blindness, by virtue of the cognitive and transforming power of Reason. And Reason can fulfill this function only as post-technological rationality, in which technics is itself the instrumentality of pacification, organon of the 'art of life'. The function of Reason then converges with the function of Art.
>
> (Marcuse 1964: 23)

And the function of art, according to Marcuse, is to provide us with a realm of ends in virtue of which the desirability of present actions can be judged – that is, precisely what is lacking in a context saturated with instrumental reason. 'The artist', he says, 'possesses the ideas which, as final causes, guide the construction of certain things' (Marcuse 1964: 23), and so the aesthetic realm is a space from within which to resist the spread of instrumental reason.

Solution 4: The emancipation of the senses: nature as subject

One strategy towards pacifying our relationship with the natural world has been to try to treat it as a subject in its own right. There is a sense in which the animal rights movement, for instance, has grounded itself in the subjecthood of certain animals, arguing that if we as subjects feel entitled to dignified treatment then we can hardly deny similar treatment to animals admitted to subjecthood. For those who want an ethic which covers vast swathes of the environment, and not just some animals similar in certain ways to human beings, this does not go far enough. Given standard conceptions of subjecthood, though, it is hard to argue convincingly that even trees are subjects, let alone trickier cases such as mountains and wildernesses. In any case, ethical Greens are nearly always placed in the position of merely appealing for a different ethical sensibility, without being able to give any good grounds for why we should, for instance, think of nature as subject. Critical theory can perhaps help here because, borrowing from Marx, it generates the subjecthood of nature from the nature of human beings as practical (specifically, labouring) creatures.

Marx theorized the relationship between subject and object in a potentially helpful way (from an ecological point of view) in his *Economic and Philosophical Manuscripts of 1844*, and Marcuse makes significant use of this work in *Counter-revolution and Revolt*. Horkheimer pointed the way in 1946 by writing that the problem was that 'subjective' (that is, instrumental) reason, 'made nature a mere object, and that it failed to discover the trace of itself in such objectiviza-tion, in the concepts of matter and things no less than in those of gods or spirit' (Horkheimer 1946: 176). This opens the way to a recognition of the subject in the object by seeing the subject's trace in the object, but it is an *ideal* trace in that it is only there by virtue of conceptualization. Marcuse tries to get closer to a material account of the extent of the object's subjecthood.

Referring to the *Manuscripts* he notes Marx's assertion that, 'the *senses* of the social man are *other* than those of the non-social man' (Marcuse 1972: 64). Marcuse agrees with this, particularly in the context of advanced capitalism where sense experience, he believes, is conditioned 'to "immunize" man against the very unfamiliar experience of the possibilities of human freedom' (Marcuse 1972: 62). Human emancipation, then, presupposes 'the emergence of a new type of man, different from the human subject of class society in his very nature, *in his physiology*' (Marcuse 1972: 64, my emphasis).

The emancipated sense, claims Marcuse, would 'guide the "human [pacified] appropriation" of nature' (Marcuse 1972: 65) – and this in two ways. First, they would apprehend the natural world as an arena for the practice and fulfilment of distinctly human faculties: the 'creative, aesthetic faculties' (Marcuse 1972: 64). This would amount to a resistance to the sway of instrumental reason because, as we have seen, the aesthetic faculty (as end-oriented) constitutes an antidote to the means-oriented nature of instrumental reason. In this sense, nature has to be seen as 'an ally in the struggle against . . . exploitative societies' (Marcuse 1972: 59) because its liberation would involve the 'recovery of the life-enhancing forces in nature' – its 'sensuous aesthetic qualities' (ibid.: 60).

Second, the emancipated senses would (in the words of Marx), 'relate them-selves to the thing for the sake of the thing' (quoted in Marcuse 1972: 65). And according to Marcuse's reading of the *Manuscripts* they would do this because, and inasmuch as, 'the thing itself is objectified human *Verhalten*: objectification of human relationships, and is thus itself humanly related to man' (Marcuse 1972: 65). For Marcuse this provides the basis for a more convincing materialist account of the relationship between human subject and material object, understood in respect of the centrality of labour: 'it grasps the world of things as objectified human labour, shaped by human labour' (Marcuse 1972: 65). So in the terms used by Horkheimer above, the trace of the subject in the object is that of the labour of the subject on the object. Marcuse would argue that while Horkheimer's notion of trace is ideal (the concept), his own is material (the worked object). The outcome of this is that nature as object has now become 'subject–object' – a 'life force in its own right', and therefore (again in Marx's words) has 'lost its mere utility' (Marcuse 1972: 65).

Greens might applaud this attempt to work out a basis for the subjecthood of the natural world ('a subject with which to live in a common universe' – Marcuse 1972: 60) but I suspect that, in Marcuse's case, they would baulk at founding it in human labour. Two years after Marcuse published *Counter-revolution and Revolt*, Fritz Schumacher's *Small is Beautiful* appeared. There, Schumacher wrote that, 'we are estranged from reality and inclined to treat as valueless everything that we have not made ourselves. Even the great Dr Marx fell into this devastating error when he formulated the so-called "labour theory of value" ' (Schumacher 1974: 11). Schumacher goes on to point out that while it is true that much of the capital we use (knowledge of all types, infrastructure, machinery, etc.) is produced by labour, 'Far larger is the capital provided by nature and not by man – and we do not even recognise it as such' (Schumacher 1974: 11).

The problem is that if the subject can only recognize the trace of itself in the object upon which it has worked, what is to become of the unworked object; will it be disallowed subjecthood? This is particularly a problem in a context close to green hearts – the defence of wilderness. It is wilderness precisely because it has been (more or less) free of the influence of human beings. If one were to adopt Marcuse's labour-based materialist account of the subjecthood of nature, one could get into the ludicrous position of supporting the mineral exploitation of Antarctica because only then would we apprehend the icy waste as 'humanly related to man'.

There are, of course, various ways in which Marcuse might respond to this putative green criticism. He might, for example, suggest that under emancipated conditions what he calls post-technological rationality would rule out exploitative use of wilderness. He might also (or simultaneously) point out that labour can take many forms, and, particularly in view of his notion (borrowed from Marx) of the senses as practical or 'active, constitutive' (Marcuse 1972: 63), he would suggest that the exercise of 'radical sensibility' (ibid.: 63) is itself a form of labour.

In other words, one does not need to labour only in a traditional sense of the word in order to apprehend our human relationship with nature. In this context it is interesting to read in Bill McKibben's widely read *The End of Nature* that we have ended nature by globally changing the weather and thus making 'every spot on earth man-made and artificial' (McKibben 1990: 54). McKibben reads this negatively, but Marcuse might say that we have at last fulfilled the historical condition for the complete and total human apprehension of the subjecthood of nature, in that we can now say (for the first time in history) that we have performed work on every single part of our environment.

OBSTACLES TO A PACIFIED RELATIONSHIP WITH
THE NATURAL WORLD

The biggest problem with critical theory's notion of social change in general, and of the move towards a pacified relationship between human beings and the natural world in particular, is that it presupposes just what it claims to be missing – that is, what Horkheimer calls 'independent thought'. Marcuse writes in *One-Dimensional Man* that what is needed is a 'new historical Subject' – one 'liberated from all propaganda, indoctrination and manipulation, capable of knowing and comprehending the facts and of evaluating the alternatives' (Marcuse 1964: 252), but as he himself says:

> At the present stage of development of the advanced industrial societies, the material as well as the cultural system denies this exigency. The power and efficiency of this system, the thorough assimilation of mind with fact, of thought with required behavior, of aspirations with reality, militate against the emergence of a new Subject.
>
> (Marcuse 1964: 252)

The problem is that if the context within which we work is thoroughly saturated with instrumental reason, then critical thought becomes impossible because there is no untainted place from which to shout the critique. The world as we live it has been made possible by the spread of instrumental reason, and this means that survival and progress in that world requires the individual marshalling and deployment of (more) instrumental reason. In the context of the natural world, writes Horkheimer, the implications are both obvious and potentially disastrous: 'The more devices we invent for dominating nature, the more must we serve them if we are to survive' (Horkheimer 1946: 97).

Our actions in the world, therefore, have the characteristics of a positive feedback mechanism: one is locked into a system where every action taken serves to strengthen and exaggerate the system's characteristics. 'Self-preservation', as Horkheimer puts it, 'presupposes [one's] adjustment to the requirements for the preservation of the system' (Horkheimer 1946: 96). In the totally administered society no action is possible that does not serve to produce and reproduce administration, and even in a society somewhat less than totally administered, most of our actions go towards making it so. Once this nightmare is assimilated, the search is on for untainted space from which to speak – and this, I believe, is the progressive political element in post-modern concerns for the marginal and 'peripheral': relatively untainted zones from which alternative forms of apprehension and action are, in principle, possible.

The question, then, is: Is advanced industrial society totally administered (from critical theory's point of view) or is there space for Horkheimer's 'independent thought'? The answer to this question in critical theory varies from text to text, although the overwhelming impression is that such space is extremely limited and even – on some readings – non-existent. We have already identified the aesthetic realm as one where a different sort of rationality operates, but Horkheimer, for one, mourns the passing of historical moments when genuinely speculative thought was possible – even if only for a privileged few. Now, he writes, such thought is 'altogether liquidated' as 'meditation' is superseded by 'pragmatic intelligence' (Horkheimer 1946: 103).

Horkheimer believes indeed that such pragmatic intelligence (in the form of what he here calls 'subjective reason') is a fundamental and ineradicable aspect of the human condition. He writes that, 'the social need of controlling nature has always conditioned the structure and form of man's thinking and thus given primacy to subjective reason' (Horkheimer 1946: 175), and that, 'From the time when reason became the instrument for domination of human and extra-human nature by man – that is to say, *from its very beginnings* – it has been frustrated by its own intentions of discovering the truth' (Horkheimer 1946: 176; my emphasis). Critical theory's project, then, cannot be one of erasing instrumental reason, but of building self-conscious awareness of the nature and reach of such reason, and of its inadequacy as a guide to living a fully human life, at peace (as far as possible) with the natural world.

One might imagine that the work of critical theorists themselves amounts to testimony that properly *critical* theory is possible, but of course this would be naïve. How are critical theorists to be sure that they are not 'spoken' by the administered society, and that critical theory itself is not turned, in some diabolical twist, to instrumental advantage? Marcuse, for one, appears pessimistic when he suggests that no path to liberation can be advertised because, 'The critical theory of society possesses no concepts which could bridge the gap between the present and its future' (Marcuse 1964: 257). In other words, the very nature of the critique of critical theory is such that we cannot take it at face value; we cannot be sure that we are not spoken (instrumentally) as we (try to) speak (substantively).

Indeed, of course, the overwhelming tone of critical theory in these respects is pessimistic. There is a strong sense that the nature of modern industrial society is such that radical change cannot be brought about. Critical theory cannot provide Greens with a sophisticated theory of social change because it gives us, instead, a sophisticated theory suggesting its impossibility.

But perhaps at this point Greens have more to say to critical theorists than the other way round. The latters' pessimism is based on their belief that the human subject in modern society is condemned to follow the dictates of the system for reasons of survival within it. And the system itself, geared towards capital accumulation, tends towards ever-increasing rationalization and the ever-widening deployment of instrumental reason. Critical theorists cannot see this spiral being broken. Yet the green phenomenon is arguably itself an expression of an attempt to break the spiral in at least two significant directions.

First, the post-materialist aspects of green politics demonstrate the possibility of founding a politics in late-capitalist society based on a refusal of capital accumulation. If capital accumulation is what drives the spread of instrumental reason, then its refusal in green politics invites the suggestion that such a politics is itself an expression of the critical thinking that critical theorists believed to be increasingly impossible.

Second, green theorists' determination to see the environment as having value in itself amounts to a resistance to the spread of instrumental reason. True, the green movement often seems divided against itself in this respect, with some sections suggesting that the non-human natural world needs to be defended in terms of its usefulness to human beings, while others argue for its intrinsic value. But the very fact that this latter view is advanced indicates the existence of a redoubt against the spread of instrumental reason, and, at the same time, holding such a view amounts to a substantive and subversive act of resistance.

CONCLUSIONS

I began this chapter with two hypotheses in respect of green politics and critical theory. The first was that useful comparisons might be drawn, and this has largely been borne out. The discrepancies between the two are instructive; critical theory tells Greens that we cannot go back in history, that human beings must be seen as apart from as well as a part of nature, and that we should place some faith in reason as salvation.

The significant thing about these conclusions is that they all point to a solution of the environmental crisis from within modernity. There has been some confusion as to whether the contemporary green movement is a modern movement, or a movement whose critique and aspirations take it outside modernity. This debate involves the need to clear up the confusion between modernity and modernization. Green politics has much more obviously called into question the modernizing strategies of 'advanced industrial societies' than it has the central tenets of modernity itself, although in respect of the latter, those who call (for example) for moves involving the re-enchantment of the natural world argue from within pre-modern parameters. Likewise, critical theory's concern is with the dark side of modernization rather than with modernity as such, and its aspiration is the redemption of modernity's promise rather than its abandonment. This is not the place to discuss whether critical theory is right in these respects, but if it is true to say that policies for environmental sustainability will emerge from modernity rather than in a complete break with it, then the critical-theoretical message is surely worth listening to.

The second hypothesis was that critical theory might provide a historical and material analysis of the relationship between human beings and the natural world, together, perhaps, with a non-Utopian resolution of the contemporary difficulties with this relationship. This has not been borne out. Throughout, critical theory's stress is on the identification and practice of a new form of reason, without much of an indication of the material conditions required for it and even less on the strategies that might bring them about. In large measure, naturally, this reflects the status and aspirations of critical theory itself. Critical theory set out principally to analyse and explain the survivability of capitalism and it accomplished this task to the point at which capital accumulation seemed an untranscendable horizon. But perhaps, as I suggested above, green politics itself calls the bluff of critical theory. If so, and if it is to do so successfully, then the findings here suggest that it needs to concentrate fully on two themes which most conspicuously challenge late capitalism's instrumentalized and administered society: post-materialism and the intrinsic value of the environment.

NOTE

1 Capra's quotations are from Merchant (1980), p. 169.

BIBLIOGRAPHY

Adorno, T. and Horkheimer, M. (1973) *Dialectic of Enlightenment*, London: Allen Lane.
Alford, C. (1985) *Science and the Revenge of Nature*, Gainesville and Tampa: University Presses of Florida.
Capra, F. (1985) *The Turning Point*, London: Fontana.
Eckersley, R. (1990) 'Habermas and Green political thought', *Theory and Society*, no. 19: 739–76.
Feuer, L. (ed.) (1976) *Marx and Engels: Basic Writings on Politics and Philosophy*, Glasgow: Fontana.
Fox, W. (1986) *Approaching Deep Ecology: A Response to Richard Sylvan's Critique of Deep Ecology*, Tasmania: University of Tasmania.
Habermas, J. (1982) 'A reply to my critics', in J. Thompson and D. Held (eds), *Habermas: Critical Debates*, London: Macmillan.
Horkheimer, M. (1946) *Eclipse of Reason*, New York: Oxford University Press.
Icke, D. (1990) *It Doesn't Have to be Like This*, London: Green Print.
Irvine, S. and Ponton, A. (1988) *A Green Manifesto*, London: Macdonald Optima.
Kemp, P. and Wall, D. (1990) *A Green Manifesto for the 1990s*, Harmondsworth: Penguin.
Luke, T. and White, K. (1985) 'Critical theory, the informational revolution, and an ecological path to modernity', in J. Forrester (ed.), *Critical Theory and Public Life*, Cambridge, Mass. and London: MIT Press.
McKibben, B. (1990) *The End of Nature*, London: Penguin.
Marcuse, H. (1964) *One-Dimensional Man*, Boston: Beacon Press.
—— (1972) *Counterrevolution and Revolt*, London: Allen Lane, The Penguin Press.
Mathews, F. (1991) *The Ecological Self*, London: Routledge.
Merchant, C. (1980) *The Death of Nature*, New York: Harper & Row.
Naess, A. (1989) *Ecology, Community and Lifestyle*, Cambridge: Cambridge University Press.
Porritt, J. (1984) *Seeing Green*, Oxford: Basil Blackwell.
Schumacher, E. F. (1974) *Small is Beautiful*, London: Abacus.
Tokar, B. (1987) *The Green Alternative*, San Pedro: R. & E. Miles.
Trainer, F. (1985) *Abandon Affluence*, London: Zed Books.

12

GREEN BELIEFS AND RELIGION

Michael Watson and David Sharpe

Much has been made of the radical nature of green[1] political, economic and social proposals, less of the analysis of what lies behind, or has motivated humanity's forward march into its contemporary environmental predicament. Our concern in this chapter is with the beliefs concerning the fundamental nature of the crisis, in particular its primary cause in human attitudes to nature and religion's role in this respect. As we shall see, this role has been ambiguous or implicit, but recently has been changing. But first of all, some background.

The Club of Rome's *The Limits to Growth* report of 1972 (Meadows *et al.* 1972) has been seen as a watershed for green beliefs about the crisis. Previously, environmental problems – population growth, environmental deterioration and depletion of non-renewable resources – were largely treated individually with one of the problems being given more importance than the others.[2] Such an approach helped to create the belief that the problem emphasized could be solved by diverting resources from other sectors. This assumption was challenged by the *Limits* study (see Ophuls 1977: 47). The problems now came to be seen by environmentalists as being strongly interrelated. They started to consider all the contributory factors and thus came to conclude that our present mode of existence was unsustainable. Discussion of environmental problems began to take place within the context of a critique of modern industrial society. Edward Goldsmith (1977: 15), for instance, argued that 'the principal defect of the industrial way of life with its *ethos* of expansion is that it is not sustainable' (our emphasis). What formed this ethos was clearly of crucial importance.

Closely related to this change in perception, was the politicization of environmentalists. Until *Limits*, as William Ophuls (1977: 2) notes, some of the most prominent environmentalists appear not to have understood 'the social, economic and political implications of the predicament'. They now came to see that the elements of the predicament that they had discussed were not the causes they had believed them to be, but merely symptoms.[3] This led them to investigate the causes, which resulted in a growing politicization of groups and individuals. Barry Commoner, for instance, redirected his research from examining the nature of technology to looking at who controlled it. As David Pepper notes, 'Commoner displayed a tendency which several environmentalists showed during the 1970s . . . they focussed on fundamental social relationships and processes which were seen to cause the phenomena with which environmental deterioration is associated' (Pepper 1989: 21). Religion takes its place as one of those fundamental social processes.

The change in the way the environmental predicament was perceived and the politicization of environmentalists were essential steps in the development of green beliefs as the basis of a political ideology. These steps involved a diagnosis of what were now seen as symptoms in order to establish fundamental causes, so that proper solutions and strategies for change of a green nature could take shape. What is of special interest to us is religion's place in this, its causal role and where it now stands in respect of green beliefs.

THE RELIGIOUS ROOTS OF THE CRISIS

To our knowledge, the first person to argue that the symptoms of humanity's environmental predicament were not the causes they were widely held to be, was Lynn White, Jun., in the influential article, 'The Historical Roots of Our Ecologic Crisis'. White argues that the beginning – approximately four generations ago – of the increased impact of humanity on its environment was the result of the 'marriage' of science and technology. He notes:

> The emergence in widespread practice of the Baconian creed that scientific knowledge means technological power over nature can scarcely be dated before 1850. Its acceptance as a normal pattern of action may mark the greatest event in human history since the invention of agriculture, and perhaps in non-human terrestrial history as well.
>
> (White 1967: 1203)

However, despite its importance, the marriage of science and technology is not, for White, the sole root of humanity's predicament. The problem runs deeper than this and requires an examination of the medieval view of humanity and nature. White believes that

> since both our technological and our scientific movements got their start, acquired their character, and achieved world dominance in the Middle Ages, it would seem that we cannot understand their nature or their present impact upon ecology without examining fundamental medieval assumptions and developments.
>
> (White 1967: 1204–5)

White proceeds to describe two developments he takes to indicate a fundamental change in humanity's relationship with and assumptions about nature. The first development is a change in agricultural practice that had occurred by the end of the seventh century in northern Europe. Certain northern peasants abandoned ploughs that 'merely' scratched the sod for ones able to cut a furrow, slice under the sod, and turn it over. These, White argues, 'attacked the land with such violence' that humanity's relationship to nature was profoundly changed: 'Formerly man had been part of nature; now he was the exploiter of nature' (White 1967: 1205). The second development is a change, which he dates 'slightly' before AD 830, in western illustrated calendars. 'In older calendars', he notes, 'the months were shown as passive personifications.' Later Frankish calendars were very different: 'they show men coercing the world around them – ploughing, harvesting, chopping trees, butchering pigs. Man and nature are two things, and man is master' (White 1967: 1205).

While White describes these developments at some length, they are only developments indicative of a more profound change, a change in humanity's beliefs about its nature and destiny. In short, the developments were indicative of the victory of Christianity over paganism. A victory that White describes as 'the greatest psychic revolution in the history of our culture'. He asserts this on the basis that Christianity introduced to western culture the ideas of progress and of time as something linear – ideas 'unknown either to Greco-Roman antiquity or to the Orient'. In addition to this, White holds the Christian story of creation – that Man was made in God's image and that he should 'fill the earth and subdue it, and have domination over every living thing' – equally, if not more, responsible for our present predicament. Prior to Christianity natural objects were protected from humanity by the belief that they all had spirits. With the victory of Christianity over paganism, 'the spirits in natural objects, which formerly had protected nature from man, evaporated. Man's effective monopoly on spirit in this world was confirmed, and the old inhibitions to the exploitation of nature crumbled.' These beliefs taken together 'not only established a dualism of man and nature but also insisted that it is God's will that man exploit nature for his proper ends'. Thus White comes to conclude that Christianity is significantly responsible for humanity's present predicament (White 1967: 1205–6).

When White's article was first published it was greeted with both sympathy and criticism. Some writers repeated the charge that the humanity versus nature relationship was largely responsible for humanity's predicament and that Christianity consequently bore much of the blame. Ian McHarg, for instance, argued that 'Judaism and Christianity have been long concerned with justice and compassion for the acts of man to man but have traditionally assumed nature to be a mere backdrop for the human play' (McHarg 1973: 174). As with White, McHarg's argument is based on the story of creation. He notes: 'apparently, the literal interpretation of the creation in Genesis is the tacit text for Jews and Christians alike – man exclusively divine, man given dominion over all life and nonlife, enjoined to subdue the earth' (McHarg 1973: 174). This exclusive concern with the story of creation was questioned in one of the main types of criticism made of White's thesis. In general, the main criticisms made were of of three types.

One of the most vocal critics of White's thesis was Lewis Moncrief. In his reply to White, he suggests, concerning the favourable response of several

prominent theologians, that 'the wide acceptance of such a simplistic explanation is at this point based more on fad than on fact' (Moncrief 1973: 32). He
draws attention to the fact that humanity has been dramatically altering its
environment since antiquity – a fact to which White also draws attention.
White's own examples, Moncrief believes, weaken his thesis. He notes that
White draws attention to the probably significant 'unnatural' changes in
humanity's environment brought about by its intervention, in the periodic
flooding of the Nile River basin and the fire-drive method of hunting of pre-
historic man. Another possible example that White or Moncrief could have
cited, and that other critics did, is the destruction of the fertility of the Near
East by early agricultural activity.

The trouble with these criticisms – and others that similarly argue that
Christian cultures are not the only cultures to have adversely affected their
environments – is that to some extent they miss the point. White does not
maintain that Christianity was the single root of humanity's present predicament. This much becomes apparent just from the title of his article (referring
to 'Historical Roots') and even more from the attention he gives to the part
played by modern science and technology. It is explicit in the reply to his
critics – 'continuing the conversation' – where he writes 'no sensible person
could maintain that all ecologic damage is, or has been, rooted in religious
attitudes' (White 1973: 44). The point is, as Osborn argues in *Stewards of
Creation*, 'not that western Christianity is the exclusive historical cause of our
environmental crisis; but that its beliefs were peculiarly well adapted to
encouraging the exploitation which has led to the present situation' (Osborn
1990: 9).

The second type of criticism made of White's thesis is also flawed. A representative example is provided by René Dubos. He believes that the *root* of
humanity's present predicament is not to be found in the west's Judeo-
Christian tradition, since

> the ecological crisis . . . has its *root* in our failure to differentiate between
> the use of scientific technology as a kind of modern magic and what I shall
> call modern religion, namely, knowledge as it relates to man's place in
> the universe and, especially, his relation to the earth.
>
> (Dubos 1973: 44; our emphasis)

Similar to Moncrief he gives examples of environmental deterioration in
which the Judeo-Christian tradition surely played no part. For instance, he
points out that 'one does not need to know much history to realize that the
ancient Chinese, Greek, and Moslem civilizations contributed their share to
deforestation, to erosion, and to the destruction of nature in many other ways'
(Dubos 1973: 46).

More important, Dubos notes that 'the Judeo-Christian attitude concerning
the relation of man to nature is not only expressed in the first chapter of
Genesis'. There are themes in the tradition other than the dominion theme
found there. He points out that

the second chapter of Genesis states that man, in the Garden of Eden, was instructed by God to dress it and to keep it – a statement which has ecological implications. It means that man must be concerned with what happens to it.

(Dubos 1973: 46–8)

However, like the first type of criticism, this second type again seems to miss the point. White himself draws attention to alternative biblical themes when he proposes St Francis as a patron saint for ecologists. White, though, is not so much concerned with the alternative themes as with how the themes have been interpreted and which have tended to dominate the hearts and minds of believers. This concern is made clear in the reply to his critics when he distinguishes between the 'wants' of Christians and those of historians:

The Christian wants to know what Scripture says to him about a puzzling problem. The historian wants to know what Christians in various times and places have thought Scripture was saying to them. The history of Biblical exegesis is sometimes troubling. So, if one points to the fact that historically Latin Christians have generally been arrogant toward nature, this does not mean that Scripture read with twentieth-century eyes will breed the same attitude.

(Dubos 1973: 60–1)

Drawing attention to alternative themes of the relationship between humanity and nature in the Judeo-Christian tradition is not, then, enough to discredit White's thesis. He himself admits that 'scattered through the Bible . . . there are passages that can be read as sustaining the notion of a spiritual democracy of all creatures' (White 1973: 28). Of more importance when trying to establish the causes of humanity's present predicament, though, is which of the various themes have dominated Christian hearts and minds. As White observes, while alternatives to the theme are to be found, especially in the Old Testament, 'the point is that historically they seem seldom or never to have been so interpreted' (Dubos 1973: 61).

Criticisms of White's thesis that attempt to question whether Christianity has played a significant part in our present predicament would, then, appear to be forlorn. To assert the Judeo-Christian tradition is not a cause is to deny that Christianity has influenced the development of western civilization – a denial which seems absurd. Worthy of more serious consideration is the third type of criticism of White's thesis – that criticism which draws attention to other possibly more important causes of humanity's predicament.

Since the contemporary environmental crisis was first documented, many causes for it have been advanced and the role of the Judeo-Christian tradition should not be over-emphasized.[4] After all, Christian ideas and values have been a powerful influence on western civilization for about 1,700 years while its present predicament has only recently materialized. Returning to one of the earlier critics of White's thesis, Lewis Moncrief argues that it seems tenable to affirm that the role played by religion in man-to-man and man-to-environment relationships is one of establishing a very broad system of allowable beliefs and behaviour. In other words, it defines the ball park in which the game is played, and, by the very nature of the park, some types of games cannot be played. However, the kind of game that ultimately evolves is not itself defined by the ball park.

(Moncrief 1973: 33)

He contends thus, that while religious belief systems are important, other causes have almost certainly played a larger part in bringing humanity to its present predicament.

In common with many green theorists, Moncrief believes that humanity's predicament has economic and social causes. Drawing attention to the two revolutions – the French and Industrial Revolutions – that have directed the west's present political, economic and social development, he suggests that the profit motive, the private ownership of resources, technological developments and urbanization have all contributed decisively to the predicament. These causes associated with western capitalism are not clearly related, he argues, to the Judeo-Christian tradition whose influence at most is indirect.

Lewis Moncrief's criticism of White's thesis was first published in *Science* on 30 October 1970. In the first half of the 1970s, White's thesis and the criticisms like that of Moncrief's that it generated, appear to have been eclipsed by the appearance of the Club of Rome's *The Limits to Growth*. Although the shift from examining symptoms to investigating causes of the environmental predicament gathered momentum around that time and played a vital part in the development of ecologism as a distinct political ideology, it is a shift that has been largely ignored, especially where the analyses of White and others are concerned. Much of the flood of literature on green politics in recent years concentrates on policy solutions to the various elements of the predicament and on strategies for change; causes of the predicament in terms of beliefs and values get relatively little attention and have to be deduced as underlying assumptions.

However, the deep causes that can be identified in green literature as to why humanity now finds itself in a predicament can be broadly arranged into three principal groups: our anthropocentric world view; the modern techno-scientific paradigm; and economic ideology (market or state capitalism). The identification of the first has led many Greens to argue that humanity should reorganize its lifestyle to take account of nature and the ecological lessons – the importance of diversity, interdependence and longevity – to be learnt from it, and for a smaller number to urge the adoption of a biocentric ethic. The identification of the second type of cause has resulted in Greens being mistrustful of the scientific method – with its tendency to examine parts instead of wholes – and of the associated 'high-impact' technology. The identification of the final group of causes has led Greens to question many current economic orthodoxies – such as the desirability of continuous economic growth and accounting practices that define the health of a society in terms of the rate of GNP increase.

In respect of these three groups of causes, religion, at least in the shape of the Judeo-Christian tradition, has been implicated directly in the first, as we have seen, indirectly but significantly in the second, and less so in the third – and then mainly through the first and second. Whatever the specific view of Christianity's responsibility, the charge has been taken seriously by theologians and the churches, not least perhaps because concern with spiritual matters, or 'spirituality', is an important aspect of the green movement itself and of its approach to overcoming the crisis (Dobson 1990: 18, 20–1, 143–5; Porritt 1985). The question arises, then, of how religion has responded or how it 'shapes up', as it were, on the issue.

In the first place, it is Christian theology which has been centre stage, following the accusations of its eco-cidal culpability. One of the basic points made in this respect is that, indeed, theology – at least of the western Church – has something to answer for, at any rate in the sense of a sin of omission. In the last three or four hundred years it has concentrated on the redemption and salvation of humanity, often at a purely personal level – and the Church's role in that – rather than on God's creative dimension and the role of the Holy Spirit in this regard (McDonagh 1986, Osborn 1990). Basically, natural history – the explanation of the natural (non-human) world and the causes in terms of its functioning – was left to scientists following the Copernican revolution. This gave rise, under the leading impulse of Bacon, Descartes and Newton, to the mechanical paradigm as the basis for the understanding, and utilization, of the natural world. Nature became objectified and quantified, not possessing 'any vital inner life force . . . [so] the stage was set for the technologists, the captains of industry and the generals to manipulate [it] in whatever way they pleased, to satisfy human needs' (McDonagh 1986: 68) – and, as we now know, to extend these apparently endlessly.

In the mechanical paradigm there was still a place for God, as designer and prime mover but exclusively transcendent (Bacon, Descartes and Newton were, after all, not irreligious men, though it is clear, as in Bacon's *New Atlantis*, that their prime fideistic enthusiasm was for science and 'the effecting of all things possible'). More or less parallel with the birth of modern science was the Reformation, which made its own contribution to theology's and religion's abdication from concern with the natural world (or even, at the limit, simply with this earthly world). This followed from the Protestant doctrine of justification by faith and the granting of God's grace to the individual human conscience, at least if the doctrine was treated in an exclusive fashion as it tended to be. The focus was on redemption from personal sin through Christ crucified and the promise of salvation through resurrection to eternal life. More specifically, Protestantism rejected Catholic natural theology, as elaborated by Aquinas and the Scholastics, in favour of revealed theology – an almost total Christological concern.

The overall tendency of these developments was to a dualism sustained in particular by Cartesian science and rationalized, later, by Kantian philosophy. Most important from the green perspective, spirit and matter were separated, religion became confined to the 'subjective' world of human existence, and non-human nature became desanctified and objectified (indeed, progressively this has applied, too, to the human body including the brain, leaving such concepts as 'mind' and 'spirit' of doubtful status). Moreover, this objectified nature became the touchstone of what was real, the 'objective' knowledge about it, obtained by scientists from an exterior 'detached' position, taking precedence over knowledge obtained by experience or any other 'interior' way (in effect, the scope of knowing being significantly narrowed, thereby seriously downgrading religious and spiritual understanding – and leaving ethical reasoning apparently on shaky foundations).

Of course, for this world view to be put vigorously into practice, it needed some further impetus even though, as Bacon and Descartes indicated, it had its own in-built instrumentalist commitment. Such an impetus was provided, some would say decisively, by the emergent bourgeois commercial and capitalist economy – whose ethos was wonderfully captured, and promulgated, by Mandeville (in the *Fable of the Bees*) in early eighteenth century England (see Goldsmith 1985, Macfarlane 1987: 119–21). In some ways the Catholic Church was a stumbling block to this ethos while its influence remained preponderant – for example, in the case of its opposition to usury. On the other hand, there is little doubt that Protestantism, at least in some of its more radical Calvinistic expressions, assisted functionally, rather than directly causally, in the development of capitalism (Osborn 1990: 8–9, Macfarlane 1987: ch. 8) – namely, its beliefs were well adapted to facilitating the ethos of enterprise, accumulation and investment (it is surely more than coincidence that the Latin Catholic region of Southern Europe lagged behind in capitalist industrialization).

Protestantism may also be said to have made an important functional contribution to the new order in its theological individualism; although in the key case of England, the leading historical scholar, Alan Macfarlane, has considerably shaken the conventional understanding of the rise of individualism by tracing it back to well before the 'watershed' of the sixteenth century (Macfarlane 1978) – indeed, suggesting its origins lay, if in any one source, in the Germanic peoples who settled in England after Rome's fall. However, Christianity certainly contained within it a very important seed of individualism, not least in comparison with Judaism: for Christ, God was God of each and everyone, and not simply of the people of Israel; for God, each of us was unique, a person in His own image (not just 'humanity', a 'people', generically in that image) and thus fully worthy of salvation – and each had freedom of choice in that respect (thus all individuals got what they really desired as reflected in that fundamental existential choice). The Reformation was centrally to do with the recovery and reassertion of this cardinal truth of the Christian religion; yet in the circumstances of Europe at that time, and especially Northern Europe, this theological reorientation contributed, clearly

217

in an unintended sense, to the new economic and political order.

Where western Christianity in its fifteenth-century 'renewal' was not in some sort of complicity, theologically, with the emergent new order, it tended to build a wall around itself, to conserve its tradition and institutional existence – namely, as the Catholic Church. With the old order disintegrating under the impact of historical events, it is perhaps not surprising that Catholic theologians, too 'focused exclusively on human history' (and almost wholly from the Fall and Redemption perspective of Augustinianism), and so the spiritual tradition 'abandoned any real wrestling with the mystery of creation' (McDonagh 1986: 108). Moreover, as McDonagh puts it, 'the understanding of salvation tended to reject the world of nature and concentrate on redeeming people and very often just the soul, *from* the natural world' (McDonagh 1986: 108). In this light, Christianity's 'contribution' to the contemporary ecological crisis is certainly not negligible even if it is mostly roundabout, diffuse and not conscious or purposive. One other factor that should also not be overlooked is the failings of the Church as an institution leading up to the turning point of the fifteenth century: how it had become excessively worldly, too, many – though by no means all – of its 'servants' being preoccupied with matters of state, of power, of wealth and with conserving in effect its temporal position (even if this sometimes took *apparently* religious forms, as graphically shown in Umberto Eco's *Name of the Rose*).

CHRISTIAN BELIEF AND NATURE

However, neither 'complicity' nor 'withdrawal', as these bear on the degradation of abuse of nature (non-human and human), has been accepted as inherent in Christianity, notwithstanding such critiques as Lynn White's, or *Time*'s broadside of 2 January 1989.[5] Since the late 1960s, at least, theologians have been returning in growing numbers and seriousness to the 'creation' theme and, more significantly, in practice so have the churches. 'Creation' is the preferred concept for its evident theological content, but it encompasses what is generally referred to as 'nature' (when this is taken to include humans) or 'bio-physical environment' or 'global ecosystem' – except that it also comprises the whole cosmos or universe.

One of the first aspects of the eruption of creation theologizing in the 1970s, and especially the 1980s, was the clarification of the medieval contribution. In this, Christianity had a stance less negligent of the natural world. St Thomas Aquinas, as the leading theologian of the period, had a major interest in the cosmological dimension. He undertook a comprehensive synthesis which situated Christian belief and thought in relation to the main elements in European cultural attainment in his epoch – his Christianity was not to be closed in on itself, in a sort of hot-house of religiosity. His cosmology and natural theology (what nature revealed of God's order) was based on the biblical account, notably of Genesis, interpreted through Aristotelian categories. He emphasized that natural diversity was to be valued as 'the manifestation of divine goodness', so that 'the whole universe participates in the divine goodness . . . and represents it better than any single creature whatever' (see McDade 1990: 434–5).

Aquinas certainly propounded a hierarchical view of the cosmos, expressed in terms of the Platonic idea of a 'Chain of Being', in which human beings (and in particular, men) were placed only a 'little lower than the angels' and the rest of creation was thus subordinate to them. But all was seen in stable, unchanging terms and man was not encouraged to adopt an interventionist, exploitative approach to nature. Indeed, according to Edward Echlin, 'It is partly through Aquinas that Christians have preserved a sense of God's abiding presence in creation' (Echlin 1989: 10). The special rational faculty of humans was to be used primarily for pursuing theological and spiritual understanding and illumination. In fact, this view had been largely held by St Augustine. Although much more preoccupied with the 'fallenness' of nature, especially human nature, and thus the need for a theology of personal salvation, he considered that the natural order was to be understood as God's 'great book written without ink', so that it had 'a derived dignity as the handiwork or art of God' (Ayers 1986: 157). When account is also taken of St Francis of Assisi – whom Lynn White, indeed, excepted from his strictures on the anti-environmentalism of Christianity – and Ignatius Loyola,[6] the influential founder of the Jesuits, then the basis emerges for the assertion of the 'Man and Nature' report of the Church of England (the first such collective Church response, it seems) that 'Much of the older religious and meta-physical thought of Europe was as . . . contemplative in its emphasis as Indian thought' (Montefiore 1975: 7) – that is, it scarcely provided a significant attitudinal basis for the modern western-led assault on the environment.

Nevertheless, as we have seen, there are certain question marks about Christianity's position which are bound to remain. Of course, the main thrust of its accusers is usually based on the creation story in Genesis; thus Ian McHarg has referred to Genesis's injunction to 'have dominion' and 'subdue' the earth as a 'declaration of war on nature' (see General Synod 1986: 21). Before exploring this aspect, which has been a principal focus of resurgent creation theology in the past 15 to 20 years, it is worth mentioning the distinction that has been drawn between western and eastern Christianity. This may be of greater significance now in the light of political developments in Eastern Europe (not least given the role of the Orthodox Church in the World Council of Churches, whose important contribution to the reorientation to creation criteria is considered later). It can be said that, at an early stage, 'among the Western Fathers a more rational understanding of creation supplanted the mystical one of the Eastern Fathers' (McDonagh 1990: 167). It is this, it has been strongly argued by Philip Sherrard (1987), that opened the way for the emergence of modern science – and also for the loss of an essential dimension of spirituality and religious culture. Notwithstanding the significance attached to creation and nature by Augustine and more especially

Aquinas, it is held that they prepared the ground for the desanctification of nature integral to modern science and technology.

The characteristics of post-Cartesian science – notably nature viewed as a self-contained entity deprived of all qualitative elements, 'as so much dead stuff' (Sherrard 1987: 99) – were implicit in the western Christian theological matrix in which the sacramental quality of nature became very largely obscured. By sacramental, it is meant here that creation is the self-expression of the Divine, in which there is an integration (though not fusion) of the material and spiritual,[7] involving a unity in diversity. God does not act simply on nature from without, and certainly not once and for all, but is active within it (in terms of the Christian doctrine of the Trinity, as Holy Spirit). This theology, with its 'cosmic' dimension of God incarnate in human and created existence, was that of the early Greek Church but has continued down to the present day as a major element in the Orthodox tradition.

A first shift away from this came notably with Augustine. For him the need for grace was paramount and only came as God's gift, as an addition. Creatures, including humans, did not participate intrinsically in divine grace; there was no 'divine light' within, no inner spiritual potentiality, and created things/beings remained separate from God. In fact, with sin (the Fall) creatures did not have the possibility of even extrinsic participation in grace, and salvation could only be communicated through the Church (as Christ's earthly body). A radical separation thus emerged of the sacred from the profane or secular, defined as every being/thing outside the Church or in nature, deprived of grace and incurably corrupt, in which the activity of the Spirit was denied.

Against this Augustinian background, Aquinas sought to 'save' nature, understood now in the Aristotelian sense of physical reality. However, the idea of separation between the natural and the spiritual spheres was so deeply embedded that the way he proceeded to free nature from its Augustinian state of corruption was in effect to dissociate it from theological evaluation. He envisaged that there was 'a double order in things' (Sherrard 1987: 107), in which nature needed no grace because it followed its own inherent laws and was efficacious in this respect (whereas in the spiritual/religious realm, of primary concern to humans, grace was paramount). Indeed, in addition to autonomy, these laws were characterized by rationality, and man shared in them through his reasoning faculties, which thus also had a status of their own unrelated to any spiritual element or source (the autonomy of reason was thereby affirmed). God appeared in relation to nature as the author and, while his 'signature' could be discerned in nature by applying the rational faculties to it through observation, he was no longer considered as immanently present in it.

In effect, Aquinas did probably help to preserve a certain sense of God's presence in nature – namely, its intrinsic goodness or merit. Moreover, he kept reason in its place by maintaining that its conclusions must ultimately conform to those of faith, since God was the supremely rational being.

MICHAEL WATSON AND DAVID SHARPE

However, for A. N. Whitehead (1953: 18) the insistence on the rationality of God and nature lay at the origin of the development of modern science, and, it may be said, determined its course. According to Sherrard, Aquinas was led into this 'insistence' by his adoption of Aristotelian categorical and abstract thinking. Theology thus moved away from being 'regarded as the expression of a given reality which had to be confirmed in actual personal experience', notably 'through a life of prayer and contemplation' (Sherrard 1987: 48–9). Aquinas himself maintained a delicate balance between nature conceived as an integral part of the divine order and nature conceived as a self-contained entity, autonomous and operating according to its own laws and premises: a balance that proved too precarious to survive long. With the conceptions of the spiritual and natural spheres having been completely divorced as distinct and separate categories in line with Aristotelian logic,[8] they increasingly drifted apart and tended to move into opposition. Contemporary recognition of the significance of this for the ecological crisis has led to a growing concern for their reconciliation. This has, indeed, been looked for in terms of a 'new consciousness in science and religion' (Schilling 1973). From the Christian side, a major forerunner has been Teilhard de Chardin, though amongst both believers and scientists his ideas have been controversial.

Following Aquinas, the tension between soul and body arising from his Aristotelian-inspired dualism was resolved in favour of the soul as the only reality for religion (thus western Christianity's overriding task was the saving of souls), with desanctified matter as the only reality for post-Cartesian science (matter as mechanism, including human 'matter', and therefore available for manipulation). At the root of this was the pre-eminence given to a certain logical rationality in Greek philosophy, especially when as with Aristotelianism it was to move from having a purely 'contemplative' to include an 'applied' status and purpose. A crucial and related problem with practical consequences in western Christianity's theology, in the wake of Augustine and Aquinas, concerns an incomplete doctrine of the Holy Spirit, or put in different but overlapping terms, 'Christomonism' (Tinker 1989). The result has been a downgrading of concern for and importance of creation in the Church. Moreover, it has led to a ready acceptance amongst Christians of the modern scientific view (Cartesian) of nature.

The dominant theological paradigm in the post-medieval west, as George Tinker sums it up, '*begins* with "God's reconciling act in Christ Jesus" [which] violates the traditional Trinitarian confession of Christianity and hence tones down the significance of doctrines of creation' (Tinker 1989: 530). In effect, the Spirit is not considered an equal in the Trinity, but only as active through Christ and its presence dependent on the saving grace of Christ, which only human beings are regarded as capable of receiving (through faith, or faith and works). The special difficulty with such a formulation, from a creation viewpoint, is its exclusivity. While theologically Christ's grace may be seen as necessary for human wholeness, it is clearly not sufficient in the above sense for creation in its entirety. Sherrard states: 'The "cosmic" significance of

221

Pentecost in which the revelation of the Father and Son is consummated in that of the Spirit, was attenuated' in western Christendom (Sherrard 1987: 111).

This deficiency in the doctrine of the Holy Spirit, unlike in the Orthodox Church,[9] vitiated any sacramental regard for nature by obstructing recognition of the continuing activity of the Spirit in nature or of any real participation of nature in the divine. Instead, creation became simply an originating divine act complete in itself (in some sense); so God is always wholly outside it, other than in Israel's history and then, supremely for all people, in his incarnation in Christ; hence theology's focus is on human history abstracted from the rest of creation. There is, too, a sense – eschatological – in which *that* history alone is developing and progressive while nature in itself is not. Undoubtedly this theology has been an important element, if in subterranean fashion, in the development of modern western political and social ideologies with their similar focus.

THE CREATION ACCOUNT

The crucial theological question from an ecological perspective is not whether there was an original divine act of creation culminating in humanity, but whether God's interest in creation is continuing, notably through the presence of the divine spirit 'in all things'. If the latter is not the case, then it appears that humanity has been left, as it were, to 'take up the running' and therefore do what it wills with nature without divine concern (whilst the need for humanity's redemption to 'enter heaven', or the kingdom,[10] is recognized). At the extreme this leads to apocalyptic visions of the 'end of the world', when some humans are 'saved'. Another way of putting this might be to ask whether divine providence concerns only humans or creation as a whole. What is at stake here is the religious basis for humanity's attitude to and relationship with the rest of creation. Does it allow or even support, in a direct way, an exploitative and manipulative practice? In this respect the creation 'story' in the Bible and how it is told are clearly of central significance, as Lynn White recognized. Not least, it shapes the Church's approach to ecological issues.

At least in the west the biblical creation account has been seen, and been used (not necessarily by Christians), as a justification for an anthropocentrism setting man apart from (not to say arrogant towards) nature, and for reducing non-human nature simply to a human utility ripe for unlimited exploitation to meet our material wants. However, in recent decades theologians, the churches, and lay Christians have increasingly returned – as a result of the development of scientific knowledge (biological and ecological notably) and/or the spur of environmental issues – to a thorough re-examination of the Bible from a creation perspective. In general the 'justification' for treating nature as at humanity's disposal to do with just as it pleases, has been considered to rest on a partial or faulty understanding.[11] To consider, then, the major points made concerning the Genesis account. In the first place, creation is God's and humans are simply a part of it. Nature is seen as a whole, interdependent in its

MICHAEL WATSON AND DAVID SHARPE

basic diversity and variety. Human beings, like other creatures, are created 'out of the earth'. The most ecologically contentious concepts, however, are those of human beings created in God's image and being given dominion over the earth along with the injunction to fill, replenish and subdue it.

In respect, first, of the 'image' characteristic, the contemporary consensus is that while this attributes special qualities and potentialities to humans, these go with special responsibilities. While there is an anthropocentrism inherent in humanity's privileged position in relation to the rest of nature, it is not undiluted. Above all, it is constrained by the belief, strongly affirmed at the World Council of Churches' 1990 World Convocation on Justice, Peace and the Integrity of Creation (JPIC), 'that the earth is the Lord's'. What 'image' indicates is humanity's particular calling 'in reflecting God's creating and sustaining love' (WCC 1990b: 18–19). So the Christian view is, more properly, theocentric. This means, moreover, that any 'claim to the possession and mastery of the world', on the part of human beings, is 'idolatrous' (WCC 1990a: 20). It has to be remembered, too, that the human being is formed from the earth and is thus placed in a similar category to other creatures: a common dependence on the earth is indicated, and an original vegetarianism is proclaimed.

There is substantial agreement that the 'image' attribute places humanity, in the tradition of royal language to which it was related in those biblical times, in a viceregal relationship to God. Following from this, 'there is an essential link between the "image" and the charge to rule (dominion) over other creatures': it signifies rule 'understood to be exercised under responsibility' to God, and therefore according to God's 'justice, mercy and true concern for the welfare of all' (Murray 1990: 425–6). This seems to agree with the conclusion of the WCC's major consultation in 1988 on the creation theme, that 'dominion refers specifically to the task of upholding God's purposes in creation rather than imposing humanity's self-serving ends'.[12] The paradigmatic, or ideal, picture of this put into practice in Genesis is in humanity's role in the Garden of Eden, to tend and keep it.

STEWARDSHIP AND DEVELOPMENT

Humanity's position is thus not seen as one of passivity in the face of a natural determinism. The Bible's symbolism of garden and gardening is of considerable significance in this respect. A later exemplification of this could be seen in the Benedictine approach to non-human nature. René Dubos (1976: ch. 8), for one, preferred this to the Franciscan position, which was too contemplative to live up to the notion of stewardship (which he saw as necessary for human well-being, in a rounded sense). In fact, stewardship is today the generally accepted understanding within Christianity, put in a more modern guise, of the role given to humanity in creation, in its relations with the rest of nature. This can be interpreted as co-worker with God in creation, but in no sense as co-equal. For it signifies that humanity's position is that it is tenant and not owner, that it holds the earth in trust, for God and for the rest of creation, present and to come. Thus, besides the interdependence inherent in all creation and therefore affecting humanity, there is an important sense in which it is accountable for its activity.

The emphasis on the limitations which stewardship implies is further reinforced by biblical teaching as to human fallibility; this is seen in the effects of reaching for divine status in Eden and at Babel. Knowledge and technological prowess represent temptations to human deification, which itself leads to disaster, including at the Fall for nature as a whole, since humanity's proper, responsible role is abandoned. In this light, the Promethean myth associated with much of modern scientific, technological and industrial development, and with modern political ideologies, is a poor guide and inspiration – Prometheans should remember what happened to Prometheus. The most recent papal encyclical dealing with these matters (Holy See 1988) sees development in a non-Promethean manner, in which stewardship concerns are a key element; for otherwise, 'nature rebels against [humanity] and no longer recognises [it] as its "master" '. D. J. Hall (1985) goes rather further in noting, from Isaiah, that as stewards of creation, rather than masters/ possessors or slaves, humans are 'neither ultimately authoritative nor irreplaceable'. The steward's concern is with creation in terms of 'wholeness' and 'holiness' – 'there is a wholeness of holiness' – involving the matter of 'our relationship to God, to our neighbour and to planet earth'. Five principles to guide practical stewardship are enunciated: responsibility for the whole earth; solidarity of all people[13] (ecumenism in religion); the community basis for stewardship, with stress on the individual's role as a participant; ecological criteria; disassociation from capitalism (first, a critique of philanthropy; second, more politically, of the dominant economic order); and taking the longer view.[14]

Stewardship involves responsibility as a central element in human relations with nature; if these are not seen as being based on mutual interdependence, then waste and degradation of resources become likely (Church of Scotland 1987: 101). Thus humanity 'filling' the earth has to take cognizance of its ecological capacity in the long run and does not mean over-filling it to the detriment of other species. The WCC World Convocation emphasized the meaning of 'replenish' as including the need to 'release the earth to regularly replenish its life-giving power' (WCC 1989: 2). This relates to the Sabbath concept, which applies to every seventh year as well as day; and it is also associated with the biblical provision for a Jubilee Year every fiftieth year, when it was re-affirmed that ownership was God's and humans were tenants of the land who should not therefore acquire it as a possession indefinitely – so in that year land that was not yours fifty years previously had to be given up and you had a right as 'tenant' simply to the land that you worked personally. All these ideas are linked to the recognition that stewardship calls for a different sort of development to that narrowly identified with economic growth based on giving overriding priority to capital accumulation (whether private or public).

The Church of Scotland has underlined that 'the pinnacle of creation in Genesis was not the making of man, but the day God rested, when all creation was living together' (Church of Scotland 1987: 5). There is concern that instrumental value needs to be strongly counterbalanced by commitment to the importance of inherent and intrinsic values in our attitude to nature (the value it has to us, notably aesthetic, as it is, and the value it has in itself independent of human views of its use or beauty). Indeed, it seems the Church should emphasize the latter in that in post-medieval western Christianity 'a recurrent theme has been that nature exists for the benefit of humanity' (Church of Scotland 1987: 3). The earlier Anglican report concluded that this was biblically incorrect: creation 'exists for God's glory', which is what gives it a meaning and worth beyond that seen from a human point of view; thus to believe that it exists 'solely for man's use and pleasure is a mark of folly' (Montefiore 1975: 67). In this light, stewardship would be debased if it were considered to any extent as 'management' – at least in the business sense.

Other major characteristics of human relationships with the rest of nature in Christian thought are trusteeship (or custodianship) and companionship; the former emphasizes conservation, the latter 'being in this together' and sharing space through time (Church of Scotland 1987: 11–13). These need to be included within stewardship as integral aspects of it in order to produce 'a balanced relationship with what is not human' (Church of Scotland 1987: 13) and to enable all three values of nature to be served in varying degrees as appropriate – for example, in rich countries the emphasis would be on custodial, non-developmental stewardship; in poor countries on the responsible development of resource use as required to raise living standards on a long-term basis. So the Benedictine model does not exclude the Franciscan one and vice versa.

There is thus general agreement among mainstream Church leaders and activists that a crucial requirement in overcoming the environmental crisis is a reformulation of what development involves. The Brundtland Report's approach is widely referred to – and Gro Brundtland played a leading part in the WCC's 'Integrity of Creation, an Ecumenical Discussion' in 1988 – but more is called for, notably in the sense of a stewardship of caring for creation's ecological integrity. This means, above all, subjecting the development process to a moral understanding, which starts from the fact that

> side-by-side with the miseries of underdevelopment, themselves unacceptable, we find ourselves up against a form of super-development, equally inadmissible . . . which consists in an excessive availability of every kind of material good for the benefit of certain social groups, [and] easily makes people slaves of 'possession' and of immediate gratification.[15]
>
> (Holy See 1988: 48)

Development limited only to its economic element is thus viewed as a demonstrable failure and in particular as not serving solidarity and respect for the inherent dignity of human beings and the rest of creation; it has produced a contradiction between 'having' and 'being' which is incompatible with the meaning of development. In contrast, development with a moral character, whilst certainly looking to a proper, sustainable material provision, seeks beyond that to take account of the role of culture, religion, community (social and political), the good earth, and, altogether, the web of relationships central to the fullness of existence.[16] Powerful obstacles stand in the way, as the WCC and Catholic Church both recognize. These are the biblical 'principalities and powers' thwarting the full advent of God's kingdom. They exist certainly in personal sin, but today are consolidated and embedded in institutionalized 'structures of sin' (Holy See 1988: 69ff, WCC 1988: 3.2, WCC 1990a: 16–19). In the face of these structures, the way forward is seen first and foremost in the solidarity of, and with, the oppressed and deprived. In this the churches are called to play their part – corporately, educationally and politically – as symbolized by the phrase adopted by both the Catholic Church and the World Council of Churches: 'the preferential option for the poor'. Justice, Peace and the Integrity of Creation is the mobilizing theme.

NOTES

1 The term 'green' is used in this chapter in the sense established by Andrew Dobson (1990) in *Green Political Thought*, as synonymous with the radical ideology of ecologism (as opposed to the broader and vaguer 'environmentalism').

2 See, for example, the work of Barry Commoner and Paul and Anne Ehrlich.

3 Some people were already aware of this. Lynn White, Jun.'s influential essay, 'The Historical Roots of Our Ecologic Crisis', first appeared in the journal *Science*, in March 1967.

4 In *Green Political Thought*, Andrew Dobson refers to approximately a dozen distinguishing characteristics of the western industrial way of life that have been put forward as causes of the present predicament.

5 'Thus the spread of Christianity, which is generally considered to have paved the way for the development of technology, may at the same time have carried the seeds of the wanton exploitation of nature that often accompanied technical progress' (*Time*, 2 January 1989; reproduced in Osborn 1990: 7).

6 On Loyola's belief about creation, see E. Echlin (1989: 11); Sophie Jakowska also comments: 'Loyola viewed the world in a somewhat Franciscan tradition, seeing God in all things', in Hargrove (1986: 131).

7 Thus 'the difference between the activity of the Spirit in nature and the activity of the Spirit outside [it] is one of degree only, not of kind' (Sherrard 1987: 93).

8 Aquinas accepted the Aristotelian conception of form and matter as primary substances, and therefore as completely separate and self-contained categories of existence. He located God as the principle of form, so matter had to be understood as outside God, its 'being' reduced to a potentiality to receive form. By its finitude, nature clearly shared in matter and was thus necessarily excluded from any divine quality (hence it was desanctified).

9 In eastern Christianity, the Spirit is considered the 'Creator of life', issuing from God and constantly involved in perfecting creation (WCC 1989: 6.1).

10 'The kingdom' can be taken to refer to a collective earthly existence, in which God's justice, peace and love, as manifested in Christ, govern human affairs – but in respect of which there is often little consideration given to non-human nature.

11 A range of major sources illustrating this include the World Council of Churches

documentation and reports on *Justice, Peace and the Integrity of Creation*; Roman Catholic encyclicals (esp. that of 1988), pastoral letters, Justice and Peace and development agency reports (for example, CAFOD in the UK); *Faith in the Environment, Peace Beyond Conflict*, and *Adfent* (May 1990), of the Church in Wales; *JPIC: A Call to Christians*, the Council of Churches for Wales; *Our Responsibility for the Living Environment*, and *Man and Nature: The Report*, of the Church of England; *JPIC: First Things First*, British Council of Churches/Christian Aid; *While Earth Endures*, Scottish Churches Council; *Making Peace with the Planet*, Methodist Church; *Survival or Extinction*, St George's House, Windsor; *Peace with Justice for the Whole Creation*, Official Report of the Basel Assembly, Conference of European Churches.

12 Fifty representatives from the Orthodox, Protestant, and Roman Catholic Churches from all parts of the world were there, including Christian indigenous people, as well as a number of Buddhists, Hindus, Jews, Muslims and Sikhs (WCC 1988: ch. 3.2).

13 This is also stressed in the papal encyclical *Sollicitudo Rei Socialis* including the 'preferential option for the poor' (Holy See 1988: 75ff, 84–7).

14 *Sollicitudo Rei Socialis* also insists that the Church's social doctrine is not 'a third way' between liberalism and collectivism but constitutes a category of its own (Holy See 1988: 83ff).

15 This is associated with 'one of the greatest injustices . . . [that] of the poor distribution of the goods and services originally intended for all' (Holy See 1988: 50). The Catholic view is that there is close connection between the development and ecological crises (see Davies 1990).

16 'Development which is not only economic but must be measured and oriented according to the reality and vocation of man seen in his totality' (Holy See 1988: 51).

BIBLIOGRAPHY

Ayers, R. H. (1986) 'Christian realism and environmental ethics', in E. C. Hargrove (ed.), *Religion and Environmental Crisis*, Athens, Ga.: University of Georgia Press.

Barbour, I. G. (ed.) (1973) *Western Man and Environmental Ethics*, Reading, Mass.: Addison-Wesley.

Church of Scotland (1987) 'While the earth endures', *Report on the Theological and Ethical Considerations of Responsible Land Use*, St Andrews: Quorum Press.

Davies, B. (1990) 'Renewing the earth: ecology and justice', *The Month*, November: 467–72.

Dobson, A. (1990) *Green Political Thought*, London: Unwin Hyman.

Dubos, R. (1973) 'A theology of the earth', in I. G. Barbour (ed.), *Western Man and Environmental Ethics*, Reading, Mass.: Addison-Wesley.

—— (1976) *A God Within*, London: Abacus.

Echlin, E. (1989) *The Christian Green Heritage*, Nottingham: Grove Books.

General Synod of the Church of England (1986) *Our Responsibility for the Living Environment*, London: Church House Publishing.

Goldsmith, E. (1977) *A Blueprint for Survival*, Harmondsworth: Penguin Books.

Goldsmith, M. M. (1985) *Private Vices and Public Benefits*, Cambridge: Cambridge University Press.

Hall, D. J. (1985) *The Steward: A Biblical Symbol Comes of Age*. Abridged for the Anglican Diocese of Oxford, Hinksey: Church House.

Hargrove, E. C. (ed.) (1986) *Religion and Environmental Crisis*, Athens, Ga.: University of Georgia Press.

Holy See (1988) *Sollicitudo Rei Socialis*, London: Catholic Truth Society.

McDade, J. (1990) 'Creation and salvation: green faith and Christian themes', *The Month*, November.

McDonagh, S. (1986) *To Care for the Earth*, London: Geoffrey Chapman.
—— (1990) *The Greening of the Church*, London: Geoffrey Chapman.
Macfarlane, A. (1978) *Origins of English Individualism*, Oxford: Oxford University Press.
—— (1987) *The Culture of Capitalism*, Oxford: Oxford University Press.
McHarg, I. (1973) 'The place of nature in the city of man', in I. G. Barbour (ed.), *Western Man and Environmental Ethics*, Reading, Mass.: Addison-Wesley.
Meadows, D. H., Meadows, D. L., Randers, J. and Behrens, W. (1972) *The Limits to Growth*, New York: Universe Books.
Moncrief, L. W. (1973) 'The cultural basis of our environmental crisis', in I. G. Barbour (ed.), *Western Man and Environmental Ethics*, Reading, Mass.: Addison-Wesley.
Montefiore, H. (1975), *Man and Nature*, London: Collins.
Murray, R. (1990) 'The relationship of creatures within the cosmic covenant', *The Month*, November.
Ophuls, W. (1977) *Ecology and the Politics of Scarcity*, San Francisco: W. H. Freeman.
Osborn, L. (1990) *Stewards of Creation*, Oxford: Latimer House.
Pepper, D. (1989) *The Roots of Modern Environmentalism*, London: Routledge.
Porritt, J. (1985) *The Green Movement: Making Whole*, London: Lucis Press.
Schilling, H. K. (1973) *The New Consciousness in Science and Religion*, London: SCM Press.
Sherrard, P. (1987) *The Eclipse of Man and Nature*, West Stockbridge, Mass.: Lindisfarne Press.
Tinker, G. E. (1989) 'The integrity of creation', *The Ecumenical Review*, October.
White, L., Jun. (1967) 'The historical roots of our ecologic crisis', *Science*, March; also reproduced in I. G. Barbour (ed.), *Western Man and Environmental Ethics*, Reading, Mass.: Addison-Wesley.
—— (1973) 'Continuing the conversation', in I. G. Barbour (ed.), *Western Man and Environmental Ethics*, Reading, Mass.: Addison-Wesley.
Whitehead, A. N. (1953) *Science and the Modern World*, Cambridge: Cambridge University Press.
WCC (World Council of Churches) (1988) 'Integrity of creation, an ecumenical discussion', *JPIC Resource Materials* 3.2, Geneva.
—— (1989) 'Orthodox perspectives on creation', *JPIC Resource Materials* 6.1, Geneva.
—— (1990a) 'Between the Flood and the Rainbow', *JPIC World Convocation Documentation*, Geneva.
—— (1990b) 'Now is the time', *JPIC World Convocation Final Document*, Geneva.

AFTERWORD[1]

In their introduction to *The Nature of Political Theory*, David Miller and Larry Siedentop write that one of the most striking features of political theory since the 1930s has been, 'the absence of any major *new* ideology' and, apparently as a partial consequence, 'the extent to which disputes about values and concepts could still be placed within a framework of inherited ideologies – notably, Conservatism, Liberalism and Socialism, which had been bequeathed to the twentieth century by the nineteenth' (Miller and Siedentop 1983: 4). To the extent that this was true at all then (and one wonders why feminism gets no mention), it is certainly not true today, for there exists a political ideology whose prescriptions and propositions cannot wholly be spoken in the language of the three ideologies Miller and Siedentop mention. The ideology is ecologism. Entire books are being devoted to it (Dobson 1990, Atkinson 1991, Dickens 1992, Eckersley 1992, Goodin 1992), and editors and writers of new textbooks on political ideologies see themselves as increasingly obliged to include a chapter on it (Ball and Daggar 1991, Heywood 1992, Macridis 1992, Vincent 1992).

But while ecologism might fulfil the three criteria normally set out for a collection of ideas to comprise a political *ideology* (that is, an analysis of political reality, a picture of the Good Life, and a theory of political action or strategy), can we say that the green perspective sheds new light on the territory occupied by political *theory*, properly speaking? In other words, can we say that green concerns lead us to reflect on the standard themes of political theory in particular ways and for particular – that is, green, rather than socialist, liberal and conservative – reasons? In anticipation of what follows, I shall suggest that the answer to this question is 'yes', and that the consequences cover much wider swathes of the study of political theory than might be suspected.

Specifically, I shall argue that green concerns influence three important areas of political theory, and that once it is accepted that they do, then a new field of enquiry with its own particular problems is opened up: green political theory itself.

The first area concerns two related questions: what can we legitimately consider to be sites of political activity? and who or what should we include in the list of members of the political community? As for the first question, some theories of politics have a narrow conception of politics, while others draw the boundaries much wider. As David Held points out in his introduction to *Political Theory Today*, the whole question of what to include in the realm of the political has usually arisen on the basis of critiques of the narrow liberal conception of politics as an arena distinct from, say, economy or culture. As Held notes, Marxism, for example, argues that, 'The key source of contemporary power – private ownership of the means of production – is . . . ostensibly *depoliticized* by liberalism' by viewing the economic realm as a non-political one (Held 1983: 5). On this reading, Marxism demands a widening of the frame of reference of the 'political' to encompass areas of public life refused the title by other theoretical perspectives.

Similarly, some strands of feminism take liberalism (and Marxism itself) to task for being too narrow in its conception of the political. The feminist proposition that the 'personal is political' amounts to an argument that the nature of one's personal life is 'structured by relations of power' (Phillips 1991: 92) and so, since politics is about power, the personal is unequivocally a political arena. So both feminists and Marxists, in their different ways, seek to widen the scope of the political, and they may even argue that these previously depoliticized areas are in fact the unsung sources of capitalist and patriarchal power, respectively. In this sense, depoliticization has an ideological function.

Green theory spreads 'the political' by arguing that the natural world – normally 'invisible' to political theory – affects, and is affected by, political decisions in a way which makes it necessary to consider it a site of political activity. Economists have been among the first to recognize the implications of this for their work by arguing that the environment can no longer sustainably be viewed as a free good, and must rather be taken into account (by pricing or some other mechanism) when economic decisions are made (see Dietz and van der Straaten, Ch. 7 this volume). This is a direct consequence of making visible what was previously invisible. The nature of the 'political', then, is a proper and contested subject for political theorists, and it is the first area of political theory to which green theory contributes in a novel way.

For green politics makes two simultaneous moves, both of which are relevant to its effect on political theory. First, it brings the non-human natural world to the foreground of our concerns, and second, it decentres the human being. It is the first move that is important in the context of the reach of the political. Once the non-human natural world is brought into the public arena as a legitimate context of debate, it and its constituent parts become potential members of the political community in the sense of potential recipients (for example) of distributive justice (see Wissenburg, Ch. 1 this volume). So we need to ask the same questions of these new members of the community that we ask of more established ones. We need to ask, for example, what our proper relationship with them should be, what rights they might have, what duties we might have towards them, and so on.

Green politics, then, brings the non-human natural world to our attention in such a way that it appears both to be a site of political activity, mostly invisible to other traditions, and a source of new members for the political community. In the same way in which our personal lives are political for feminism, and our economic lives are political for Marxism, so our dealings with the natural world have a political dimension for ecologism. In this respect, green politics makes an original contribution to a fundamental theme of political theory: the question of 'the scope of politics as a practical activity' (Held 1983: 7).

In a similar context, David Held remarks that political theory and its concerns have traditionally been located in the nation-state, such that 'concepts of the political good have been elaborated at the level of state institutions and practices' (Held 1983: 8). He believes that this focus is becoming increasingly inadequate in view of 'the growth of complex interconnections and interrelations between states and societies' – a phenomenon he refers to as 'globalization' (Held 1983: 9). The onus is on political theorists, he argues, to 'theorize the changing form of the modern polity in its global setting' (Held 1983: 9).

Green politics makes the need even more pressing, and particularly if we define globalization as Held, following Anthony Giddens, does: 'the intensification of worldwide social relations which link distant localities in such a way that local happenings are shaped by events occurring many miles away and vice versa' (Held 1983: 9). There is a clear sense in which the global linkages that Held wants theorized and taken into account are not only 'social' but ever more obviously ecological. In other words, ecological constraints comprise an important element of the conditions under which not only national but international politics are made, and therefore will need to be taken into account in any putative theorizing about 'globalization'.

The second area of political theory that green politics affects is the study of concepts such as rights, duties, legitimacy, freedom, equality, power, autonomy and democracy. More particularly, the green frame of reference helps to put a certain 'spin' on these concepts (although this is contentious: see Saward (Ch. 4) and Wissenburg (Ch. 1), this volume). For example, concomitant with the extended reach of politics, green theory suggests that we need to think about the rights not just of members of present populations but those of future generations too. Further, it suggests that we need to deploy the concept beyond the human context to that of animals and even non-sentient nature. Just how this should be done is not an issue here and is, properly speaking, a subject for green political (or, at least, ethical) theory (see Benton, Ch. 9 this volume). Yet our thoughts about rights are affected by the green agenda, and to this extent that agenda has a particular bearing on an important area of political theory.

Similarly, the decentring of the human being to which I referred earlier apparently has the effect of stressing our duties over our rights. The existence of values that transcend the individual has always had the effect of displacing rights in favour of duties (for example, in the context of nationalism), and green politics is no different. The obligation to preserve natural variety (for

231

example) might lead us to forgo any number of rights – to travel when, how, and where we will, for example – and the general tenor of this perspective is to demand that the exercise of rights be justified in the face of apparently overriding obligations.

Indeed, in general, in the face both of the urgency and the scale implied by the green analysis of our environmental predicament, the legitimacy of political decisions might be judged more in the light of their consequences than the way they are reached. Green theory seems so inexorably driven towards an end-oriented theory of the good (Goodin 1992) that it is, precisely, a problem internal to green political theory as to how the means can be made to matter in a way that most Greens want. Once again, then, the green perspective raises particular questions about political-theoretical concepts such as democracy (see Saward (Ch. 4) and Achterberg (Ch. 5), this volume). Similar remarks could be made about power, freedom, autonomy and equality (for example) and all this is enough to indicate the way in which green politics and its concerns influence the second area of political theory to which I wanted to refer.

The third area relates to what is normally referred to as the history of political thought – that is, the study of political theorists themselves. Ecologism will affect this in either or both of two ways: first, by bringing previously buried political theorists to our attention, and second, by forcing us to reassess the work of canonical theorists such as Hobbes, Locke, Rousseau and Marx (see, for example, Grundmann 1991). Both these effects have a precedent in what feminism has done to the study of the history of political thought. Feminism has brought to our attention previously marginalized theorists, such as Mary Wollstonecraft and Harriet Taylor, and simultaneously revealed unsuspected dimensions in the thought of canonical theorists (see, for example, Pateman 1989).

As far as the latter is concerned, one study might involve an examination of the way in which theorists have deployed the natural world in such a way as to create or reinforce certain views about human relations. In this way the natural world is seen to have performed an ideological role, functional for the production and reproduction of power relations. It is well known, for example, that women have been closely associated with the natural world throughout history (see Evans, Ch. 10 this volume). It might emerge that (some) theorists have taken the already subordinate position of the natural world and used women's association with nature to legitimate and deepen their subordination with respect to men. This kind of study would be a direct consequence of ecologism's making visible the non-human natural world and having us take account of it in an explicit way in our studies of political thought.

Similarly, the ecological perspective might enable us to take alternative views on the adequacy of the work of political theorists. Following the introduction of the non-human natural world to the political arena, we need to take account of it in our deliberations. Increasingly we will encounter theoretical assumptions which create blind-spots that disable the natural world. Robyn Eckersley, for example, has suggested that Jurgen Habermas is 'unable to work the interests of nonhumans into his theory in any theoretically meaningful way because his theory is grounded in *human* speech acts' (Eckersley 1990: 760). This assessment – while itself debatable (see Lucardie, Ch. 2 this volume) – would not have been possible without the grounding provided by the ecological point of view.

Once again, then, green politics can be seen as enriching an area of political-theoretical endeavour. Remarks made earlier suggest that it does so, too, in the context both of questions as to the nature and reach of the political, and considerations of standard political-theoretical concepts. If all this is right, then ecologism can be mobilized to make an impact on the study of political theory. Any one of the areas of study mentioned above could constitute a programme for research – indeed they already do, as the chapters in this volume testify.

A number of questions remain, however. One, briefly, concerns an area of political theory to which I think ecologism is unlikely to make a contribution. Ecologism as such cannot address the twin issues of the nature of political theory, on the one hand, and how to go about it, on the other. In other words, it is unlikely that the ecological perspective can help resolve difficulties over what makes (say) political theory distinct from political philosophy, nor whether we should best go about it by rigorously contextualizing political concepts, like Quentin Skinner, or refusing the possibility of such rigour, like William Connolly. These are arguments internal to political theory which might be affected by some politically informed perspectives (such as Marxism), but which seem mostly unaffected by ecologism.

Another question concerns green political theory itself. I have already said that the green influence on the areas of political theory outlined above suggests that there are issues internal to green theory that need pursuing. I have referred, for example, to the need to develop a green theory of value, and the associated discussion as to whether particular political forms and strategies can be 'read off' from it (see Goodin, 1992). Greens might subscribe to a particular normative version of democracy, for example, but do they do so for reasons that can be derived from green principles or is such support imported from other political traditions? Similarly, Robyn Eckersley's contention that a 'lasting solution to the ecological crisis must include a shift from an anthropocentric to an ecocentric orientation towards the world' (Eckersley 1990: 740) needs further argument and clarification. Again if, as deep ecologists hold, we should reject the picture of human beings-in-environment in favour of the view of us as 'organisms as knots in the biospherical net or field of intrinsic relations' (Naess 1973: 96), what does this mean for theories of agency or, more specifically in the context of political theory, autonomy? (see Lucardie, Ch. 2 this volume). All these are questions that emerge from within green theory itself. There are many more, and the chances are that discussion of them will, in time, amount to a corpus of reflections that will go by the name of green political theory.

In conclusion, the green perspective bears on three features of political theory in a particular way. It widens the realm of political debate and introduces new members to the political community. It casts its own peculiar glow on political concepts, and it provides a new dimension within which to assess the history of political thought and the status of political theories. All of this will ensure an enduring green influence on the future of political theory.

Andrew Dobson
Keele University, 1993

NOTE

1 The views expressed in this afterword are mine alone and no other contributor to this collection should necessarily be associated with them.

BIBLIOGRAPHY

Atkinson, A. (1991) *Principles of Political Ecology*, London: Belhaven.
Ball, T. and Daggar, R. (1991) *Political Ideologies and the Democratic Ideal*, New York: Harper Collins.
Dickens, P. (1992) *Society and Nature: Towards a Green Social Theory*, Hemel Hempstead: Harvester–Wheatsheaf.
Dobson, A. (1990) *Green Political Thought*, London: Routledge.
Eckersley, R. (1990) 'Habermas and green political thought', *Theory and Society*, no. 19: 739–76.
—— (1992) *Environmentalism and Political Theory: Toward an Ecocentric Approach*, New York: State University of New York Press, and London: University College of London Press.
Goodin, R. (1992) *Green Political Theory*, Oxford: Polity Press.
Grundmann, R. (1991) *Marxism and Ecology*, Oxford: Oxford University Press.
Held, D. (1983) *Political Theory Today*, Cambridge: Polity Press.
Heywood, A. (1992) *Political Ideologies: An Introduction*, Basingstoke and London: Macmillan.
Macridis, R. (1992) *Contemporary Political Ideologies* (5th edn), London and New York: Harper Collins.
Miller, D. and Siedentop, L. (1983) *The Nature of Political Theory*, Oxford: Clarendon Press.
Naess, A. (1973) 'The shallow and the deep, long-range ecology movement. A summary', *Inquiry*, no. 16: 95–100.
Pateman, C. (1989) *The Sexual Contract*, Cambridge: Polity Press.
Phillips, A. (1991) *Engendering Democracy*, Cambridge: Polity Press.
Vincent, A. (1992) *Modern Political Ideologies*, Oxford: Blackwell.

NAME INDEX

SUBJECT INDEX

holism 9, 14, 21–35, 65–6, 76, 196
housing 154
hunting *see* blood sports

individualism 21–35, 161–76, 185, 217
industrial mode of production 105–16
Industrial Revolution 121–2, 132, 134, 215
industrialization 105–16, 122
instrumental reason 193–4, 198–9, 201–9
intensive stock rearing 173–5
interrelationism 30
intrinsic value 5, 14, 28, 65–6, 76, 85, 87, 97, 196, 202, 209

Judaism 212, 217
justice 3–20, 27, 53, 92–9, 151, 230

labour theory of value 133, 205
Law of Diminishing Returns 120
liberalism 68–9, 76, 83, 89, 91, 94, 99, 161–76, 182, 185, 187–8, 230
liberty 93–4, 96, 166

market (economy) 90–1, 93, 96, 119–23, 133–4
Marxism 40–3, 54–6, 131–4, 141, 153, 166, 179, 183, 187, 192–3, 203–5, 230–1, 233
materialism 59, 199–201, 205
mobility 88–9
mysticism 23, 219

Netherlands, The 85–9, 98; Green Party (Groenen) 22; National Environmental Policy Plan (NEPP) 85–8, 98; Nature Policy Plan (NPP) 85–8, 98
non-reductionism 29–30
non-violent direct action (NVDA) 49–54, 58, 60

Orthodox Church 219–20, 222, 227

pacifism 39, 49–54, 58, 60
participatory democracy 47–8, 50–4, 57, 76, 78; *see also* direct democracy
patriarchy 185
plants 12, 27–8

pluralism 40–3, 55, 94
pollution 125–33, 135
post-industrial society 108, 115, 152
post-materialism 200, 207–9
post-modernism 185, 206
pragmatism 76–7
productive forces *see* forces of production
progress 121, 132, 195, 206
Protestantism 216–17

rational choice theory 59, 129–30
religion 210–28
rights 161–76
Russia 56–7

self-reliance 152–3, 155
social democracy 153
social rationality 147, 153–4
socialism 39–40, 132, 148, 153, 164, 169, 172, 179, 182, 187
state (theories of the) 40–5, 54–9
stewardship 223–6
stoics 9, 13
sustainable development 84–91, 95–6, 98–9, 115–16, 128–9, 134–8
sustainability *see* sustainable development

technocentrism 54
technology 39, 45, 48–9, 50–4, 60, 109, 190
teledemocracy 73–5, 78
theology 216–22
Third World 58, 109–11, 116, 134, 152, 187
transmission principle 98–9

unemployment 108, 116, 154–5
USA, the 56–7, 109–11, 148, 150, 152, 154
utilitarianism 11, 162, 170–1

voluntary simplicity 151

welfare 147, 154–7
welfare state 148, 152–3
World Council of Churches 219, 223–6
World Commission on Environment and Development (WCED) 58, 85–6, 134, 146